THE HUNGARIAN COOKBOOK

THE
HUNGARIAN
COOKBOOK

with a note on wines by CHARLES G. DERECSKEY

drawings by GEORGE KOIZUMI

THE PLEASURES
OF HUNGARIAN
FOOD AND WINE

SUSAN DERECSKEY

wm

WILLIAM MORROW
An Imprint of HarperCollins*Publishers*

A hardcover edition of this book was originally published by Harper & Row, Publishers, Inc.

THE HUNGARIAN COOKBOOK. Copyright © 1972 by Susan Derecskey. Illustrations copyright © 1972 by Harper & Row, Publishers, Inc. Foreword copyright © 1987 by Susan Derecskey. All rights reserved. Printed in the United States of America. No part of this book may be used or reproduced in any manner whatsoever without written permission except in the case of brief quotations embodied in critical articles and reviews. For information, address HarperCollins Publishers, 195 Broadway,New York, NY 10007. Published simultaneously in Canada by Fitzhenry & Whiteside Limited, Toronto.

First PERENNIAL LIBRARY edition published 1987.

Designer: Sidney Feinberg

Library of Congress Cataloging-in-Publication Data

Derecskey, Susan.
    The Hungarian cookbook.

    Reprint. Oringinally published: New York : Harper & Row,
1972. 1st ed. With a new preface by the author.
    Includes index.
    1. Cookery, Hungarian.   I. Title.
TX723.5.H8D47   1987   641.59439   87-45135
ISBN 0-06-091437-8 (pbk.)

    20 21 LSC 30

For Charles

Contents

Foreword

There is a mystique about things Magyar, a forbidden city of the soul that remains forever closed to outsiders. Fierce and proud, the Hungarians have convinced the world that their culture is as impregnable as their language. Perhaps, but not when it comes to Hungarian cuisine.

Much has changed—in Hungary, in America, in politics and in the kitchen—since I wrote those words fifteen years ago in the foreword to my Hungarian cookbook, but they are as true today as they were then.

Since the government of Hungary reopened the country's border to the West, millions of foreigners have discovered Hungary and sampled the pleasures of its table. It does not matter, it seems, if tourists do not speak the language: they can always manage somehow to read a menu and point out the piece of cake they want. And with the fine Hungarian wines and foodstuffs that used to be scarce in the West being freely exported, it has become easy for people to duplicate at home the dishes and desserts they enjoyed in Hungary.

My family and I have made many trips to Budapest and the Hungarian countryside since this book was first published. I still spend much of my time there browsing in the markets and food shops (and stopping for a restorative coffee and cake, of course). I never cease to marvel at how much sophistication has been restored to Hungarian cuisine. Whether I am in a state-subsidized luxury restaurant or a family-owned storefront pastry shop, I find the level of accomplishment remarkable. And it is an achievement won against considerable odds, for supplies remain limited and unpredictable.

At the same time, another kind of gastronomic revolution has taken place in the United States. To an extraordinary degree, Americans have focused their attention on food. Few home kitchens are without a food processor and powerful electric mixer—items that were strictly restaurant tools fifteen years ago—and a shelf of specialized cookbooks. And whereas a decade ago serious cooks had to shop in ethnic enclaves for special ingredients, today they can easily find them at the local supermarket or in the gourmet emporiums that have sprung up all over the country. In fact, if I were writing this book today, I would be more generous with the paprika, since it no longer has to be hoarded.

The recipes in this book have stood the test of time. Many of them were given to me by Hungarian grandmothers and mothers who figured out how to adapt traditional dishes to American ingredients and conditions. All the recipes were tried out in my kitchen before publication, and they have since been tested—over and over again—by loyal readers. Now, I hope, these recipes will appeal to a new generation of cooks, including some of those intrepid culinary explorers who are not afraid to venture into uncharted terrain, as well as young people of Hungarian origin who want to cherish and preserve their heritage.

They are right to do so, and not only for sentimental reasons. Hungarian cuisine is unique and on a par with the world's great cuisines. Historical circumstances worked together to make Hungarian cuisine unique. The first of these was the juxtaposition and mingling of many different cultures through the centuries. Then there was the long isolation of much of Hungary from the West. As a result, cooking styles that can be traced back to the early Magyar tribes, who settled the land in the ninth century, have survived virtually intact. And the influence of the Turks, who occupied Hungary for nearly a hundred and fifty years, still lingers on, most notably in paprika and rétes (strudel), which they introduced. Since then, peasant and bourgeois cooking alike have been slowly refined into some truly magical dishes. In Hungary as in few other places, the fruits of the earth have been transformed by the force of the imagination into culinary art.

Obviously, the gastronomic history of Hungary would make a volume in itself. But I leave that to others to write. My desire is to pass on to my readers some of the joy the Hungarian kitchen has brought to our home. Whether those readers are Hungarian by blood or by temperament, I hope they will find their own pleasures in these pages.

SUSAN DERECSKEY

Washington
February 1987

Special Equipment, Techniques, and Ingredients

Happily, Hungarian cooking does not need any costly one-purpose utensils or odd pots that would not be found in any well-stocked kitchen. Heavy-bottomed flameproof casseroles in different sizes for stews and large pots for soups and dumplings will get a lot of use. A potato ricer comes in handy, and a chestnut roaster or *Spätzle* mill will speed the galuska making considerably.

With a few vital exceptions, there are no special techniques for Hungarian cooking either. The commonsense rules, like adding hot —even boiling—stock to a simmering pot of stew or soup, or beating whipped cream ice cold, still apply. The right-size pot should be used and the appropriate utensil. But above all, the cook should use her intelligence in the kitchen.

BACON. The bacon used in Hungarian cooking is smoked bacon, the kind that is sold by the piece (about 5 inches square) in butcher shops and, lately, supermarkets. Thick-sliced breakfast bacon may reluctantly be substituted.

BREAD CRUMBS. In Hungary, bread crumbs are made at home from stale zsemle (club rolls). Here, some family bakeries sell bread crumbs they make from stale rolls and French or Italian bread, and a few premium brands of all-white, nonflavored bread crumbs can be found on the market. If neither is available, make your own or try a substitute some Hungarian-American cooks swear by, namely crushed cornflakes.

BUTTER. Sweet butter should always be used in Hungarian cooking. When it is not available, substitute salt butter and decrease the amount of salt in the recipe.

CARAWAY SEEDS. A few crushed caraway seeds enhance the flavor of the paprika, much as salt brings out the flavor of other foods.

COOKING FAT. Real lard is the cooking medium in Hungary itself, but a good-quality vegetable oil may always be substituted. In fact, many Hungarian émigrés prefer it because it is far lighter and much more healthful. American packaged lard is also quite acceptable. Whichever you use, skim any excess off the dish before serving.

ONIONS. The slow "stewing" of chopped onions in hot fat until they turn soft is a fundamental technique of Hungarian cooking. Use enough fat, keep the heat very low, and never allow the onions to brown.

PAPRIKA. There is no alternative to imported Hungarian paprika. It makes all the difference. The real thing sometimes shows up on a supermarket exotic foods shelf even in the most out-of-the-way places. If you cannot find it, order it from one of the food specialty stores listed at the end of the book.

SAUSAGE. Smoked Hungarian cooking sausage is very hard to get. The more widely found Polish Kielbasy sausage can be used in its place.

SOUR CREAM. Hungarian sour cream is thinner and tarter than the American commercial product. Before adding it to a dish, beat it lightly with a fork. Even better, thin it with buttermilk (2 to 3 tablespoons per ½ cup of sour cream). Never mix cold sour cream directly into a hot sauce; it will curdle, ruining the texture and appearance of the dish. Cool the sauce somewhat, and have the sour cream at room temperature. Stir a bit of sauce into it first, and gradually add that mixture to the sauce. And always use sour cream sparingly —many a good dish has been spoiled by a milky sauce.

TOMATOES. Canned vegetables are or ought to be taboo in the kitchen, but an exception can be made for tomatoes used for cooking. By all means use garden tomatoes when they are in season; the rest of the year, canned whole tomatoes give far better results than the hothouse varieties. Where tomato sauce is called for, the canned kind, especially the one that has bits of tomato in it, is an acceptable substitute for homemade sauce.

Pronunciation Guide

If you are going to cook it right, you might as well say it right.

As an aid to pronunciation, a phonetic transcription of the Hungarian name of each dish appears at least once. Generally speaking, the stress in Hungarian is on the first syllable of a word, with a lighter stress on the first syllable of the second word of a phrase. For example, csirke paprikás would be pronounced CHEER-ke PAH-pree-kahsh. Vowels may be short or long, and with the following exceptions consonants are pronounced as in English.

 c soft, like ts . . . in oats
cs like *tch* . . . . . . in church
 g hard, like *g* . . . in good
gy like *dge* . . . . . . in edge
 j like *y* . . . . in you
 s like *sh* . . . . in sugar
sz like *s* . . . . in sardine
 z like *z* . . . . in zing
zs like *zh* . . . . in pleasure

A Note on Wines

My earliest wine memories reach back to happy times spent in our own vineyard in the foothills of Transylvania: to the days when I was first permitted to handle the lopótök (the wine thief) to draw wine from a barrel; to the outdoor lunches under the old walnut trees at harvest time; to the stoking of the all-night fire under the huge bubbling cauldron making plum brandy.

Growing up in an ancient winegrowing area leads to attitudes toward wine and a code of etiquette which are not always understood by others. My American friends, for example, find it hilarious that I would return to a liquor store with just the cork in my pocket to claim a refund for a bottle of bouchonné wine. And I now make sure no one is watching when I knock back a measure of Hungarian barack brandy, since the day I was told that I do it exactly like Erich von Stroheim in *The Grand Illusion*.

That vineyard of ours is long since gone. The trees were cut down and the earth leveled in anticipation of a World War II battle that never came. But the habits acquired many years ago linger on with the memories. And after drinking many wines in many places, it was a pleasure to find the tastes reminiscent of a somewhat distant past right here in New York City.

Hungarian wines are now available in the United States. Few, to be sure, and not the little wines from the vineyard of a relative, or friend, or friend's friend, or trusted supplier—some of those very ordinary and some really great—that many Hungarians in the old country still drink.

On a recent trip to Hungary, we dropped in to visit a writer who lives on the shore of Lake Balaton. The host opened a bottle of so-called export-quality wine, sent by the mayor of the winegrowing village, with his compliments, to do honor to the guests. The same wine, held in high esteem and a rarity in its homeland, is readily available in any of the larger liquor stores in the United States. Such "export-quality" wines are supplied to a few restaurants catering to tourists in Hungary and are shipped abroad to earn foreign exchange.

They are *real* wines, as distinct from the concoctions that often go under that name. They rank several notches below the *Grand Crus* of France, but they are as good as any of the better light table wines of quality.

Hungary is one of the historic winegrowing areas of the Old World. Barrels of Hungarian wines traveled on oxcarts and were towed upstream on Danube barges to faraway lands to be praised by popes, poets, emperors, and various princes of the day and age. Actually, viticulture in what has become Hungary antedates the arrival there of the Magyar tribes in the ninth century. A somewhat obscure Roman emperor, Probus (A.D. 276–282), ordered his legions who were stationed in the area, then called Pannonia, to plant and cultivate grapes. Perhaps they resented the unmartial activity, for Emperor Probus ended up on the wrong side of a legionnaire's blade in a Pannonian vineyard. But by that time the deed was done: to this day, wine is produced on the ancient spots cultivated by Roman legionnaires.

That viticulture requiring such intensive care survived in Hungary through the centuries is a sort of miracle in itself. It had to weather a rich assortment of historic and natural disasters—a Mongol invasion, 150 years of rule by nondrinking Turks, wars of subjugation and liberation, siege and pestilence, and the onslaught of a vicious little plant louse called phylloxera that swept Europe and devastated most of Hungary's vineyards in 1875. Relief came from the New World when it was found that hardy American vine stock, even when grafted, resisted the fatal pest. A fair repayment, it would seem, for the work of a nineteenth-century Hungarian exile named Ágoston Haraszthy, who organized modern large-scale methods of winegrowing in the state of California.

More recently, following World War II, the Hungarian vineyards survived the collectivization drive, although only barely, until a compromise with independent winegrowers was hammered out. Today, there are some large cooperatives, lots of privately owned small vineyards, and so-called hill communities—a very loosely organized cooperative formula combining private ownership subject to strict quality control and common marketing. Significantly, the term itself was borrowed from the thirteenth century, when it granted special privileges to its winegrower members.

The science of viticulture has been pursued in Hungary for a long time, with pampered state institutions traditionally taking a leading role. A fine tradition has developed and has been maintained. As a result, today the quality of Hungarian wines traveling abroad is as good as if not better than it has ever been.

Annually, close to half a million bottles of Hungarian wine arrive in the United States. They include the following varieties:

TOKAY (*toh-koi*). For centuries Tokay Aszú (*toh-koi ah-sū*) has thrilled the palates and the imagination of Europeans, east and west. It is the wine Mephisto offered Faust, the one the court of Louis XIV doted on, a favorite of Tsar Peter the Great, who bought himself a vineyard in the Tokaj hills to be sure of a steady supply. It financed a Hungarian war of independence against the Hapsburg emperor in the eighteenth century, and it was Franz-Joseph's annual birthday gift to Queen Victoria in the next. And it remains one of the world's best-known wines, even though tastes have been shifting to drier wines.

Tokay Aszú is a full-flavored, sweet dessert wine of golden color, believed by many connoisseurs to be in a class by itself. It is definitely not a table wine. For the uninitiated it might be a revelation to have Tokay Aszú instead of port or brandy and liqueurs after a substantial meal, or to sip a heady glass with sweets. The other Tokay wines, Tokay Szamorodni (*toh-koi sah-mo-rod-nee*) and Tokay Furmint (*toh-koi fur-mint*) are also dessert wines but less rich than the Aszú.

All Tokay wines come from the gentle hills (Tokaj-Hegyalja) of northeastern Hungary where wine has been produced for more than a thousand years, and which now comprise a district of some 25 winegrowing villages. Tokay Aszú is made of Furmint grapes brought into Hungary by French settlers in the eleventh century and a lesser amount of native Hungarian Hárslevelű grapes. They ripen unevenly, and the sun-shriveled (aszú) berries, covered with a "fine rot," are picked separately as for some late-harvest Rhine wines. They are pressed into pulp, but unlike anywhere else, this precious sweet pulp is then added to the general run and treaded once again in cloth bags. It takes the Tokay Aszú four to eight years to mature in traditional small barrels (Gönci hordó), each containing 30 to 35 gallons of wine. The wine keeps practically indefinitely, improving with age. Bottles are marked by the number of puttony—containers—of aszú pulp that have been added to the barrel, 3, 4, or 5 Puttonyos as the case might be. The higher the number, the sweeter and better the wine is supposed to be. The 6 Puttonyos and the 1 and 2 Puttonyos are seldom made, and the most concentrated variety of all, Tokay Esszencia, is not marketed.

Tokay Szamorodni is made of the whole cluster of grapes, without first picking off the shriveled aszú berries. It varies in quality and sweetness, depending on the proportion of overripe to just-ripe grapes. Tokay Furmint is harvested earlier than the other two and processed like any other wine.

EGRI BIKAVÉR (*e-gree bi-ka-vehr*), Bull's Blood of Eger. Named for its dark red color and the ancient little town in the hills of eastern Hungary, this is a full-bodied, velvety red wine, with a surprising twangy twist; dry enough to go well with steak, for example, and a number of Hungarian dishes. It rivals the best of the Spanish clarets, and it is, next to Tokay, the best-known Hungarian wine in Europe. Egri Bikavér looks back on a colorful history and triumphs. For a long time it was widely believed that real bull's blood was mixed into the wine by Eger's close-mouthed winegrowers—who deny such rumors to this day. The ultimate test of Egri Bikavér's potency came in 1552, when the Turkish armies of Ali Pasha took the fortress of Eger under siege. Inside, some 2,000 valiant Hungarians—fortified, no doubt, by manly portions of Egri Bikavér from the labyrinth of underground cellars that still serve to store the wine—withstood the siege of more than 100,000 Turks for several months.

SZEKSZÁRDI VÖRÖS (*sek-sahr-dee vu-rohsh*), Szekszárd Red. A pleasant country wine with the smell of the wooden barrel about it, Szekszárdi Vörös is the driest of Hungarian red wines and recalls the best of Italian reds. It comes from southwestern Hungary, from the low hills surrounding the little town of Szekszárd, called Aliaca in Roman winegrowing times. The grapes, Kadarka, are ancient Hungarian stuff that produce a variety of different red qualities depending on the region in which they grow. Some people, including the Derecskeys, actually prefer the coarser and drier Szekszárdi Vörös to the mellower Egri Bikavér. Franz Liszt was another devotee of this wine and a regular visitor to Szekszárd as a result.

NEMES KADAR (ne-mehsh kuh-dahr), Noble Kadar. This red wine might come from a number of winegrowing places in Hungary, since Kadarka grapes, a native Hungarian variety, from which it is made, are grown in at least a fourth of the country's winegrowing areas. They are a major component of Egri Bikavér from northeastern Hungary, and the grape for Szekszárdi Vörös from the southwest, among others. Nemes Kadar, as the available export variety is known, tends to be sweetish, but it is light enough to serve as an excellent companion to game meats.

LEÁNYKA (lay-ahny-ka), Little Girl. Egri Bikavér's partner from the same rolling hills of the Eger region. It is a delicate white wine, dry, but with full bouquet and a quality of freshness about it that easily makes it into a favorite. It equals or even surpasses the better-known white table wines of the Lake Balaton area in western Hungary. Leányka is one of those wines that can stand on its own, at any time of the day with a snack or a meal.

BADACSONYI KÉKNYELŰ (bah-dah-tchohn-yee kayk-njeh-lŭ). Badacsony is the name of a strange flat-topped volcanic hill on the northern shores of Lake Balaton, where Roman legionnaires broke ground for vineyards long ago. Kéknyelű (literally, "blue-stalked") is the name of the grape whose origin is lost in the mist of history; it is considered one of the ancient local varieties. This wine has the distinction of being the driest of Hungarian white wines, a delightfully light and playful but smooth wine of distinction that goes with virtually everything requiring the accompaniment of white wine.

BADACSONYI SZÜRKE BARÁT (*bah-dah-tchohn-yee sŭr-ke bah-raht*), Grey Friar of Badacsony. A wine from the same rich wine-producing volcanic soil, the protected southern slope of Badacsony hill on Lake Balaton, as the Badacsonyi Kéknyelű. The grapes that go into it are the Pinot Gris that do not manage to produce anything of distinction in their native France. Hungarian writers rave about the combination of warmth and sunshine reflected by the great lake and the volcanic soil that brings forth the grape's hidden qualities. Whatever the reason, the very ordinary Pinot Gris blossomed in its Hungarian habitat into a somewhat sweetish but well-rounded, semilight white wine with a wholesome bouquet.

HUNGARIAN RIZLING (*reez-ling*). A transplanted Italian Riesling spelled the Hungarian way, and a pleasant enough light white wine with a "green," sour tinge. It is what the French would call a *petit vin*, unpretentious, not for occasions, but good enough to accompany a simple meal. It is produced mainly near Lake Balaton, with even quality control imposed on the export variety, and it is less expensive than other Hungarian wines. The Rizling's taste evokes memories for Hungarians of those scratchy everyday wines in bars around the corner, and makes them reach for club soda to mix with it for one of the most popular in-between-meals drink, the fröccs.

DEBRŐI HÁRSLEVELŰ (*deh-broi-yee hahrsh-le-ve-lū*). The small wine district of Debrő, comprising but three villages in northern Hungary, and an ancient native Hungarian variety of grapes lend their names to this unique white wine. Debrői Hárslevelű is a proper antidote to concoctions pouring out of wine factories. It is a savory wine with the aroma of fresh hay about it, a real country wine with somewhat rough edges, the kind travelers probably used to find in country inns.

BARACK PÁLINKA (*bah-rahtsk pah-lin-kah*). Not a wine, but a fiery Hungarian apricot brandy of well-deserved fame from the flat Kecskemét peach- and apricot-growing region in southern Hungary. Barack is a more sophisticated cousin of plum brandy, better known hereabouts as slivovitz (Szilvorium in Hungarian), and has just as many uses for brandy devotees. It is rich in aroma, and should be sniffed lovingly before tossing it back. Barack is strong stuff that burns its way down to the stomach, spreading that feeling of well-being for which it is appreciated. On cold winter mornings in the Hungarian countryside a drink of barack is a favorite way to fortify oneself before facing the elements. An urban use of the same brew is to have it as an apéritif, with a few morsels of something like cheese straws before meals. There was hardly a Sunday dinner at my father's house without apricot or plum brandy first being served to the men standing about. A shot or two, it is believed, properly sets one up for a leisurely meal.

A Hungarian meal and ambience is unthinkable without wine, be it Hungarian or not. An old-fashioned Hungarian toast wishes, "Bort, buzát, békességet, szép asszony feleséget!"—Wine, wheat, peace, and a beautiful woman for a wife—in that order, make no mistake about it.

CHARLES G. DERECSKEY

THE HUNGARIAN COOKBOOK

Soups
Levesek
(LE-VE-SHEK)

$\mathcal{S}$oup is the soul of Hungarian cuisine, its very breath of life. For me, as a Hungarian only by marriage, this concept has been as difficult to comprehend as it is for a convert to Catholicism to accept the Trinity as an article of faith. But bow we must to the wisdom of the ages: I now hear myself talking about soups like a native-born Magyar. Erőleves and Újházy tyúkleves are hardly different from the bouillons and chicken soups of other cultures; the vegetable soups, however, are a phenomenon quite apart. Their range of ingredients and of impact is simply marvelous, and I imagine that if I had pressed my research to its logical conclusion, I would have found a manioc soup invented by a Hungarian living on the Equator and a milkweed soup invented by one in the Adirondacks. Even without such exotica, there is a soup for every menu, one for every occasion. Try it and see: the worst that can happen is that you will never again get away with opening a can of condensed soup and pretending it is the real thing.

✌ Bouillon
ERŐLEVES
(*e-ru-le-vesh*)

Cooking is a bit like skating: what you learn when you're young stays with you all your life, but it is very hard to start when you grow up. By the time I was fifteen, I could make a lumpless white sauce, a flaky piecrust, and a tender, juicy roast chicken. It took me the next fifteen years to learn to make a good meat soup.

The basic principles are so few and so simple, I can't imagine why, except that no one ever told me what they were. All it takes is a little bit of care and a lot of patience to make a good soup. First of all, never boil it—start it cold and keep the flame low from the very beginning. Second, remove the scum as soon and as fast as it forms. And third, cook the soup for a long, long time. I have found, too, that it is worth a special trip to the butcher for soup meat and bones. All too often, what is sold as such in large urban supermarkets is barely one level above garbage. If you trust your supermarket or have no alternative, try to get flanken or short ribs and marrow bones: they make the best soup. The marrow itself is a delicacy. In our house the men of the family have it for a little *Vorspeise* to keep them going until suppertime. There must be a more elegant way to eat it than standing around the stove, but they report it tastes best like that.

1 pound soup meat
1 or 2 pounds bones in 3-inch pieces, preferably marrow bones
2 cloves
1 onion
2 carrots
2 parsnips or white turnips
2 small kohlrabies, if available
1 or 2 leeks, if available
2 leafy halves of celery stalks
2 sprigs of parsley
1 clove garlic
12 peppercorns
1 bay leaf
1 tablespoon salt
1½ cups uncooked fine egg noodles (optional)
Dara gombóc (farina dumplings, page 23), 2 or 3 per person
   (optional)

Wash the meat and bones and place them in a large, heavy-bottomed pot. Cover them with cold water and slowly bring to the simmer, uncovered. Remove the scum as fast as it forms. Do not boil the soup: the fat and scum will break up in the broth, spoiling its appearance and taste. Continue cooking and skimming the broth for about 1 hour. Stick the cloves into the onion, then add it, the thoroughly cleaned vegetables, and the seasonings to the soup. Cover partially and simmer at least until the meat is tender, about 1 to 1½ hours, or longer. Place a sieve in a large bowl and pour the soup through. Set the broth aside to cool. Remove the marrow from the bones, mash and lightly salt it, and serve it immediately on fresh rye bread or white toast. (One pound of bones gives one or two servings.) Discard the bones, the onion and cloves, the celery, parsley, garlic, peppercorns, and bay leaf, as well as any loose bones or fat from the meat. Cut up the remaining vegetables and pieces of meat. Degrease the broth and correct the seasoning: it may need considerably more salt. If the egg noodles are going to be cooked in the broth, heat it to a simmer and drop them in. After 10 minutes, return the vegetables and meat to the broth, and continue simmering until the noodles are done. Prepare the dumplings separately and add them to the soup just before serving. Serve very hot.

৺ Stock
CSONT LEVES
(chohnt le-vesh)

The secret ingredient of many fabulous soups and stews is a good stock. Hungarians call it csont leves or bone soup because they make it without meat, and it is as much a part of the kitchen furniture as the wooden spoon and the mixing bowl: no self-respecting cook would be without it. For those of us who are lazier than we ought to be about such matters, there are, fortunately, several excellent canned stocks that can be substituted with confidence. When making homemade stock, though, be sure to buy the bones from a reliable butcher. They can be mixed in an all-purpose meat stock, but I prefer to keep them separate and make a specific stock that I have more control over. Instructions for making all kinds of stock follow. The proportions are for a large quantity, but there is no logical reason not to make a smaller amount if that is all you will be needing.

> **5 pounds beef or veal bones in 2- to 3-inch pieces, or 3 pounds chicken backs and necks**
> **1 tablespoon salt**

2 carrots
2 onions
2 leafy celery stalks
1 parsnip
4 parsley sprigs
2 cloves garlic
1 bay leaf
6 peppercorns

Wash the bones or chicken pieces, and place in a large stock pot. Pour on enough cold water to cover by 2 to 3 inches, and slowly bring to barest simmer. Skim off all the scum as soon as it forms. (In the case of veal stock, continue cooking until the foam stops forming, then discard the water, wash the bones, put them back in the scrubbed pot, and start all over again with cold water.) After simmering 1 hour, add the salt and cleaned vegetables and the remaining ingredients. Continue simmering, partially covered, for about 5 hours or until the bones seem "cooked out." Spoon off the fat and scum from time to time, and add more hot water as needed to keep the bones covered. When you feel the stock is done, strain it into a bowl and let it stand. Skim off all the fat, and taste the broth. If the flavor is too thin, boil off some of the water; the stock may also need additional salt. Let the stock cool completely, then refrigerate it. It will keep almost indefinitely if you boil it twice a week to kill any bacteria. Stock may also be frozen, preferably in pint-size containers for easier handling later on.

⋅⋞§ Goulash Soup
GULYÁS LEVES
(gū-yahsh le-vesh)

This poor peasant brew has been so manhandled and abused over the years that it is a miracle anyone still gives it a second look. And yet, when it comes to soups, few rank higher than a wholesome hearty gulyás. So suppress the memory of all those god-awful goulashes in quaint foreign restaurants and high school cafeterias and try gulyás just one more time—according to this proven formula. It is a rich, spicy concoction, just the thing for a cold day or a buffet supper. Diced potatoes are usually cooked in gulyás leves along with a kind of half-noodle, half-dumpling called csipetke.

3 tablespoons lard or cooking oil
1 medium onion, finely chopped
½ pound soup meat, cut in 1-inch cubes
Salt
1 teaspoon paprika
Pinch of caraway seeds, crushed with the back of a spoon
4 cups beef stock or canned beef broth and water
1 clove garlic, peeled and stuck on a toothpick
½ medium green pepper, cut in ½-inch strips
2 small tomatoes, preferably canned
½ pound (about 2 medium) potatoes
Csipetke (pinched noodles, page 22) (optional)

Heat the lard or oil in a large, heavy-bottomed pot. Sauté the onion until it turns translucent, then add the meat and brown it lightly on all sides. Sprinkle with 1 teaspoon of salt, the paprika, and caraway seeds, and add 2 cups of the stock or broth and blend thoroughly. Add the garlic, green pepper, and tomatoes, and bring to the simmer. Cover and simmer for 1 hour, adding more stock or broth as necessary to keep the meat covered. Peel and dice the potatoes in ½-inch pieces, and add them to the soup along with 1 teaspoon of salt and enough stock to cover them. Simmer until the potatoes are done (about 25 minutes), remove the soup from the heat and let it stand. Discard the garlic, skim off most of the grease, and correct the seasoning (more salt may be needed). Stir in the csipetke, bring the soup back to the simmer and serve.

⇜ Chicken Soup
ÚJHÁZY TYÚKLEVES
(*u-ee-hah-zee tyūk-le-vesh*)

In the early years of the century, there was a famous actor in Budapest named Ede Újházy. So great was his fame that people followed his fiacre throughout Budapest and gathered daily at Gundel's restaurant in the zoo to watch him eat lunch. Besides being a great friend of Gundel, he was a gourmet in his own right, and his favorite dish was chicken soup. In time, he created his own version: by substituting a cock for the hen that was generally used then and adding a variety of vegetables and garnishes, he developed the rich, golden soup that still bears his name. The whims of fortune are such that Ede Újházy spent his last years in misery, a poor and forgotten idol of the stage. Today no one remembers the laughter, the tears, the bravos: it is the chicken soup that turned out to be his finest performance. A genuine Újházy tyúkleves has everything in it: chicken, vegetables, and one, two, even three garnishes. In America it is best to make it with a three-pound fryer chicken, which is sure to be fresh. As for garnishes, the standby is fine egg noodles. Májas gombóc (liver dumplings) and dara gombóc (farina dumplings) are both classic. In my opinion, though, Újházy soup is in itself a triumph of man over nature: the noodles and dumplings are merely a bow to the civilization that made it all possible.

> 3-pound chicken, split or quartered
> 1 pound chicken wings or backs and necks (optional)
> 2 carrots
> 2 parsnips or white turnips
> 2 small kohlrabies, if available
> 1 leek, if available
> 1 medium onion
> 2 leafy halves of celery stalks
> 2 sprigs of parsley
> 1 clove garlic
> 6 peppercorns
> 1 tablespoon salt
> Dumplings: májas gombóc (page 24) or dara gombóc (page 23),
>   2 or 3 per person (optional)
> 1½ cups uncooked fine egg noodles
> ¼ pound thinly sliced mushrooms (optional)
> Eggs, 1 per person (optional)

Wash and clean the pieces of chicken and place them in a large, heavy-bottomed pot. Clean the vegetables thoroughly, cut up the carrots, parsnips or turnips, and kohlrabies, and lay them with the leek, onion, celery, and parsley on top of the chicken. Add the garlic, peppercorns, and salt, and enough cold water to cover everything. Slowly bring to the simmer, cover partially, and simmer until the chicken is tender—about 1 hour for a fryer, 2 hours or more for fowl. Place a sieve in a large bowl and pour the soup through. Set the broth aside and let it cool. Discard the celery, parsley, garlic, and peppercorns as well as any loose chicken bones or skin. Cut up the remaining vegetables and pieces of meat. Degrease the broth and correct the seasoning. Return the vegetables and meat to the broth, and bring it slowly back to the simmer. If dumplings are to be cooked in the soup, add them at this point. When the soup returns to the simmer, add the noodles. Five minutes later, add the mushrooms if you wish to use them. Continue simmering until the dumplings are done, then lift them out and keep them warm in a side dish. If you are serving eggs with the soup, add them to the broth for poaching. When they are done (about 3 minutes) place them in the side dish. Pour the soup into a large tureen and carefully float the eggs and dumplings on top. Serve immediately.

VEGETABLE SOUPS
ZÖLDSÉG LEVESEK
(*zuld-shayg le-ve-shek*)

Given a bit of time to experiment, a determined Hungarian cook could—and probably would—make a soup from any vegetable that grows on the planet earth. Even within the confines of the temperate zone, Hungarians have produced a variety of vegetable soups that is simply staggering. Of the scores that I have heard or read about, I selected several that are especially successful under conditions of modern life. In principle, they should be made with meat or chicken stock, but I have found store-bought vegetables to be so pale and fatigued after their cross-country journey that they are overwhelmed by the broth. This is particularly true of cauliflower and green beans. Garden vegetables are another story altogether; they seem to improve when cooked in stock, and all their flavor and nutritional value are preserved. Whether you decide to use water or stock in these recipes, be sure to try them all and make more converts from the can.

ᴇᴈ Asparagus Soup
SPÁRGA LEVES
(shpahr-ga le-vesh)

1 pound asparagus, cleaned and cut in 1-inch pieces
4 cups veal or chicken stock or water or a mixture of stock and
   water
1 teaspoon sugar
2 teaspoons salt
2 tablespoons butter
2 tablespoons flour
2 tablespoons chopped parsley
½ cup milk
Galuska (dumplings, page 21) (optional)

Drop the asparagus into boiling stock or water, and add the sugar and salt. Simmer, uncovered, for about 5 minutes, or until the asparagus is nearly tender. Make a roux by heating the butter in a heavy-bottomed saucepan and stirring in the flour and parsley. Cook it, stirring constantly, for about 3 minutes, and dilute with milk. Blend thoroughly to be sure there are no lumps, and gradually mix in 3½ cups of asparagus broth. Add the asparagus pieces, correct the seasoning, and simmer for 5 more minutes, or until the asparagus is done. If galuska are to be added, prepare them separately, making one-third of the recipe on page 21, and drop the cooked galuska into the soup just before serving.

Cream of Asparagus Soup
SPÁRGA KRÉM LEVES
(shpahr-ga kraym le-vesh)

For a gilded-lily kind of soup, try spárga krém leves some day. Follow the preceding recipe for asparagus soup, and when it is done, purée the soup, using an electric blender or, preferably, a food mill. Just before serving, reheat the soup to the barest simmer and remove it from the heat at once. Let it cool for about 3 minutes. Meanwhile, whisk together 1 egg yolk and ½ cup of sour cream in the bottom of a soup tureen or large bowl. Blend 2 tablespoons of soup into this liaison, then carefully add the rest of the soup a little at a time, stirring constantly. Garnish with pirított zsemle kocka (croutons, page 25) and serve immediately.

⋟ Bean Soup

BAB LEVES

(bab le-vesh)

½ pound dried navy or pea beans
1 teaspoon salt
1 carrot
1 leek (if not available, use an onion)
1 clove garlic, peeled and stuck on a toothpick
¼-pound piece of smoked bacon or half a smoked knuckle or
  ham hock (optional)
2 tablespoons cooking oil
2 tablespoons chopped onions
1 teaspoon paprika
2 heaping tablespoons flour
1 tablespoon chopped parsley
¼ cup sour cream, at room temperature (optional)
2 teaspoons vinegar

Wash the beans and soak them overnight in cold water to cover. (Or use the quick soaking method: boil vigorously for 5 minutes, turn off heat, cover, and soak 1 hour.) Drain and rinse the beans and put them in a large pot. Add the salt, carrot, leek, garlic, and piece of smoked meat. Pour on enough water to cover the beans and meat by 2 inches, and bring to the simmer. Cook slowly, partly covered, for 2½ to 3 hours, or until the beans are tender, adding more water as necessary to keep them well covered. When they are done, discard the garlic, and remove the meat to a side dish. Make a roux as follows: melt the oil in a heavy-bottomed saucepan and gently sauté the onions in it until they wilt. Stir in the paprika and then the flour, and let it froth for 2 to 3 minutes. Add the parsley. Thin the roux with ½ cup of broth from the bean soup, then slowly pour the roux into the soup. Let it simmer for 10 minutes: if the soup is too thick, slowly add hot water and simmer 2 or 3 minutes longer; if it is too thin, let it simmer another 5 to 10 minutes. Take the soup off the heat and let it cool. Blend some soup in the sour

[11]

cream to keep it from curdling, then slowly stir the sour cream into the soup. Mix in the vinegar and taste for seasoning. Cut the meat into bite-sized pieces and stir them into the soup. Reheat before serving.

ৼ§ Cauliflower Soup
KARFIOL LEVES
(kahr-fee-ohl le-vesh)

1 small (5-inch) head of cauliflower
6 cups veal or chicken stock or water or a mixture of stock and
   water
1 teaspoon salt
2 tablespoons butter
2 heaping tablespoons flour
1½ tablespoons chopped parsley
½ cup sour cream, at room temperature

Wash the cauliflower and separate it into flowerets, all more or less the same size. Place them in a large heavy-bottomed pot and cover with stock or water, add salt, and slowly bring to a gentle boil. Cook, partially covered, for about 7 minutes, or until the cauliflower stalk is firm but can easily be pierced with a knife. In a small saucepan make a roux by heating the butter and adding the flour and parsley. Thin the roux with about ½ cup of the cauliflower broth, and gradually pour it back into the soup. Simmer for another 10 minutes, or until the cauliflower is done and the soup has lost all floury taste. Cool thoroughly. Pour about 2 tablespoons of soup into the sour cream and blend thoroughly, then slowly mix the sour-cream mixture back into the soup. Correct the seasoning. Reheat just before serving.

Cream of Cauliflower Soup
KARFIOL KRÉM LEVES
(kahr-fee-ohl kraym le-vesh)

To make cream of cauliflower soup, proceed as for cauliflower soup (preceding recipe), blending in the roux and letting it simmer for 10 minutes. Then, pass the soup and vegetable through a food mill or blender (preferably a food mill, which gives a far more interesting texture). Whisk together 1 egg yolk and ½ cup of sour cream (at room temperature) in a soup tureen. Just before serving, pour the warm—not hot—soup very slowly into the tureen, mixing it thoroughly with the egg-cream liaison. Taste for seasoning and serve immediately.

⋐§ Green Bean Soup
ZÖLDBAB LEVES
(*zuld-bab le-vesh*)

1 pound fresh green beans, cleaned and cut in 1-inch pieces
4 cups veal or chicken stock or water or a mixture of stock and water
2 teaspoons salt
1 clove garlic, peeled and stuck on a toothpick
1 teaspoon vinegar
2 tablespoons butter
1 small onion, chopped fine
1 teaspoon paprika
2 tablespoons chopped parsley
2 tablespoons flour
¼ cup sour cream, at room temperature

Drop the beans into boiling stock or water and add the salt, garlic, and vinegar. Simmer, uncovered, until the beans are nearly tender, about 15 minutes. Remove from the heat and prepare a roux as follows: Heat the butter in a heavy-bottomed saucepan and sauté the onion in it until it turns translucent. Add the paprika, parsley, and flour, and cook, stirring constantly, for about 3 minutes. Dilute with ½ cup of the green-bean broth, then stir in 3½ cups of the broth, adding more water if necessary. Add the beans and simmer for 10 minutes or until the beans are tender. Take the soup off the heat and let it cool. Remove the garlic. Mix 2 tablespoons of soup into the sour cream, then slowly pour that mixture into the rest of the soup. Correct the seasoning, bring back to the simmer, and serve.

✑ Kohlrabi Soup
KALARÁBÉ LEVES
(ka-la-rah-bay le-vesh)

1 pound (about 4 or 5 small pieces) kohlrabi
½ cup cooking oil
2 tablespoons flour
2 tablespoons chopped parsley
1 teaspoon salt
Freshly ground black pepper
4 cups veal or chicken stock or water or a mixture of stock and
 water
¼ cup sour cream, at room temperature

Peel the kohlrabies and cut in ½-inch dice. If a kohlrabi looks veined and woody, use only the top half. Heat the oil in a heavy-bottomed 3-quart saucepan and sauté the kohlrabi pieces until golden. Sprinkle them with flour and continue cooking until light brown. Add the parsley, salt, and pepper. Stir in the stock, bring it to the boil, and simmer, partially covered, for 45 minutes or until the kohlrabi is tender. Remove from the heat and let the soup cool. Dilute the sour cream with 2 tablespoons of soup, and then slowly pour the mixture into the soup. Bring the soup back to the simmer and serve.

✑ Lentil Soup
LENCSE LEVES
(len-che le-vesh)

1½ cups (about ¾ pound) dried lentils
1 tablespoon salt
2 leafy celery stalks
2 carrots
1 leek or medium onion
2 cloves garlic, peeled and stuck on toothpicks
3 peeled tomatoes, preferably canned
½ medium green pepper, cut in ½-inch strips
2-ounce piece of smoked bacon
3 frankfurters, sliced

Wash the lentils in cold water and pick them over, discarding any shriveled or black ones. Place them in a large, heavy-bottomed soup pot, and add 6 cups of cold water and the salt. Simmer, covered, for 45 minutes. If desired, purée all or some of the lentils at this point, or leave them whole. Add the cleaned vegetables to the pot as well as the smoked bacon. Bring back to the simmer and continue cooking for about 45 minutes or until the lentils are tender. Remove the celery, onion, garlic, and bacon from the soup and discard them; remove the carrots and leek, slice them in ½-inch pieces, and put them back in the soup. The tomatoes should have dissolved; if not, mash them with a fork. About 15 minutes before serving, bring the soup back to the simmer and add the frankfurter slices. Cook at least 10 minutes, and serve the soup.

⊷§ Mushroom Soup
GOMBA LEVES
(gohm-ba le-vesh)

½ pound fresh mushrooms
2 small onions, finely chopped
4 tablespoons lard or cooking oil
6 cups beef stock or canned beef broth and water
1 teaspoon salt
Pinch of freshly ground black pepper
2 heaping tablespoons flour
2 tablespoons chopped parsley
½ cup sour cream, at room temperature

Wash the mushrooms and slice them: there should be about 2 cups. In a heavy-bottomed 3-quart saucepan, sauté the chopped onions in 2 tablespoons of lard or oil until they wilt. Add the mushrooms and sauté them until they turn limp. Slowly pour in the stock, scraping up any pan juices. Season with salt and pepper and gently simmer for 5 minutes while preparing a roux. For the roux, heat the rest of the lard or oil in another 3-quart saucepan and sprinkle on the flour. Cook for 3 minutes, stirring constantly, then add the parsley. Pour in the hot soup, stirring all the while. Cover partially and simmer for 10 minutes. Taste the soup: if it seems flat, add more salt; if it tastes floury, let it simmer a few more minutes and taste it again. When the soup is done, set it aside to cool. Then mix 2 table-spoons of lukewarm soup into the sour cream to keep it from cur-dling and slowly pour the mixture into the soup. Bring back to the simmer and serve.

Cream of Mushroom Soup
GOMBA KRÉM LEVES
(*gohm-ba kraym le-vesh*)

To make a distinctive cream of mushroom soup, follow the recipe for mushroom soup (preceding recipe) up to the point of adding the sour cream. Then, set aside 3 or 4 mushroom slices per serving and pass the rest of the soup through a food mill. (For a smoother but less interesting texture use an electric blender.) Just before serving, mix together 1 egg yolk and ½ cup of sour cream in the bottom of a soup tureen or large bowl. Reheat the soup just to the simmer, remove it from the heat, and let it stand for about 3 minutes. Carefully blend a couple of tablespoons of soup into the egg and sour cream liaison, then slowly pour in the rest, stirring all the while. Float the mushroom slices on top of the soup and serve immediately.

✑ Sauerkraut Soup
KORHELY LEVES
(*kor-hay le-vesh*)

Hungarians swear by the restorative powers of sauerkraut soup much as the French keep the faith in *soupe à l'oignon* as a wee-hours antidote to too much champagne. Korhely is, in fact, an archaic term for drunkard. But you don't have to be tipsy to enjoy korhely leves: we had it for the first time one autumn evening after spending the day in the woods. I was looking for something to make in a hurry to warm us up and fill us up, and korhely leves (made with canned sauerkraut that time) did the trick. I would not, however, care to pass judgment on its other attributes, hangover cures being so sub-jective and culturally conditioned.

1 pound sauerkraut, canned or fresh
¼ pound bacon
1 small onion, finely chopped

¾ cup tarhonya (egg barley)
1 tablespoon flour
1 teaspoon paprika
½ pound smoked sausage
¼ cup sour cream

If fresh sauerkraut is used, cook it in its juice plus 2 cups of water for 1 hour. Canned sauerkraut may be added directly to the soup. Dice the bacon in ¼-inch pieces, and slowly fry them until they start to render fat. Add the chopped onion and sauté until it turns translucent. Add the tarhonya and, stirring constantly, cook it until it swells and turns golden brown. Sprinkle with flour and paprika, and continue to sauté for 2 to 3 minutes, stirring constantly. Add the sauerkraut and enough liquid to make a thick soup (about 6 cups). Simmer for half an hour or until the sauerkraut and tarhonya are nearly done. Slice the sausage rather thinly (about ¼ inch) and add it to the soup. Simmer for 10 minutes more, then let the soup cool somewhat. Blend about 2 tablespoons of soup into the sour cream, then slowly stir the sour-cream mixture into the soup. Taste and add more salt if needed—the soup should be very sharp and sour. Reheat if necessary and serve hot.

⋙ Cream of Savoy Cabbage Soup
KELKÁPOSZTA KRÉM LEVES
(kel-kah-poh-sta kraym le-vesh)

8 cups beef stock or canned beef broth and water
1 small head (about 1½ pounds) Savoy cabbage
2 tablespoons butter
¼ cup minced onions (1 small onion)
2 heaping tablespoons flour
Salt
Freshly ground black pepper
½ cup sour cream, at room temperature
½ cup grated Swiss cheese

Bring the stock to a boil in a large pot while cleaning and shredding the cabbage. Add the cabbage to the stock, bring it back to the simmer, and cook, uncovered, for about 12 minutes. Remove from the heat and make a roux as follows: Heat the butter in a

3-quart saucepan and sauté the onions until they are translucent. Sprinkle with flour and cook for 3 minutes, stirring constantly. Stir about 4 cups of hot soup into the roux, then pour the mixture back into the rest of the soup. Blend thoroughly and let the soup simmer for 10 more minutes. Pass it through a food mill and season it with salt and pepper. Let the soup cool. Stir some soup into the sour cream first, then slowly pour the mixture into the soup. Just before serving, reheat to the simmer and stir in the cheese. Serve immediately.

✑§ Sorrel Soup
SÓSKA LEVES
(*shohsh-ka le-vesh*)

1 pound sorrel
3 tablespoons cooking oil
1 medium onion, sliced in thin rings
4 cups veal or chicken stock or water or a mixture of stock and water
1 teaspoon sugar
2 teaspoons salt
2 tablespoons butter
2 tablespoons flour
¼ cup sour cream, at room temperature
Pirított zsemle kocka (croutons, page 25) (optional)

Clean the sorrel and cut the leaves into chiffonade (¼-inch-wide shreds). Heat the oil in a heavy-bottomed 3-quart saucepan and sauté the onion rings until they go limp. Add the sorrel and cook it, stirring constantly, until it wilts. Heat the stock to boiling, pour it on, and add the sugar and salt. Simmer, uncovered, for 30 minutes. In another saucepan, melt the butter, sprinkle with flour, and cook about 3 minutes, stirring constantly. Dilute this roux with ½ cup of sorrel broth, gradually blend it into the rest of the soup, and simmer 10 minutes longer. Remove the soup from the heat and let it cool. Mix 2 tablespoons of soup with the sour cream, then slowly pour it into the soup. Correct the seasoning and bring back to the simmer. Garnish with croutons and serve.

Garnishes for Soups and Stews

Levesbe Valók és Körítések

(LE-VESH-BE VA-LOHK AYSH KU-REE-TEH-SHEK)

Soups and stews are at the very heart of Hungarian cuisine, and to do them justice, one should always serve them with their traditional garnishes. The origins of some of the classic combinations are lost in antiquity, but, as is so often the case, it makes good sense to respect the lore of the kitchen. Cream of asparagus soup is too monotonous without the croutons; csirke paprikás without galuska is a shameful waste of sauce. And certain stews that are perfectly acceptable with mashed potatoes or rice taste infinitely better with tarhonya or puliszka. Most of these garnishes require little extra effort—croutons, for example, take less than five minutes to make—which is justified when it enhances a dish that it may have taken a lot of thought and attention to prepare.

⋙ Soft Dumplings
GALUSKA
(*gah-lūsh-kah*)

Of all the recipes in this book, I would say if you can't cook galuska, you can't cook Hungarian. Without galuska, csirke paprikás might as well be arroz con pollo. So, galuska is a must. Despite all the mumbo jumbo surrounding it, this dumpling is quite simple to master (though it may take more than one try) particularly if you use a *Spätzle* machine or a chestnut roaster. The following recipe will serve six generously; for experiments and soups, stick to one cup of flour/one egg proportions.

3 cups sifted all-purpose flour or 2½ cups granular
(instant-blending) flour
1½ teaspoons salt
3 eggs
2 tablespoons butter or oil

Mix the flour and salt together in a large mixing bowl. Make a
well, add the eggs, and beat with a wooden spoon. Add as much
cold water as necessary (about ½ cup) to hold the dough together.
Beat vigorously until the dough comes away from the sides of the
bowl and starts to blister on the surface. Let the dough rest for at
least 45 minutes. Turn it out on a wet breadboard and, using a
knife or the edge of a soup spoon, cut off irregular pieces about
½ inch long and the thickness of a pencil. Drop the pieces into a large
pot of rapidly boiling water. You can also force the dough through
a *Spätzle* machine or a chestnut roaster directly into the water.
Galuska are done seconds after they rise to the surface. Skim them
off the top of the water with a slotted spoon or drain in a colander.
Turn the galuska into a bowl, add the butter or oil, and serve.

⋐§ Pinched Noodles
CSIPETKE
(*chi-pet-ke*)

Csipetke is the missing link between the noodle and the dumpling, a bit of each but not quite either. It is the classic garnish for
gulyás, gulyás leves, and hamis gulyás leves. To avoid boiling the
soup or stew, cook the csipetke separately in water and stir it in
just before serving.

1 cup sifted all-purpose flour or 1 cup minus 2 tablespoons
granular (instant-blending) flour
½ teaspoon salt
1 egg
1 tablespoon oil

Mix the flour and salt and add the egg. Stir to make a stiff
dough, sprinkling on a few drops of cold water if necessary. Knead
until smooth. Let the dough rest for at least 30 minutes. Then flatten

[22]

it a bit at a time between your floured palms (or roll it out ⅛ inch thick on a floured board) and pinch off pieces slightly smaller than a dime. Drop them into rapidly boiling salted water and cook until tender, about 15 minutes. Drain and rinse the csipetke, and stir them directly into the stew or soup, if ready. Otherwise, turn the csipetke into a bowl, coat with oil, and set aside in a warm place until ready to use.

৵ঌ Farina Dumplings
DARA GOMBÓC
(*dah-rah gom-bohts*)

Dara gombóc should make anyone reconsider our cultural custom of leaving farina for infants and invalids. These fluffy puffs are the perfect embellishment for homemade chicken soup or bouillon. The following method was devised by Margaret Simon, formerly of Budapest, and passed on to me by her daughter-in-law Dorothy, who like myself grew up in blissful ignorance of gombóc, dara and otherwise. Unlike the other recipes I have tried, Margaret's method works well with American farina, even the so-called instant kind. For best all-around results, do not cook the dumplings directly in the soup you plan to serve: heat up a pot of stock (or canned broth diluted with water) and use that instead. The following recipe makes about 15 small dumplings.

1 egg
½ teaspoon salt
About ½ cup farina, "quick" or "instant"
3 quarts stock or canned broth and water

About 45 minutes before serving time, separate the egg, putting the white in a shallow soup dish with the salt. Beat the white with a fork until it is frothy. Quickly blend in the yolk. Slowly add the farina, stirring constantly with the fork until the batter is very thick. Use as much farina as the egg will hold. Let the dough stand until it gets hard, at least 10 minutes. Meanwhile, bring the cooking liquid to the simmer. Using a teaspoon, form almond-shaped dumplings and drop them one at a time into the broth. Do not crowd the dumplings. When the surface of the broth is covered with them, put the lid on and simmer gently for 2 minutes if "instant" farina was used, for 5 minutes if "quick" farina was used. Remove one dumpling with a slotted spoon and taste it. It should be neither gummy nor hard; if it is too moist, let the others cook an extra minute or so. Then carefully transfer them to the soup that will be served or keep them in a bit of warm broth on the back of the stove. Continue until all the batter is used up. The dumplings should be eaten as soon after cooking as possible.

⊷ Liver Dumplings
MÁJAS GOMBÓC
(mī-yahsh gom-bohts)

Liver dumplings provide a splendid enrichment to a clear meat or chicken soup. Done properly, they are quite delicate, being nothing more than a lightly spiced liver paste poached in broth. Májas gombóc can be made with any kind of liver, though calves' liver does seem too expensive and chicken livers have a rather strong flavor. Beef or pork liver might be a better choice. As with dara gombóc, it is advisable to cook the dumplings separately in stock and add them to the soup before serving. This recipe will serve six, with two to three dumplings each.

> ½ cup dry bread crumbs
> 5 tablespoons milk
> 2 tablespoons lard or cooking oil
> 1 small onion, sliced in thin rings
> ¼ pound liver, cut in ½-inch pieces
> ¼ cup flour
> 1 teaspoon chopped parsley
> ¼ teaspoon salt
> Pinch of dried marjoram
> Pinch of black pepper
> 1 egg
> 3 quarts stock or canned broth and water

About an hour before the soup is to be served, pour the bread crumbs into a small bowl, moisten them with milk, and set aside. Heat the lard or cooking oil in a small skillet and sauté the onion rings until they start to wilt. Add the pieces of liver and brown them quickly on all sides. Chop the liver and onions together, using a food chopper (medium blade), a hand chopper, or a large kitchen knife. Mix together the flour, parsley, salt, marjoram, and pepper, and blend in the chopped liver. Beat the egg until frothy and add it to the bread crumbs and milk, then stir that batter into the liver mixture. Bring the stock to a simmer. Form round dumplings with a wet teaspoon and drop them one at a time into the stock. When you have one layer of dumplings in the pot, put the lid on and simmer for 3 minutes. Taste one of the dumplings to see if it is done: it should be cooked through. If not, put the lid back on and simmer 2 more minutes. Taste again, and when the dumplings are done, carefully remove them from the broth with a slotted spoon and put them in the soup or in a small pot of warm broth. Keep making dumplings until all the liver paste is used up. Serve the soup and dumplings as soon after cooking as possible.

✌§ Croutons
PIRÍTOTT ZSEMLE KOCKA
(pi-ree-tot zhem-le kohts-kah)

There can be no doubt that fresh-made croutons raise certain soups (cream of asparagus, for one) to another power. As a garnish, they are so quick and easy to prepare that they really ought to be at every cook's fingertips. In Hungary, croutons are made from zsemle, a hard roll that resembles a good American club roll. But they can just as well be made from ordinary white bread that has been left out overnight or dried for 20 minutes in a warm oven. Allowing 3 slices of dry bread for six servings, trim off the crusts and cut the bread into ½-inch cubes. Melt ½ cup (1 stick) of butter in a skillet. As soon as it stops foaming, drop the bread cubes in and fry them quickly on all sides, being careful not to let the butter burn. Drain the cubes on paper toweling and set them aside until ready to use.

ᴇᏅ Potato Dumplings
KRUMPLIS GOMBÓC
(*krump-lish gom-bohts*)

Fear of failure kept me from making potato dumplings for many years. When I finally decided to take the plunge, I called on my Aunt Loretta, whose dumplings are legendary. Her directions started with the comment "Take nine potatoes for six people: once they taste the dumplings they want more." As for how much flour to use, she said, "Just enough, you know." In fact, the amount of flour depends on how moist the potatoes are, and there is no way to measure it exactly—it varies from one time to the other. Using bread crumbs in the dough is her innovation, and it does seem to make the dumplings a lot lighter than those made with flour alone. There is undoubtedly more to it than that, so in this recipe I have tried to be as precise as possible about the quantities and techniques to use to produce light, fluffy dumplings that, as my dear aunt said, always taste like more.

> 2 to 2½ pounds (9 medium) potatoes
> ¾ cup butter (1½ sticks), at room temperature
> Salt
> Pinch of nutmeg or pepper
> 2 eggs
> 3 cups sifted all-purpose flour (or 2 cups flour and 1 cup dry
>   bread crumbs)
> 1 cup dry bread crumbs

The night before serving, cook the potatoes in their jackets in salted water until done (when they can be pierced easily with the point of a paring knife). Drain, and as soon as potatoes are cool enough to handle, peel them and force them through a ricer. Spread the riced potatoes out on a cookie sheet and let them stand uncovered overnight, to dry them out. When you are ready to make the dumplings, transfer the riced potatoes to a large bowl (there will be about 4 to 5 cups, loosely packed). Beat in ½ cup (1 stick) of butter, 1½ teaspoons of salt, and the nutmeg or pepper. Then blend in the eggs. Using your hands, work in 2 cups of flour (or 1 cup of flour and 1 cup of bread crumbs), and as much of the other cup of flour as needed to make a dough that can be handled: it should be quite sticky but able to hold its shape. Start forming dumplings with your floured hands. Roll each dumpling in additional flour after shaping it. (You should have 18 to 20 dumplings 2 inches in diameter, 24 or more dumplings 1½ inches in diameter.) Just before serving, drop them one at a time into plenty of boiling salted water. Do not crowd them in the pot. After a minute or so, give the dumplings a jog with a wooden spoon to keep them from sticking to the bottom. Let them cook gently for 5 minutes, uncovered, after they rise to the surface. Taste one: it will be firm and not gummy in the middle when done. Do not overcook. While boiling the dumplings, quickly brown 1 cup of dry bread crumbs in ¼ cup (½ stick) of butter. As the dumplings are ready, lift them carefully out of the water with a slotted spoon, roll them in the browned bread crumbs, and keep them warm until all are done. Serve immediately.

Potato Dumplings with Croutons
ZSEMLE GOMBÓC
(zhem-le gom-bohts)

Many Hungarians cannot abide potato dumplings without croutons, and they have a point. The sweet, crunchy taste of the fried bread cubes nicely offsets the smooth, bland texture of the dumplings. Zsemle gombóc are particularly good with meat prepared like game (vadas hús and birkahús vadasan, for example). To transform krumplis gombóc into zsemle gombóc, make croutons (pirított zsemle kocka, page 25) from 3 slices of white bread, and fold them into the dough just before forming the balls; then continue with the recipe.

◦§ Egg Barley
TARHONYA
(tahr-hohn-yah)

Tarhonya is one of the few ancient foods that have survived intact: it was a staple of the nomads and it is a staple in the modern kitchen. In my mother-in-law's day, a year's supply of tarhonya was prepared each August to see the Derecskeys through the winter. Huge quantities of egg-and-flour dough were mixed, sieved, and set out to dry in the late-summer sun. Then the tarhonya was put in white cloth sacks and stored in the pantry. Nowadays that kind of industry hardly seems necessary: the packaged kind of tarhonya is good and widely available. It is known as egg barley in English, and it is distributed by several noodle manufacturers. It has all the virtues the nomadic people appreciated: it is nourishing, economical (3¢ per serving at the time of writing), compact—a one-pound box, which serves 16 persons quite amply, takes up the room of a thick paperback book—and it lasts forever. Tarhonya can be boiled in salted water, but it tastes far better when braised like pilaf rice. It is the traditional garnish for a number of stews, and is an unusual and particularly apt side dish to serve with roast beef or steak. The following recipe will serve six people.

> 1 small onion, finely chopped
> 2 tablespoons butter or cooking oil
> 1 cup packaged tarhonya
> 2 cups beef or chicken stock or water
> 1 teaspoon salt

Use a small saucepan with a tight-fitting lid, and sauté the onion in the butter or oil until transparent. Add the tarhonya and cook, stirring constantly, until all the pieces are coated with fat and start to lose their opaque look. Add the stock or water and salt, stir, and bring to the boil. Reduce the heat and cover tightly. Simmer for a total of 25 to 30 minutes, checking after 15 minutes to add more liquid if necessary. When done, the tarhonya should be neither hard nor soggy but fluffy like rice.

⋖§ Yellow Corn Meal Mush
PULISZKA
(pu-lees-kah)

Over the years, Hungarians from Transylvania have acquired a liking for mammaliga, the Rumanian national dish. It is, quite simply, yellow corn meal mush. Hungarians call it puliszka, and their enjoyment of it is something of a cultural secret vice. Among themselves, Transylvanians often eat puliszka, both as a side dish and in typically Hungarian adaptations like túrós puliszka (baked with cheese). They would probably not, however, admit to such low cravings when in mixed company with Hungarians from the plains or from Budapest, many of whom regard corn as food for pigs. But they are mistaken: puliszka is the ideal accompaniment to certain stews, notably erdélyi tokány, the Transylvanian beef stew with bacon, whose smoky flavor is enhanced by the sweet rich taste of corn. (Be sure to use coarse stone-ground yellow corn meal, which can be found in health-food shops and some grocery stores.)

1 cup stone-ground yellow corn meal
1 teaspoon salt
2 tablespoons butter

Stir corn meal into 1 cup of cold water. Bring 3 cups of water to a boil in a heavy-bottomed 2-quart saucepan, and add salt. Gradually pour corn meal mixture into boiling water, stirring constantly until it starts to bubble. Cover partially and simmer 8 to 10 minutes, stirring occasionally. Add more salt if necessary: mush tends to taste very flat if undersalted. Beat in butter and serve.

Snacks and Luncheon Dishes

Előételek és Egytálak

(E-LU-AY-TE-LEK AYSH EDGE-TAH-LAK)

Because of the primacy of soup in the Hungarian menu, appetizers are not considered as important as they are elsewhere. The snack, however, is a different story. It might be just a few slices of salami and kolbász and double-smoked bacon with a bit of bread; it might be a couple of stuffed kohlrabies (p. 171) or cabbage rolls (p. 149). For the tízórai (the midmorning break) and the ritual glass of wine that is the cement of social relationships, a bite of something good to eat is essential. Traditionally, in fact, cafés used to serve hot kis pörkölt (a small helping of pörkölt) and szalontüdő (sour lungs) on Sunday mornings when the men of the town met to pass the time between church and Sunday dinner over a glass of wine or beer or barack (apricot brandy). Some of these dishes might be elaborated upon to make a light lunch or supper, and many other favorites appear elsewhere in this book: kocsonya (jellied pork, p. 83), tojásos borjú velő (brains with eggs, p. 99), krumpli paprikás (potato stew, p. 175), and lecsó with sausages (p. 168). None are exactly convenience foods; neither are the dishes that follow. But there are times when cold cuts or hamburgers or hot dogs are no longer appreciated or appropriate, and for those moments a bit of Hungarian wizardry is a welcome gift.

⋖§ Cabbage Dumplings
KÁPOSZTÁS GOMBÓC
(kah-poh-stahsh gom-bohts)

Of all the experiments for this book, only káposztás gombóc made me feel like Madame Curie. The kitchen was like a laboratory for days, but I finally got what I was after. Here is a first-rate dish that will win a lot of acclaim, if not the Nobel prize.

1 small head (1 to 1½ pounds) cabbage
Salt
2 tablespoons butter
2 cups sifted all-purpose flour
1 egg
2 tablespoons lard or cooking oil
1 tablespoon sugar
Pinch of freshly ground black pepper
½ cup (about 2 ounces) grated Swiss cheese

Grate the cabbage, put it in a large glass bowl, sprinkle it with salt, and set it aside for about half an hour. Cut the butter into the flour, and add 1 teaspoon of salt, the egg, and enough water to make a soft dough. Roll it out about ½ inch thick on a well-floured board. Heat the lard or oil in a heavy-bottomed skillet and brown the sugar in it, then squeeze out the cabbage and add that. Cook, stirring frequently, until brown (about 25 to 30 minutes). Let it cool for 5 minutes, then spread it on the dough, grind some black pepper over it, and roll up the dough like a jelly roll, starting on the long side. With the side of your floured hand, cut the roll into 2-inch pieces and roll them into balls. Set them on a floured board. Then drop the dumplings one at a time into plenty of boiling salted water. Do not crowd the pot. Give them a jog so they do not stick to the bottom. The dumplings are done 3 to 4 minutes after they rise to the top. Taste one to be sure: it should be moist but not gummy in the middle. Remove the dumplings with a slotted spoon, roll them in grated cheese, and place them in a baking dish. When all are done, put the dish under the broiler to brown the top. Serve very hot.

NOODLE DISHES
LASKÁK
(lahsh-kahk)

No matter where they come from or where they've ended up, Hungarians of all ages love noodles. Given a good káposztás kocka or túrós metélt, a Hungarian far from home will surely kiss the cook's hand, for these are the dishes that mother used to make. They are seldom found on restaurant menus or served at dinner parties. Indeed, they seem to taste better at the kitchen table—but this may be an illusion. Here my own conversion to Hungarian cooking is complete. I find myself falling back on these dishes over and over again: for supper alone with the children, for lunch on a cold, wet day, and so on. And, I am certain, when my sons grow up, they too will kiss the cook who has the imagination to serve them túrós metélt rather than sirloin steak.

Noodles with Cabbage
KÁPOSZTÁS KOCKA
(kah-poh-stahsh kohts-kah)

1 medium (about 2 pounds) cabbage
1 teaspoon salt
1 tablespoon sugar
3 tablespoons cooking oil or lard
½ cup minced onions
Pinch of freshly ground black pepper
12 ounces egg noodles, preferably 1-inch squares (if not available, break up 1-inch-wide noodles)

Core and wash the cabbage, then shred it or grate it, using the large hole of the grater. You should have about 6 cups. Sprinkle with salt and let it stand about 30 minutes. Squeeze dry. Using a 9- or 10-inch frying pan, brown the sugar in oil or lard. Add the onions and cook until they start to wilt. Stir in the cabbage and sauté it, turning frequently, until it is tender (about 25 minutes). Season with black pepper. Scrape the cabbage, onions, and pan juices into a large bowl. Meanwhile, cook noodles according to package directions. Drain and rinse the noodles and quickly toss them with the cabbage. Serve immediately.

Noodles with Ham
SONKÁS KOCKA
(shohn-kahsh kohts-kah)

4 ounces (about 1 cup) cooked ham (leftover ham or smoked shoulder is ideal, but delicatessen boiled ham may also be used)

1 egg yolk
¾ cup sour cream
Pinch of freshly ground black pepper
12 ounces egg noodles, preferably ½-inch squares (if not
    available, use ½-inch-wide noodles)
2 tablespoons butter

Chop the cooked ham, using the coarse blade of the food
grinder. Stir in the egg yolk and the sour cream. Season to taste with
black pepper. Just before serving, cook the egg noodles according to
package directions. Drain and rinse the noodles and mix thoroughly
with the ham. Melt the butter in a 10-inch skillet, pour in the ham
and noodles, and heat through, about 3 minutes, turning all the
while. Transfer to a big bowl and serve immediately.

✎§ Noodles with Potatoes
GRÁNÁTOS KOCKA
(grah-nah-tohsh kohts-kah)

About 2 pounds (7 or 8 medium) new potatoes
3 tablespoons cooking oil
2 small onions, finely chopped
1 teaspoon paprika
1 teaspoon salt
8 ounces egg noodles, preferably 1-inch squares (or break up
    wide noodles)

Scrub the potatoes and boil them in their jackets until done.
Drain them and let them cool thoroughly (this may be done the day
before). About half an hour before serving, peel and dice the potatoes and set them aside. Heat the oil in a 10-inch heavy skillet and
sauté the onions until transparent. Stir in the paprika and salt. Add
the potatoes, and cook until golden brown, turning often. Prepare
noodles according to package directions. Scrape the potatoes, onions,
and fat into a large serving bowl. Add the cooked, drained noodles,
toss, and serve.

✑ Noodles with Pot Cheese
TÚRÓS METÉLT
(tŭ-rohsh me-taylt)

12 ounces egg noodles, preferably in 1-inch squares (or break
up wide noodles)
¼ pound smoked slab bacon, cut in ¼-inch cubes, or about
½ cup diced thick-sliced breakfast bacon
1 cup sour cream, at room temperature
3 tablespoons buttermilk
8 ounces pot cheese or creamed small-curd cottage cheese, at
room temperature
Pinch of freshly ground black pepper
2 tablespoons chopped fresh dill (optional)

Cook the noodles according to package directions. Meanwhile
fry the bacon until tender. Scrape the bacon and the fat from the
pan into a large serving bowl. Add the hot noodles and mix thoroughly. Thin the sour cream with the buttermilk and fold it into the
noodles, turning until all the noodles are coated. Gradually mix in
the cheese until it breaks up into small lumps. Season with black
pepper, sprinkle with dill, and serve immediately.

✑ Palacsinta
PALACSINTÁK
(pah-lah-chin-tahk)

Stuffed baked palacsinta, a tossed green salad, and a bottle of
wine—can there be a more elegant lunch? Once you have the knack
of making the palacsinta, a thin pancake, it is even easy on the cook.
They can be made the night before, stuffed in the morning, and
put into the oven while the guests are having drinks. Out of a vast
range of fillings, I would recommend four that are both delicious
and typically Hungarian: pot cheese, brains, pörkölt, and ham. The
palacsinta should be stuffed and rolled with the cheese and brain
fillings, and layered with the ham. The pörkölt filling can be used
either way.

The following recipe will make at least 20 palacsinta 6½ inches in diameter. The batter will keep for three days in the refrigerator; after that it is likely to sour. Always shake it or stir well before using it, and add the soda water at the last minute. Taste the first palacsinta: if it is too thick, add more soda water to the batter; it may also need a pinch more salt. The second palacsinta will also have to be discarded, since it will get soggy lying on the bottom of the pile. It is best to make palacsinta in a special palacsinta or French crêpe pan, which is easy to handle because it is the right size and shape. Once you have the pan, just wipe it clean with paper towels after making palacsinta and do not use it for anything else. Cooking palacsinta one at a time can be rather tedious and time-consuming at first, but it has to be done that way. Once you have the knack, though, it goes fast, and eventually you should be able to work with two pans simultaneously.

Palacsinta Batter
PALACSINTA TÉSZTA
  (*pah-lah-chin-ta tay-sta*)

3 cups sifted all-purpose flour
1½ teaspoons salt
6 eggs
1½ cups milk
6 tablespoons melted butter
About 1½ cups soda water
3 tablespoons cooking oil

Mix the flour and salt together in a big bowl. Work in the eggs, one at a time, then very gradually add the milk, beating well as you go along. Beat in the melted butter and strain the batter to remove any large lumps. Cover and refrigerate for at least 2 hours or overnight. Just before using, shake or stir the batter and pour in as much soda water as needed to make a thin batter, the consistency of light cream. Make each palacsinta separately: heat a 6½-inch crêpe pan or a small frying pan with sloping sides until very hot, then brush with cooking oil. When it starts to smoke, remove from the heat and pour 2 to 3 tablespoons of batter into the pan (work with a ladle the right size, if possible). Quickly turn the pan around so the batter flows to the sides, thinly coating the entire bottom. A palacsinta is supposed to be very thin, as thin as it can be without getting lacy. Pour any excess batter back into the bowl. Put the pan back on the heat for about a minute, then give it a couple of good jerks to loosen the palacsinta, then flip it if you can or turn it over by hand, using a spatula to lift it up out of the pan first. Cook briefly on the second side and slide it into a warm dish or pie plate. Continue making palacsinta until you have at least three per person. Keep the palacsinta warm on the back of the stove or in the warming oven, or make them several hours in advance and warm them up later.

The palacsinta batter may also be made in a blender: put the milk, eggs, salt, flour and melted butter in the jar, in that order. Blend at top speed for about 1 minute, then scrape down the sides of the jar and blend another few seconds. Cover and refrigerate for 2 hours or overnight; just before making the palacsinta, shake or stir the batter and add the soda water.

Pot Cheese Filling for Palacsinta
TÚRÓS TÖLTELÉK
(tū-rohsh tul-te-layk)

1 pound pot cheese
3 eggs
½ teaspoon salt
2 tablespoons chopped fresh dill
¾ cup sour cream
3 tablespoons buttermilk

Lightly butter several shallow oblong or oval baking dishes (as many as you need to hold all the palacsinta rolls in one layer). Strain the cheese and force it through a ricer. Beat it well with the eggs and salt, and stir in the chopped dill. Spread some of the filling on each palacsinta (page 37) and roll it up and place it in a baking dish. Thin the sour cream with the buttermilk and spread it on the palacsinta rolls. A half-hour before serving, place the baking dishes in a preheated 325° oven and bake for 20 minutes. Serve immediately.

Brains Filling for Palacsinta
VELŐS TÖLTELÉK
(*ve-lush tul-te-layk*)

Calves' brains make an excellent filling for palacsinta. Prepare them as for tojásos borjú velő (page 99), let the filling cool, and spread some of it on each palacsinta (page 37). Roll it up and place it in a lightly greased oblong or oval baking dish. About 20 minutes before serving, place in a preheated 350° oven and bake for 15 minutes. Serve immediately.

Meat Filling for Palacsinta
HÚSOS TÖLTELÉK
(*hū-shohsh tul-te-layk*)

For a spicy meat filling, make a borjú or sertés pörkölt with 1 pound of veal (page 90) or lean pork (page 72), or use leftover pörkölt. Take the meat out of the sauce and chop it in a meat grinder. Stir 1 cup of sour cream into the meat and as much sauce as needed to make a thick mush. Spread each palacsinta (page 37) with filling, roll it up, and place it in a lightly greased baking dish. Or, make a rakott palacsinta: lightly grease a round baking dish about 9 inches in diameter with high sides, and place a palacsinta in the bottom. Spread it with meat filling, cover with another palacsinta, and continue alternating filling and palacsinta until you reach the top. End with a palacsinta and cover it with a bit of sauce. In either case, about half an hour before serving, place the dish in a preheated 350° oven and cook for 20 to 25 minutes. Reheat the remaining pörkölt sauce. Cut the rakott palacsinta into wedges like a cake. Spoon some sauce over each serving.

Layered Palacsinta with Ham
SONKÁS RAKOTT PALACSINTA
(*shohn-kahsh rah-kot pah-lah-chin-ta*)

½ pound (about 2 cups) cooked ham
2 cups sour cream
½ cup buttermilk
2 eggs

Freshly ground black pepper
Butter

Chop the ham in a food grinder and thin the sour cream with the buttermilk. Beat the eggs and 1 cup of the sour cream into the ham and season to taste with black pepper. Lightly grease a 9-inch round baking dish with high sides and place a palacsinta (page 37) in the bottom. Spread some ham filling on it and cover with another palacsinta. Continue making layers of ham and palacsinta until you reach the top, ending with a palacsinta. Dot it with butter and set aside until ready to bake. About 40 minutes before serving, pour on the rest of the sour cream and place in a preheated 350° oven to bake for 30 minutes. Serve immediately, cut in wedges like a cake.

Fish
Hal

(HAL)

*H*ungary is a landlocked country, but fresh fish from its lakes and streams is served everywhere. Of these, the most famous is fogas, a delicately flavored pike-perch from Lake Balaton in the western part of the country, the only place in the world where it lives. When our oldest son was just a year old, we took him to Budapest to show him off to his grandparents. We stayed at the Szabadság, a downtown hotel, and it was not easy to feed him until we thought of fish. So every day we would call room service and order a fogas for him and me to share: it came with fried potatoes and several side dishes of cold fresh vegetables (pickled beets, cole slaw, that sort of thing). I felt virtuous for having one healthy, low-cholesterol meal a day; he feasted like the crown prince.

As any fish lover knows, there are basically five ways to cook fish. It can be poached, grilled, sautéed, baked whole or in fillets, and it can be made into soup. Hungarians use all methods, and it is possible to build a Hungarian meal around fish by starting with a good soup, adding a salad, and serving a Hungarian dessert. There are excellent white wines from the Balaton region that are perfect with any kind of fish–Badacsonyi Kéknyelű and Badacsonyi Szürke Barát—as is the lovely and dry Leányka.

Directions for poaching, grilling, and sautéing fish follow. In addition, I have picked three uniquely Hungarian recipes for baked fish fillets in sauce. And anyone who likes fish soup must try halászlé: it tastes best on the banks of the Tisza, but a creditable imitation can be made with fresh carp.

To poach fish, simmer it for about 10 minutes in fish stock or salted water to which a small sliced onion and a couple of parsley stems have been added.

To grill fish, brush it with a mixture of cooking oil, pepper, salt, and paprika and broil it an inch from the flame for about 5 to 7 minutes on each side or until it turns a golden brown.

To sauté fish, salt and pepper it and dip it in flour to which ½ teaspoon of paprika has been added. Brown it in hot oil or butter and oil, cooking it 4 to 5 minutes on each side.

Baked fish fillet dishes can be made with any fresh-water fish. A good choice, if there is a fishmonger in the vicinity, would be yellow pike. It approximates the flavor of European sweet-water fish, and it is not prohibitively expensive. Nowadays, when buying fish, one is pretty much at the mercy of the person who is selling it, so it is important first of all to find a reliable fish store, then to have some idea of how a really fresh whole fish should look. The outward signs of freshness are a clear eye, shiny skin, and firm flesh. Always buy whole fish when possible, allowing one pound of fish per person (or ½ pound of fillets per person). If the recipe calls for fillets, have the fish filleted and be sure to take the head, tails, and bones home for stock.

To make a stock, wash the bones, heads, and tails and place them in a large enameled or stainless steel pot. Add one small onion, thinly sliced, 4 or 5 parsley stems, a teaspoon of salt, and enough water to cover. Simmer, uncovered, for at least 30 minutes. Strain before using.

◄§ Fish Fillets in Green Pepper and Tomato Sauce
BADACSONYI FOGAS
(*bah-da-chohn-yee foh-gahsh*)

6 pounds whole fresh-water fish
½ cup white wine (optional)
4 tablespoons cooking oil
4 medium tomatoes, canned or fresh (about 1 pound of fresh
   tomatoes)
1 medium green pepper
1 small onion, finely chopped
1 tablespoon chopped parsley

2 tablespoons flour
1 teaspoon paprika
Boiled potatoes

Have the fish cleaned and filleted, and make a stock (page 46) with the fish heads, tails, and bones, adding ½ cup of white wine, if desired. Wash and dry the fish fillets, salt them, and place them in an oiled baking dish. If the tomatoes are fresh, scald them to peel them (canned tomatoes are already peeled). Quarter and seed them and set them aside (you should have about 1½ cups). Core and seed the green pepper and cut it into ½-inch strips. Heat the rest of the oil and sauté the chopped onion until it starts to wilt. Add the parsley, tomatoes, and green peppers, sauté for 2 to 3 minutes, then sprinkle with flour. Cook another 2 or 3 minutes until the flour starts to brown. Stir in the paprika. Pour in 2½ cups of strained fish stock, blend thoroughly, and let simmer for 10 minutes. Dilute with more fish stock if necessary, correct the seasoning, and pour over the fish fillets. Cover with a piece of aluminum foil, place in a preheated 350° oven, and bake 10 minutes. Serve hot with plain boiled potatoes.

⊷§ Fish Fillets in Paprika and Sour Cream Sauce
PONTY PAPRIKÁS
   (pont-y pah-pree-kahsh)

6 pounds whole fresh-water fish
Salt
3 tablespoons cooking oil
1 small onion, finely chopped
1 teaspoon paprika
½ cup sour cream, at room temperature
Galuska (dumplings, page 21)

Have the fish cleaned and filleted, and make a stock (page 46) with the fish heads, tails, and bones. Wash and dry the fillets, salt them lightly, and place them in a lightly oiled baking dish. Sauté the chopped onion in the rest of the oil. Stir in 1 teaspoon paprika and 1 cup of fish stock. Simmer for 10 minutes, then take the pan off the heat and let it cool to lukewarm. Blend some of the paprika sauce into the sour cream, then slowly pour that mixture back into the sauce. Taste for seasoning and consistency: if necessary, dilute the sauce with more fish stock or water. Pour the sour-cream sauce over the fillets, cover with a lid or piece of aluminum foil, and bake for 20 minutes in a 300° oven. Serve with galuska.

✑ Fish Fillets with Mushrooms in Sour Cream Sauce

BETYÁR FOGAS
(*bet-yahr foh-gahsh*)

6 pounds of whole yellow pike or other fresh-water fish
Salt
3 tablespoons butter
½ pound mushrooms
2 tablespoons cooking oil
1 small onion, finely chopped
1 teaspoon paprika
½ cup sour cream, at room temperature
Boiled potatoes or rice

Have the fish cleaned and filleted, and make a stock (page 46) with the fish heads, tails, and bones. Wash and dry the fillets, salt them lightly, and place them in a buttered baking dish. Clean the mushrooms and slice them ¼ inch thick. Heat the rest of the butter with the oil, and sauté the chopped onion until the pieces turn transparent. Add the mushrooms and sauté until golden brown. Sprinkle with paprika. Stir in 1 cup of fish stock and simmer for 10 minutes. Take the pan off the heat and let it cool to lukewarm. Pour some fish sauce into the sour cream, mix thoroughly, then slowly pour the mixture back into the sauce. Taste for seasoning and consistency: if the sauce is too thick, dilute it with fish stock. Pour the sour-cream sauce over the fish fillets, cover the dish with a lid or piece of aluminum foil, and bake in a 300° oven for 20 minutes. Serve with plain boiled potatoes or with white rice.

✌ Fisherman's Soup
HALÁSZLÉ
(ha-lahs-lay)

I had my first halászlé in a restaurant garden just a stone's throw from the River Tisza. I can still see that soup and taste it in my mouth: delicate pieces of fish swimming in a rich, sharp paprika sauce. It was served only with bread, and we ordered a bottle of white wine, which we drank with great pleasure. I have tried many times since then to duplicate that halászlé. I knew that it ought to be made with at least three different kinds of fish, one for strength, one for flavor, and one for delicacy, but it was impossible to find the right combination. For one thing, the same kinds of fish are not to be had in the United States, and what is available has not been freshly caught. The Hungarian cooks I consulted advised me to use carp instead, a fish whose bones make an excellent soup and whose meat is firm but subtle in taste. They were right. For homemade halászlé, you will need a carp about 6 pounds in size. Ask the fishman to bone it and cut it into chunks, and be sure he gives you the head and bones to use for stock. Buy some additional roe if you like it.

> **1 fresh carp, about 6 pounds, boned and cut in chunks**
> **Salt**
> **1 medium purple (Bermuda) onion, thinly sliced**
> **Carp head and bones**
> **1 tablespoon paprika**
> **1 medium green pepper, cut in ¼-inch rings**
> **1 small hot pepper (if unavailable, use Tabasco sauce)**
> **3 small peeled tomatoes, cored and quartered**
> **Carp roe or milt (optional)**

Put the pieces of fish in a large pot and salt them. Set it aside. Spread the onion slices in the bottom of a saucepan large enough to hold the head and bones comfortably. Place them on top of the onion slices and pour on enough water to cover. Sprinkle with paprika and slowly bring to the simmer. Cover partially and simmer for 30 to 40 minutes. Strain the broth into the pot containing the fish chunks, and add the green pepper rings, the hot pepper (or

Tabasco to taste), and the tomatoes. Simmer, uncovered, for 15 minutes. Shake the pot gently from time to time, but do not stir the soup. Test a piece of fish: if it flakes easily when poked with a fork, it is done. If not, cook another 5 minutes. When it is done, take the pot off the heat and let it stand at least 5 minutes to settle the soup. If roe or milt is to be added, put it in the pot after the fish has cooked for 10 minutes.

Poultry

Szárnyas

(SAHRN-YAHSH)

CHICKEN
CSIRKE
(*cheer-ke*)

An east European friend of mine married to an American tells the following story. Soon after she came to this country, she invited her in-laws to dinner. Naturally, she prepared the ultimate meal, focused on a magnificent roast chicken. No one uttered a word of praise, because chicken was too ordinary for them. After they left, she sat in the kitchen and wept. It took a while for her to figure it out, but now she knows: when she wants to impress her guests, she serves a peasant stew—that they do appreciate. Indeed, chicken is still a special-occasion dish in eastern Europe. In the West, however, factory farms and fast freezing techniques have made chicken both cheap and plentiful, and everyone seems to be looking for new ways to prepare it. The Hungarians have a deft hand with chicken dishes: the sauce may be rich and well seasoned, but the delicacy of the meat is never overpowered. When you make these dishes, avoid frozen chicken. Always use fresh-killed chicken, the 2½- to 3-pound size for fricassees and breaded chicken and the 5- to 6-pound size for roast chicken.

✑ Chicken Paprikash
CSIRKE PAPRIKÁS
(*cheer-ke pah-pree-kahsh*)

The perfect chicken paprikash can be very elusive indeed. I speak from experience. My own search lasted many years as the best Hungarian cooks the world over told me the *only* way to make it—

no two methods ever the same, of course. My quest ended finally in Gundel's restaurant at the zoo in Budapest. There before me lay the ultimate Hungarian chicken dish, pieces of golden chicken in a rose-colored sauce, delicately spiced and thickened with just the right amount of sour cream. A bowl of galuska, also just right, and a generous helping of cucumber salad, the cucumber sliced paper thin, came with it. Here was an achievement worth duplicating!

When it comes to csirke paprikás, I definitely favor spreading the wealth: everyone should know how to make this fabulous dish. It can be the focal point of any kind of meal, from the familial to the very festive, and you will never tire of it. Csirke paprikás must be accompanied by galuska and cucumber salad (page 193). It should be served with just a simple appetizer or clear soup before and a light dessert after the main course. A dry white wine goes best; a Badacsonyi Kéknyelű will make the meal an occasion.

> 2 small (2½-pound) chickens, each cut in 8 pieces
> Salt
> About ¼ cup chicken fat or cooking oil
> 1 large onion, chopped fine
> 2 teaspoons paprika
> 1 medium green pepper, cored and cut in ½-inch strips
> 3 small peeled tomatoes, preferably canned
> ½ cup sour cream, at room temperature
> Galuska (dumplings, page 21)

Wash and dry the chicken pieces. Save the livers for another dish, but make a stock with the backs, necks, wing tips, gizzards, and hearts. (Place them, plus ½ teaspoon of salt, in a small saucepan and cover with cold water. Gently bring to a simmer, partially covered, and cook slowly for 1 hour.) Heat the chicken fat or oil in a heavy-bottomed frying pan and sauté the onion until the pieces turn translucent. Add the chicken pieces, a few at a time, and sauté briefly until yellow on all sides. Do not brown the chicken or cook it long enough for the surface to get hard. As the pieces are done, put them in a side dish and keep them warm. When all are done, pour ½ cup of chicken stock into the frying pan, scrape up any bits sticking to pan, and stir in 1 teaspoon of salt and the paprika. Arrange the chicken pieces in a deep, heavy-bottomed pot large enough to hold them all: place the breasts and thighs on the bottom, the legs and wings on top. Pour on the sauce from the frying pan and as much chicken stock as necessary to bring the cooking liquid to the halfway mark. Lay the green pepper strips and tomatoes on top of the chicken, cover, and simmer 15 minutes. Rearrange the pieces of chicken, put the cover back on, and simmer another 15 minutes, or until the chicken is cooked through. (It is done when the breast can be pierced easily with a table fork.) Remove from the heat and let cool. Skim off most—but not all—of the grease. Mix 2 tablespoons of chicken sauce into the sour cream and very slowly pour the mixture back into the sauce. Taste for seasoning. Just before serving, bring the csirke paprikás back to the simmer and cook on very low heat for 2 or 3 minutes. To serve csirke paprikás, give each person a piece of chicken, dark or light meat, with a generous helping of galuska, and spoon a bit of sauce over both. Pass the rest of the sauce.

✌§ Chicken Fricassee with Mushrooms
CSODA CSIRKE
(*choh-duh cheer-ke*)

The literal translation of csoda csirke is "miracle chicken," and this is, in fact, a marvelous fricassee. But though it is very rich and savory, it is not overwhelming. My own idea of an elegant meal starts with a clear soup, then the csoda csirke with white rice, followed by a salad of Boston or Bibb lettuce, and fresh strawberries or melon for dessert. A white Badacsonyi Szürke Barát would be an excellent wine to accompany the meal.

2 small (about 2½-pound) chickens, each cut in 8 serving pieces
Salt
12 tablespoons (1½ sticks) butter
2 tablespoons cooking oil
Pepper
Sifted or granular (instant-blending) flour in a shaker
2 tablespoons minced shallots or scallions, or 1 small onion,
    finely chopped
½ pound mushrooms, sliced
1½ tablespoons chopped parsley

About ½ cup sour cream, at room temperature
White cooked rice

Wash and dry the chicken pieces. Save the liver, but make a stock with the necks, backs, wing tips, hearts, and gizzards. (Put them in a small saucepan, add 1 teaspoon salt, cover with cold water, and gently simmer for an hour. Strain and set aside.) Heat ½ cup (1 stick) of butter plus 2 tablespoons of cooking oil in a large, heavy-bottomed skillet. Sauté the pieces of chicken, a few at a time without crowding, until they turn yellow on all sides. Put all the pieces back in the pan, cover, and cook at very low heat for 10 minutes, turning once. Sprinkle with salt, pepper, and flour, roll each piece in the pan fat, cover, and cook 5 minutes, turning once (the flour will start to brown). Remove the chicken to a side dish. Pour ½ cup of stock into the pan and scrape up any bits stuck to the bottom. Arrange the chicken in a large, heavy-bottomed casserole, breasts and thighs on the bottom, legs and wings on top. Pour on 1½ cups of chicken stock, cover, and simmer 25 to 30 minutes or until done. (The chicken is done when a breast can be pierced easily with a table fork.) Meanwhile, sauté the shallots or onions in the remaining 4 tablespoons of butter until they wilt. Add the mushrooms and brown them lightly. Stir in the parsley and cook 1 minute. After the chicken has been simmering about 15 minutes, scrape the mushrooms, with all the onions, parsley, pan fat, and juices, into the fricassee. When the chicken is done, remove the pot from the heat and let it cool. Skim off most of the grease. Stir 2 tablespoons of sauce into ½ cup sour cream, then slowly pour it back into the sauce. Taste the sauce: it may need more salt and, if the chicken was especially juicy, more sour cream. Just before serving, reheat and simmer for 2 or 3 minutes. Transfer the chicken and sauce to a big bowl—or serve directly from the cooking pot. Give each person a helping of rice and a piece of chicken, and spoon some sauce over both.

❧ Chicken Fricassee with Bacon
HAJDUSÁGI CSIRKE TOKÁNY
(hĭ-dū-shah-gi cheer-ke to-kahny)

With lots of pepper and smoked bacon to give it zest, hajdusági csirke tokány can hardly be called a subtle dish. Its sauce is rich and spicy and needs mashed potatoes or rice to set it off. A tossed green salad is absolutely essential. For a sweet touch in dessert, serve madártej (floating island, page 201). One of the less dry wines, like a Badacsonyi Szürke Barát, would do the meal justice.

> **2 small (2½ pounds) chickens, each cut in 8 pieces**
> **Salt**
> **¼ pound smoked bacon, cut in ¼-inch dice (slab bacon is preferable, but thick-sliced breakfast bacon may be used instead)**
> **About 2 tablespoons bacon fat or cooking oil**
> **1 large onion, finely chopped**
> **1½ teaspoons freshly ground black pepper**
> **½ teaspoon thyme**
> **1 clove garlic, peeled and stuck on a toothpick**
> **2 small peeled tomatoes, preferably canned**
> **½ cup dry white wine**

Wash and dry the chicken pieces. Save the livers for another time, and make a stock with the necks, backs, wing tips, hearts, and gizzards. (Put them in a small saucepan, cover with cold water, and add ½ teaspoon salt. Gently simmer, partially covered, for about an hour. Strain and set aside.) In a large, heavy-bottomed skillet, fry the bacon until it starts to render fat. Add 2 additional tablespoons of bacon fat or oil, and sauté the chopped onion until it turns translucent. Push the onion and bacon to one side or transfer them to a side dish, and sauté the chicken pieces in the same pan, adding more fat or oil if necessary. The chicken should not be browned or allowed to harden: cook the pieces just long enough to turn yellow. As they are done, remove them to a side dish and sprinkle them with salt, pepper, and thyme. When all have been cooked, arrange them in a large, heavy-bottomed pot, breasts and thighs on the bottom, smaller pieces on top. Pour ½ cup of chicken stock into the skillet, scraping up any bits, then pour it over the chicken. Add the garlic and the tomatoes. Cover and simmer 10 minutes, then rearrange the pieces. Mix the wine into an additional ½ cup of stock and pour it over the chicken. Cover and simmer 20 minutes, or until done. (The chicken is done when a breast can be pierced easily with a table fork.) Put the chicken in a serving dish, discard the garlic, and let the sauce settle. Skim off most of the grease and taste for seasoning. The sauce should be rather thick: if it is not, reduce it by boiling rapidly for 2 or 3 minutes. Pour the sauce over the chicken and serve.

✑§ Breaded Chicken
RÁNTOTT CSIRKE
(*rahn-tot cheer-ke*)

There is, of course, nothing uniquely Hungarian about rántott csirke: one would be hard put indeed to say what sets it apart from Wiener Backhendl or, for that matter, American Southern fried chicken. Be that as it may, it is a basic dish in Hungarian cuisine, since it can be a keystone of a meal with any kind of soup or vegetable. And it can be chic or just as easily go to a picnic. Within a couple of months some years ago, we were served rántott csirke at a candlelit diplomatic dinner party in Bonn, the most protocol-conscious capital in the world, and in an open-air restaurant on Lake Balaton in Hungary. At home we like it best at room temperature, served informally with a salad or a creamed vegetable. A bowl of soup to start with, a piece of cake or rétes to end with, and a chilled bottle of Debrői Hárslevelű, a fruity Hungarian white wine, to sip along the way—such are the good things of life.

2 small (about 2½ pounds) chickens, each cut in 8 pieces
3 eggs
2 cups dry bread crumbs
Salt
Pepper
Sifted or granular (instant-blending) flour in a shaker
1 cup cooking oil

Wash and dry the chicken pieces. Save the wing tips, necks, backs, hearts, and gizzards for stock. Spread out the other pieces, including the livers, on a plate or sheet of waxed paper. In a flat soup bowl, beat the eggs with a fork. Put out a second plate or sheet of waxed paper, this one with a layer of bread crumbs on it. Sprinkle the chicken pieces all over with salt, pepper, and flour. Shake off any excess, and dip each piece in the beaten eggs, coating the entire surface. Lift it up to let the extra egg drip off. Dredge each piece with bread crumbs. (Breaded chicken parts may be refrigerated until ready to cook.) Using a large, heavy-bottomed frying pan, or two small pans, sauté the chicken parts in hot oil until golden brown on both sides. When all the pieces are browned, arrange them in the frying pan with the breasts and thighs in the middle, wings and legs around them. The oil should be ½ inch deep: add more if necessary. Cover, reduce the heat, and cook 20 minutes, turning the pieces once. Take the cover off and cook 5 minutes to crisp the breading. Drain on paper towels and serve warm or cool.

◁§ Roast Chicken
SÜLT CSIRKE
(shült cheer-ke)

Despite all people's efforts to claim it, roast chicken is and always will be ethnically neutral. Cooked according to this method, which is favored by many Hungarian cooks, it comes out moist and tender with a faint smoky taste—unlike anything you might have in France or Germany or the United States. To compose a Hungarian meal around it, choose a meat or vegetable soup, a vegetable side dish, mashed potatoes, and salad. A good dessert might be palacsinta with nuts (page 207). Roast chicken is greatly enhanced by wine: we prefer a light red wine, like a Szekszárdi Vörös, unorthodox perhaps but quite suitable. Among the white wines, we would choose a somewhat fruity but not sweet wine, like a Hungarian Debrői Hárslevelű.

1 roasting chicken, about 5 pounds
Salt
½ teaspoon marjoram
2 tablespoons butter
2 shallots, or 3 scallions, or 1 small onion
Thick slices of fat bacon
1 tablespoon cooking oil

Wash the chicken inside and out and dry thoroughly. Save the liver for another dish, and make a stock with the neck, heart, and gizzard. (Put them in a small saucepan, add ½ teaspoon of salt, and cover with cold water. Simmer, partially covered, for about an hour. Strain and set aside.) Preheat the oven to 400°. Rub the cavity and skin of the chicken with liberal amounts of salt. Put the marjoram, butter, and peeled shallots or onion in the cavity. Wrap the chicken in bacon, being sure to cover the breastbone and joints, and truss. Place side down in a lightly oiled roasting pan and put it on the middle rack of the oven. Reduce the heat immediately to 350°. After 25 minutes, turn the chicken over to the other side. Roast on that side for another 25 minutes, then turn the chicken breast up. Put it back in the oven for 20 minutes, then remove the bacon (since the bacon will shrink, it should not be necessary to cut the strings; if it sticks, use kitchen shears to cut the bacon away). Continue roasting for 20 minutes, basting once or twice, or until the skin is browned and the chicken is done (i.e., a drumstick moves easily in its socket). Place the chicken on a platter, remove the trussing strings, and let it stand at room temperature for 15 minutes while making the sauce. To make a European pan gravy—without flour—pour off most of the fat in the roasting pan, leaving what looks like 2 or 3 table-spoonfuls. Place the pan on a stove burner, pour 1 cup of hot chicken stock into the pan, and rapidly scrape up the browned roasting juices. Taste for seasoning, and simmer 10 minutes, stirring often. Taste again, then pour into a sauceboat. Carve the chicken, in the kitchen or at the table, and serve immediately.

DUCK
KACSA
(kah-chah)

For many people, duck—or rather duckling—is still strictly a restaurant dish, even though there is no longer any reason not to serve it at home. Fresh-killed ducklings are often available on order from the butcher, and the frozen ones are quite good. If you buy a frozen duckling, be sure to check that there are no bruises or visible lumps of ice. Contrary to many experts, I have found that a large duckling (5 to 6 pounds) is not enough for six hearty eaters; it serves four quite generously, however. For more than four at table, cook two or more ducks at the same time. If there is any left over, slice it and serve it cold with a fresh lettuce salad for a very good lunch.

✌§ Roast Duck
KACSA PECSENYE
(*kah-chah pe-chen-ye*)

This has been one of our favorite company dinners for many years: people who snub their noses at chicken turn misty-eyed when they see a roast duck, and it is virtually foolproof. Once the novelty of a fruited bird (e.g., *caneton à l'orange*) wore off, I began to appreciate the east European combination of red cabbage or sauerkraut with duck. Mashed potatoes or potato dumplings round out the meal very nicely indeed. To complement this groaning board, pick a dry red table wine, a Hungarian Szekszárdi Vörös, if possible. Boszorkányhab (page 200) would offer the gentle touch I crave for in a dessert after such a filling meal.

2 fresh ducklings (if not available, use frozen ducklings)
Salt
Pinch of black pepper
½ teaspoon dried marjoram
3 small onions
1 leafy stalk of celery
Cooking oil

As soon as you get the fresh ducks home (or thaw the frozen ones), wash them thoroughly inside and out and generously salt the cavities, rubbing the salt in with your hand, and sprinkle the insides with pepper and marjoram. Put a peeled onion in each cavity, skewer it shut, and truss the ducks. If you do not intend to use the duck immediately, wrap it loosely in waxed paper and keep it in the refrigerator. Fresh duck will keep like that for at least 2 days, a frozen duck a little less. Use the wing tips, gizzard bits, and necks to make a simple stock: put them in a small saucepan, add ½ teaspoon of salt, a peeled onion and stalk of celery, and simmer, partly covered, for 1 hour. Strain and set aside. Just before roasting, preheat the oven to 400°. Grease the roasting pan with oil and put the ducks in, breast up. Prick the thighs and lower part of the bodies with a cooking fork. Put the ducks in the oven and roast for 15 minutes. Take them out and turn them on the side. Replace them in the oven, turn the heat down to 350°, and roast for 20 to 30 minutes, depend-

[61]

ing on the size. Turn ducks over and roast on the other side for 20 to 30 minutes. Then turn the ducks breast up and roast for 15 minutes or until done. (Duck is done when the legs are loose in their sockets and the juices run yellow.) Place the ducks on a platter, cut away the trussing strings, and keep the ducks in a warm place while making a pan gravy. To make the sauce, pour off most of the fat in the roasting pan, leaving about 2 tablespoonfuls. Heat it on top of the stove, and pour in about 1½ to 2 cups of hot duck stock. Quickly scrape up the pan juices and simmer, stirring now and then, for about 20 minutes. Taste for seasoning and set aside. Reheat just before serving.

GOOSE
LIBA
(lee-ba)

My earliest memory of goose goes back to a scene in a Balzac novel that I read in my teens; indeed, I never saw a live goose until I traveled in the backwoods of Europe as a grown woman. My husband, by contrast, recalls helping the girls force-feed the geese when he was growing up in Transylvania. Remembrance of things past and more, for therein lies the secret of cooking goose. First of all, American geese are not fatted, and that means the liver is healthy and, often enough, quite unpalatable. And since goose is a luxury item, I feel I should cook it whole for special occasions as do the Czechs and Austrians, and sometimes the French, but seldom the Hungarians. In my husband's childhood, the goose was never roasted whole: the meat was cooked with beans or sauerkraut; the neck, gizzard, and heart were used in a risotto; and the skin of the breast was cut up for cracklings. All the fat, because of its unique qualities as a cooking medium, was saved; it would not be exaggerating to say it was cherished. The liver—sometimes nine inches across—was the ultimate delicacy, cooked and served cold in very thin slices. (As a matter of fact, Hungary is one of the world's largest producers of foie gras and became in recent years a major supplier of the French pâté industry.) While pretending to favor the pursuit of pleasure at any cost, in my heart I find it scandalous to cut up a goose at today's prices; on the other hand, it may be worth having a crazy goose feast just so everyone can have a go at the cracklings before he dies. Besides, the rest of the goose can be used for three exotic dishes that few of us would otherwise try: sólet, liba aprólékos rizottó, and káposztás liba. That makes four meals for six persons, and all are magnificent.

✑ Roast Goose
LIBA PECSENYE
(*lee-ba pe-chen-ye*)

Dressed goose runs about 8 to 13 pounds in weight and, in theory, serves six to twelve people, according to size. But the bird has such a large, bony carcass (like duck) that the helpings turn out to be rather skimpy. In my experience, eight hearty eaters is about as far as you can stretch a roast goose, even with stuffing. Force-fed or not, goose is extremely fatty and should, therefore, be served with something sour like braised sauerkraut or red cabbage and something bland like potato dumplings or mashed potatoes. Either a dry red wine like a Hungarian Szekszárdi Vörös or a dry white wine (a Leányka, for example) would be appropriate to drink. For dessert, I know what our Hungarian friends would like best— a gesztenye püré (chestnut purée, page 202). If that sounds a bit heavy for the meal, make an apple boszorkányhab (page 200).

1 dressed goose, 8 to 13 pounds
Salt
1 onion
1 leafy stalk of celery
1 carrot
2 or 3 sprigs of parsley

To prepare a goose for roasting, wash it thoroughly inside and out as soon as you thaw it or as soon as you get it home if you have been able to buy a fresh one. Pull out all the loose fat from the inside, wash it, and set it aside to render later. Cut off the wing tips and put them aside with the neck, gizzard, and heart for stock. Salt the inside of the cavity very generously, rubbing the salt in with your hand. Close the vent with a trussing pin or sew it up and truss the bird. Wrap it loosely in waxed paper and put it in the refrigerator until ready to roast. Stuff the goose, if you care to, just before cooking, using a favorite duck or turkey dressing recipe. About 4 hours before serving time, take the goose out of the refrigerator. Salt the skin, prick the lower part of the body front and back, and set the goose breast up in a roasting pan. Allow 2 to 3 hours cooking time depending on the size of the goose (plus another ½ hour if it is stuffed). Preheat the oven to 425°. Pour 1 cup of boiling water into the roasting pan and place the goose in the oven to roast for 15 minutes at 425°. Then take it out, turn the goose on its side, and turn the heat down to 350°. Roast for 30 to 45 minutes on each side, draining off the fat as it accumulates and adding more boiling water from time to time. Baste once every 15 minutes. Turn the goose breast up, and roast for at least 30 more minutes—it is done when the drumsticks move easily in their sockets. While the goose is cooking, render the goose fat by placing it in a small saucepan with ½ cup of water. Cover and cook slowly until all the fat melts. Uncover and cook until the fat stops sputtering (at least 1 hour). Strain it and keep it in a jar in the refrigerator to use as a substitute for lard. At the same time, make a stock with the wing tips, neck, gizzard, and heart: place them in a saucepan, add 1 teaspoon of salt, the onion, celery, carrot, and parsley, and water to cover. Simmer with the lid on until the pieces of meat are tender, at least 1 hour. Strain and set aside. When the goose is done, remove the trussing pins and strings and place it on a platter. Keep it in a warm place. Make a sauce by pouring off all but about 2 tablespoons of fat from the roasting pan. On top of the stove, pour 1 cup of hot goose stock into the pan and quickly scrape up all the bits stuck to the bottom. Taste for seasoning: it may need more salt. Simmer and add more stock as necessary to make a thick pan gravy. Pour it into a sauceboat. Carve the goose at the table: cut away the drumsticks and wings and slice the breast as thinly as you can. Be sure everyone gets a good helping of skin. Some would say that it is the best part.

✑ Goose Cracklings
LIBA TEPERTŐ
(lee-ba teh-per-tu)

In the Hungarian gastronomic lexicon, goose cracklings are just a little something to titillate the appetite, what the French would call an *amuse-gueule*. Liba tepertő is, at the same time, the last word in luxury, a sort of Magyar Peking duck, since only the breast skin of the goose is used, and then it yields barely enough for six people. Naturally, the rest of the goose should not be wasted: the neck and gizzards are the basis for an exceptionally good risotto, the breast meat can be braised in sauerkraut, and the legs cooked with beans. The fat, of course, must be rendered and saved (see preceding recipe), and the carcass makes a stock that can be used along with the fat to doctor up countless everyday dishes, like pilaf rice or beans (fehér bab főzelék, page 146). In Hungary, tepertő is usually served as a midmorning snack, but for Americans it seems more appropriate as a light weekend lunch with nothing more than a good loaf of bread and a light green salad to cut the fat.

To make tepertő, first remove the skin of the breast, leaving a thin (¼ inch or less) layer of meat attached. Cut the skin as evenly as possible into 2-inch squares and cut a small x in each piece of meat. Spread the squares of skin, skin side up, in a pan large enough to hold them in one layer, if possible. (A 12-inch chicken-fryer with high sides would be about right.) Pour on just enough liquid to cover the pieces, using a 2-to-1 mixture of water and milk, which, according to some old authors, brings out the fine, nutty taste of cracklings. Cover the pan and start cooking on medium heat; as soon as the water evaporates and the fat starts sputtering, remove the lid and turn up the fire. When the goose skin turns golden brown, take the pan off the heat and sprinkle the fat with a handful of cold water. Put the cover back on until the sizzling stops, then quickly lift the cracklings out of the fat with a slotted spoon. Press out some of the excess fat with a wooden spoon, salt the cracklings, and serve them hot.

⊷ Goose in Sauerkraut
KÁPOSZTÁS LIBA
(kah-poh-stahsh lee-ba)

Superficially, káposztás liba is a Székely gulyás made with goose. But the impact is quite different, so much so that anyone who can say after sampling káposztás liba that stewed goose is indistinguishable from stewed pork should resign as itinerant palate. To bring out the very special virtues of this dish, serve it with the plainest of boiled potatoes and a fine white wine such as a Hungarian Leányka. Apple or cherry rétes (strudel, page 212) would be a fitting dessert.

2 pounds fresh sauerkraut
3 tablespoons goose fat or cooking oil
½ cup finely chopped onions
1½ teaspoons paprika
Goose stock (optional)
1 teaspoon salt
1 goose breast, skinned and boned
2 cloves garlic, peeled and stuck on toothpicks
¼ cup sour cream
Boiled potatoes

Rinse the sauerkraut in cold water and drain it. Heat the goose fat or oil in a heavy-bottomed pot large enough to hold all the sauerkraut and meat. Slowly sauté the onions in the fat until they wilt, stir in the paprika, and cook for 2 or 3 minutes, stirring constantly. Pour in ¼ cup goose stock or water, add the salt, and mix thoroughly. Squeeze out the sauerkraut and add it, turning it in the sauce. Cut the goose meat into 1-inch cubes and bury them as well as the garlic in the sauerkraut. Add enough goose stock or water to come about three-quarters of the way up, cover the pot, and simmer gently, stirring from time to time, until the sauerkraut and meat are done (about 2 hours). Add more liquid if needed to keep the sauerkraut moist. Take the pot off the heat, let it cool to lukewarm, and remove the garlic. Stir some of the sauerkraut and sauce into the sour cream, then slowly pour that mixture into the pot. Taste for seasoning: it may need more salt. Just before serving, bring back to the simmer and cook for 2 or 3 minutes. Serve directly from the cooking pot or from a large bowl, with boiled potatoes on the side.

☙ Goose in Beans
SÓLET
(*shoh-let*)

Sólet is, one might say, the Hungarian cassoulet. Like the French equivalent, it varies widely from region to region and from kitchen to kitchen. Here, in its basic form, it is so good I for one would not want to tamper with it. Beer always seems to go best with beans, the luxury status of goose notwithstanding, and the only feasible dessert is a bowl of fresh fruits in season, like apples or pears and grapes.

> 1 pound large white beans (marrow or Great Northern)
> 3 tablespoons goose fat or cooking oil
> 1 medium onion, finely chopped
> 1 tablespoon flour
> 1½ teaspoons paprika
> 1 teaspoon salt
> 3 cloves garlic, peeled and stuck on toothpicks
> 2 goose legs and hindquarters
> Goose stock (optional)

Wash and sort the beans and soak them overnight in cold water. (Or boil 5 minutes, cover, and allow to stand 1 hour.) Drain the beans, saving the soaking liquid. In a heavy-bottomed casserole large enough to hold all the meat and beans, heat the goose fat or oil and sauté the chopped onion in it until the pieces turn translucent. Sprinkle with the flour and paprika and continue cooking for 5 minutes, stirring constantly. Add the salt and ½ cup of water, mix thoroughly, and add the beans, turning them in the sauce. Bury the garlic and pieces of meat in the beans, and pour on enough goose stock or water from soaking the beans to cover the beans exactly. Bring to a simmer on top of the stove, cover, and place in the middle of a preheated 350° oven. Bake until done, about 3 hours. During the cooking time, add more liquid if necessary but do not stir. Serve directly from the casserole, giving each person some crust, some meat, and a generous helping of beans.

◝◞ Goose-Giblet Risotto
LIBA APRÓLÉKOS RIZOTTÓ
(lee-ba ah-proh-lay-kohsh ree-zo-toh)

Describing liba aprólékos rizottó is hopeless: it is truly *sui generis*. The goose giblets have none of the cloying, heavy flavor of chicken giblets, and so the dish manages to be both light in taste and rich in effect—altogether memorable. Since it is, as one might imagine, very filling, a tossed green salad is absolutely essential. There are two schools of thought—red and white—about which wine to serve: either a Szekszárdi Vörös or a Rizling would be acceptable.

1 set of goose giblets (gizzard and heart) and the neck
1 leek, or 1 onion
2 carrots
1 teaspoon salt
6 peppercorns
½ cup goose fat
1 medium onion, finely chopped
2 cups rice, preferably short-grained
½ pound fresh green peas
½ pound sliced mushrooms
1 tablespoon chopped fresh parsley

Wash the giblets and neck (do not use the liver) and place them in a saucepan with the cleaned leek or onion and carrots. Cover with 6 cups of cold water, add the salt and the peppercorns, and simmer, partially covered, until the meats are tender, about 1 hour. Melt 5 tablespoons of goose fat in a heavy-bottomed 2½- or 3-quart saucepan and slowly sauté the chopped onion until the pieces turn translucent. Stir in the rice, coating all the kernels, and cook until they swell and turn milky. Do not let the rice brown. Pour in 4½ cups of boiling goose-giblet stock. Shell the peas (you should have about ½ cup) and add them. Cover tightly and simmer very gently. Melt the remaining goose fat in a skillet and sauté the sliced mushrooms. Cut the gizzard and heart into bite-size pieces and remove the meat from the neck. Keep the meats warm in a bit of stock. When the rice is done (about 20 minutes), carefully fluff the rice and stir in the warm mushrooms and meat with a fork. The carrots and leek or onion may be cut into ½-inch pieces and added too, but this is a matter of individual taste. Sprinkle with chopped parsley and serve.

Pork

Sertés

(SHAYR-TAYSH)

Over the centuries, Hungarians have devised hundreds of splendid ways to prepare meat. They use all the conventional methods: sautéing and braising, roasting, and, occasionally, grilling the meat. In addition, they have perfected four classic stews—gulyás, pörkölt, paprikás, and tokány. Essentially, the difference between them is this:

• Gulyás is a very thin stew. The meat, usually beef, is cut into cubes no larger than one inch in size, browned with onions, and cooked until tender in a lot of stock.

• In pörkölt, the meat is cut in cubes one inch or slightly more in size. It is browned and then braised in a small amount of stock or water. Pork and veal make the best pörkölt; beef pörkölt can be good too, but beef gulyás is considerably better.

• A paprikás stew is a pörkölt with sour cream added at the very end. The finest paprikás is made with veal or chicken meat.

• For tokány, the meat is cut into very small pieces, about 2 inches long and ¼ inch thick. Only the tiniest bit of liquid is added, and the meat literally stews in its own juice. Tokány can be made with any kind of meat or a combination of meats.

Pork is a vital ingredient in many of these stews. It is also the basis of any number of magnificent casseroles, and the cutlets when prepared Hungarian style are very fine indeed. Pork is everyday fare year in and year out for most Hungarians, and life without it would be dismal beyond reckoning. The salamis, the sausages, the bacons are more than mere food: they are an integral part of a way of life. The old customs are vanishing, it is true, but my husband and his friends still contrive to stage a traditional pig-killing every winter. A two-day orgy of pork eating may not be everyone's idea of how to spend a weekend in the country—but for them it is more than a holiday, it is a homage to home.

⌁§ Pork Paprika Stew
SERTÉS PÖRKÖLT
(shayr-taysh pur-kult)

Pörkölt can be made with any kind of meat, but it always seems to come out best with pork. The meat absorbs the flavor of the sauce and gives something back in exchange. Pörkölt really should be served only with galuska, the tiny flour-and-egg dumplings; packaged curly noodles are about the only acceptable ready-made substitute, and a poor one at that. The meal definitely must have a salad, either cucumbers or lettuce, and a sweet dessert: palacsinta (page 207) or stíriai metélt (noodle pudding, page 206) would be good. Serve the pörkölt with a chilled bottle of Badacsonyi Kéknyelű, a lovely white wine from Lake Balaton.

> 1 large onion, finely chopped
> 3 tablespoons cooking oil
> 2 pounds pork shoulder, cut in 1-inch pieces
> 1½ teaspoons salt
> 1½ teaspoons paprika
> ¼ teaspoon caraway seeds, crushed with the back of a spoon
> 1 medium green pepper, seeded and cut in ½-inch strips
> 3 small peeled tomatoes, preferably canned
> Galuska (dumplings, page 21)

In a 3-quart, flameproof casserole, sauté the onion in oil until it goes limp. Push to one side or remove to a side dish. Pat the meat dry and start browning it a handful at a time in the same pot. Remove to a side dish, and when all the meat is done, pour ½ cup of water into the pot and scrape up the juices. Stir in the salt, paprika, and caraway seeds. Put the meat and onions back into the casserole and add enough water to barely cover the meat. Simmer, covered, 30 minutes, then add the green pepper strips and tomatoes. Cover and simmer 1 hour more or until the meat is tender, adding water whenever necessary to keep the meat barely covered with sauce. Let cool a bit and skim off as much fat as possible from the surface of the sauce. Taste and correct the seasoning. Reheat if necessary. Serve directly from the casserole or from a bowl. Give each person a helping of galuska and some pieces of meat, then spoon a little sauce over both.

✑ Szekler Goulash
SZÉKELY GULYÁS
(*say-kay-y gū-yahsh*)

Nothing should be allowed to detract from this unique blend of pork, sauerkraut, and sour cream. With plain boiled potatoes to set it off and a dry white wine (preferably a Leányka) to drink with it, it makes a truly sensational main course. In fact, it is the Derecskeys' favorite Hungarian meat dish. We eat it year round in the mountains and at the shore, on festive occasions and on busy weekdays, and we never tire of it. Since the gulyás is rather rich and filling, dessert need be no more substantial than fruit-filled rétes (strudel, page 212).

> **3 pounds sauerkraut, preferably fresh or in a plastic package (if neither is available, use canned sauerkraut)**
> **3 tablespoons buttermilk**
> **½ cup sour cream**
> **2 pounds shoulder of pork**
> **1 cup chopped onions**
> **3 tablespoons oil**
> **1½ teaspoons salt**
> **1½ teaspoons paprika**
> **½ teaspoon caraway seed, crushed with the back of a spoon**
> **Boiled potatoes**

Rinse the sauerkraut and squeeze dry. If it still tastes briny, rinse a second time. Blend the buttermilk into the sour cream and set aside. Cut the meat into 1-inch cubes and pat dry. In a 3-quart flameproof casserole, sauté the onions in oil until they turn transparent. Push them to one side and start browning the meat lightly on all sides. Remove the meat to a side dish. Pour ½ cup of water into the pan and scrape up the juices, then stir in the salt, paprika, and caraway seeds. Put the meat back into the pan and spread the sauerkraut over it. (If canned sauerkraut is used, add it only after the meat has cooked 1 hour.) Pour in enough water to barely cover the sauerkraut, put the lid on, and simmer 1½ hours or until the meat and sauerkraut are tender. Add more water during the cooking period to keep the gulyás barely covered with sauce. When done, remove from the heat and let cool. Mix 2 tablespoons of sauce into the sour cream, then slowly stir the mixture back into the pot. Taste and correct the seasoning. Bring back to the simmer. Székely gulyás may be served directly from the pot or from a deep bowl. Each person should get a couple of boiled potatoes and a generous helping of meat, sauerkraut, and sauce.

⌒৯ Pork Stew with Bacon
CSIKÓS TOKÁNY
(chee-kohsh to-kahny)

Literally, the name of this dish means cowboy stew, and it is attributed to the horsemen of the Hungarian plain. They ate their meals in the open, sometimes making a stew with strips of pork meat and bacon in a bogrács or cauldron over the fire. Nowadays it is cooked in the kitchen, on a low, steady source of heat in a heavy-bottomed pot, and the tripod and cauldron figure only in dinner-table chitchat. Csikós tokány is a particularly succulent stew, and it goes equally well with mashed potatoes or galuska. It does call for a fresh salad with the meal and a pleasant white wine like a Hungarian Rizling to drink. Dessert might be a couple of nut-filled palacsinta (page 207) for each person.

2 pounds shoulder of pork
¼ pound bacon, preferably smoked slab bacon, though
    thick-sliced breakfast bacon may be used instead
1 large onion, thinly sliced
¼ cup cooking oil or additional bacon fat
1½ teaspoons salt
1½ teaspoons paprika
1 medium green pepper, cored and cut in ½-inch strips
3 small peeled tomatoes, preferably canned

½ cup sour cream, at room temperature
Mashed potatoes or galuska (dumplings, page 21)

Cut the pork shoulder and bacon into strips about 2 inches long by ¼ inch wide by ¼ inch thick, keeping the two separate. Fry the bacon strips until golden in a 3-quart flameproof casserole. Remove them to a side dish. Sauté the onion slices in the same pot until they go limp, adding cooking oil or bacon fat if needed. Put them to one side with the bacon. Pat the pork dry and start browning it a handful at a time in the casserole, using as much oil or fat as necessary. Add the pork to the bacon and onions. Pour ½ cup of water into the casserole, scrape up the pan juices, and stir in the salt and paprika. Put the bacon, onions, and pork back into the pot. Add enough water for the meat to be half in, half out of the sauce: it will be quite thick. Drop in the green pepper strips and tomatoes. Cover and simmer 45 minutes, or until the meat is tender, adding more water as necessary to keep the sauce at the halfway mark. Remove from the heat and let cool. Skim off as much fat as possible. Stir 2 tablespoons of sauce into the sour cream, then slowly stir that mixture back into the tokány. Taste and correct the seasoning. Bring slowly back to the simmer. Serve directly from the casserole (or from a deep bowl), giving each guest a helping of mashed potatoes or galuska first, with the tokány alongside and sauce spooned over everything.

✑§ Djuvetch
GYUVECS
(djū-vech)

Only the most impassioned irridentist would claim gyuvecs for Hungary. This spicy casserole of summer vegetables belongs to the Balkans, where it appears and reappears in a thousand guises. This recipe gives it a Magyar aspect; gyuvecs was obviously too good not to be absorbed into the Hungarian repertoire. Serve it hot, with a green salad and bread, and be sure to pass the sour cream as well. A chilled white wine is the ideal thing to drink, and a Debrői Hárslevelű is particularly apt. For dessert, fresh midsummer fruits—peaches, plums, melon—would be in keeping with gyuvecs's seasonal origins. (The following recipe serves four generously as a meal. To serve six or eight, double the recipe but do not add quite as much water, since the vegetables generate a lot of juice. Leftover gyuvecs can be reheated, no damage done.)

   1 pound eggplant
   Salt
   1 medium green pepper
   3 small peeled tomatoes, preferably canned
   3 medium potatoes
   ¼ cup white rice, regular or instant
   3 tablespoons cooking oil
   ½ cup minced onion (1 medium onion)
   1 pound shoulder of pork, cut in 1-inch cubes
   1 teaspoon paprika
   2 cloves garlic, peeled and mashed or chopped very fine

Peel and slice the eggplant ¼ to ½ inch thick, sprinkle with salt, and let stand 30 minutes. Core the green pepper and cut it in ½-inch strips, quarter the tomatoes, and set both aside. Peel the potatoes and slice them ¼ inch thick, cover with cold water, and set aside. Parboil the rice for 10 minutes, unless so-called instant rice is used. Heat the oil in a heavy skillet and sauté the minced onion until it turns transparent. Push to one side and lightly brown the meat, using more oil if needed. Stir in 1 teaspoon of salt, the paprika, and the garlic. Cover and simmer 15 minutes. Preheat the oven to 325°. Grease a deep 2- or 3-quart baking dish (an 8-cup soufflé mold will just about hold everything, but a somewhat larger dish is preferable). Pat the eggplant slices dry and fill the dish with layers as follows, sprinkling each layer with salt. Half the eggplant and potato slices on the bottom (use the odd pieces, saving the better-looking ones for the top layer). Next, half the rice and all the pork mixture followed by the green pepper strips, quartered tomatoes, and the remaining rice. The rest of the eggplant and potato slices should be neatly arranged on top. Scrape up the juices left in the frying pan, using ½ cup of water. Pour it over the gyuvecs and pour in more water if needed to cover the top layer. Cover the dish with a lid or piece of aluminum foil. Place in the center of the preheated oven and bake 1½ hours, or until the food shrinks away from the side of the dish. Remove from the oven and let stand for 20 minutes. Serve directly from the casserole.

⌇ Transylvanian Baked Sauerkraut
KOLOZSVÁRI RAKOTT KÁPOSZTA
(koh-lohzh-vah-ree rah-kot kah-poh-sta)

Sauerkraut is one of the pitiful orphans of American cooking: a whole generation of kids knows it only as something to put on hot dogs at the beach. What a loss! This is one of the world's most versatile delicacies. In this dish, for instance, it is baked with pork and smoked meats, and the flavors meld—especially if the dish is made in advance and reheated—in a winning combination. Rakott káposzta is a hearty, country-style casserole, and it needs nothing more than a fresh loaf of rye bread to go with it, though it could be preceded by a light soup. To drink: our choice would be a Badacsonyi Kéknyelű, or some other dry white wine, or a pale beer. Dessert should be kept light. Try meggyes rétes (sour-cherry strudel, page 212) or boszorkányhab, a rum-flavored apple froth (page 200).

3 tablespoons bacon fat or cooking oil
½ cup chopped onions
1 pound ground pork
1 clove garlic, crushed or finely chopped
1 teaspoon salt
1 teaspoon paprika
Freshly ground black pepper
¼ pound smoked bacon, cut in ¼-inch dice (or use thick-sliced breakfast bacon)
½ pound Hungarian or other smoked sausage, cut in ¼-inch slices (optional)
¼ cup white rice, regular or instant
2 pounds fresh or canned sauerkraut
1 cup sour cream
Additional sour cream for serving

Heat the bacon fat or oil in a heavy skillet and sauté the onions until they start to wilt. Add the pork and brown it thoroughly. Stir in the garlic, salt, paprika, and pepper. Cover and simmer 10 minutes. In another frying pan, cook the bacon until it starts to render fat. Add the sausage slices and cook 5 minutes or until the bacon starts to brown. Parboil the rice for 10 minutes, unless instant rice is being used. Preheat the oven to 325°. Grease a deep 2- or 3-quart baking dish (an 8-cup soufflé mold will work, but use a larger dish if you have one). Rinse the sauerkraut and squeeze it dry. Spread a third of it on the bottom. Put in all the bacon and sausage mixture, including the pan fat. Spread another third of the sauerkraut over this, and dot it with 2 tablespoons of sour cream. Sprinkle with rice. Add the pork mixture with all its pan juices. Cover with the remaining sauerkraut. Pour 1 cup of water into the pork skillet, swish it around, and pour it over the kraut. Then spread the rest of the sour cream on top. Place in the center of the oven and bake, uncovered, for 1½ hours, or until the food shrinks away from the sides of the dish and the sour-cream topping turns golden brown. Remove from the oven and let stand for 20 minutes. (Kolozsvári rakott káposzta may be made in advance and reheated; in fact, it tastes better that way.) Serve directly from the casserole and pass a bowl of sour cream for those who care to add a dollop of it.

✑ Sautéed Pork Cutlets
NATÚRSZELET
(nah-tūr se-let)

Every self-respecting cook should be able to toss off a decent pork cutlet or chop. Any fresh vegetable, cooked or raw, can be served with it, all the starchy garnishes—potatoes, rice, noodles— taste good with it, and nearly everyone likes it. It just must not be allowed to go dry. Pork cutlets, which come from the butt, stay moist and tender, no matter what. Boned loin chops, thinly sliced, may be used in this and the following three recipes.

Allow 2 cutlets or chops per person, pat them dry, then sprinkle them with salt and pepper and flour. Shake off the excess. Heat ½ cup lard or cooking oil in a heavy frying pan and lightly brown the cutlets or chops quickly on both sides. Pour in ½ cup of water, cover, and simmer about 20 minutes or until the water has evaporated. (Test the meat with a table fork; if it is tender but the water has not evaporated, boil it off by raising the heat and removing the pan cover.) Turn the meat over to brown it on the second side. Serve immediately.

[78]

✑ Breaded Pork Cutlets
RÁNTOTT SZELET
(*rahn-tot se-let*)

Breaded pork cutlets are a guaranteed success. They are tender and juicy and have a distinctive nutty flavor that has been known to win people over from the more delicate veal cutlet. In Hungary itself, it has become the universal substitute for the beloved bécsi szelet, which has hardly been seen since the war. At the very least, rántott szelet should be served with mashed potatoes and a fresh salad of some kind (green salad, cold green beans, tomatoes, cucumbers). Another hot vegetable might also be added. One of the less dry white wines, such as a Badacsonyi Szürke Barát, would make the meal very special indeed. This might be the occasion for a sweet dessert like női szeszély (page 224) or madártej (page 201).

2 pounds pork cutlets or boned, thin-sliced pork chops
2 eggs
1½ cups bread crumbs, more if necessary
Salt
Pepper
Sifted or granular (instant-blending) flour in a shaker
1 cup cooking oil

Pat the meat dry and spread the cutlets out on a plate or sheet of waxed paper. Beat the eggs thoroughly with a fork in a flat soup bowl until they start to froth. Line up the meat, the eggs, and another plate or piece of waxed paper spread with a layer of bread crumbs. Sprinkle the cutlets evenly with salt, pepper, and flour, lightly coating the entire surface. Dip each cutlet into the beaten egg and lift out to let the excess drip off. Turn the meat in the bread crumbs, coating each cutlet evenly but not too thickly. (The breaded cutlets may be refrigerated until ready to cook.) In a frying pan large enough to hold all the pieces without crowding or in two separate pans, fry the cutlets in ¼ inch of oil until golden brown on both sides. Cover, reduce the heat, and cook 20 minutes, turning the meat once. Uncover and cook 5 minutes to make the coating crisp. Drain the cutlets on paper toweling and serve.

✑ Pork Cutlets with Potatoes
PAPRIKÁS SZELET
(pah-pree-kahsh se-let)

This dish makes an excellent one-pot meal: it is hearty and it tastes very, very good. The meat, vegetables, and potatoes interact most favorably, and all that needs to be added is a green salad. A nice white wine, such as a Hungarian Rizling, would be good to drink. Only a very light dessert should be served: boszorkányhab (page 200) or almás pite (page 222), for instance.

2 pounds (about 8 medium) potatoes
1½ pounds pork cutlets or boned, thinly sliced pork chops
Salt
Freshly ground black pepper
Sifted or granular (instant-blending) flour in a shaker
¼ cup cooking oil
1 large onion, sliced thin
1 teaspoon paprika
Pinch of caraway seeds, crushed with the back of a spoon
2 cloves garlic, peeled and stuck on toothpicks
1 medium green pepper, cored and cut in ½-inch strips
2 small peeled tomatoes, preferably canned

Peel the potatoes and cut them into half-moons ¼ inch thick. (To make half-moons, cut each potato in half lengthwise, lay each half flat, and slice it ¼ inch thick the long way.) Cover them with cold water and set aside until ready to use. Pat the cutlets dry and sprinkle them with salt, pepper, and flour. Shake off any excess, then brown them quickly in hot oil in a large skillet. Transfer them to a 3-quart flameproof casserole. Sauté the onion slices in the skillet until they go limp, and add them to the cutlets. Pour ½ cup of water into the skillet, loosen up the pan juices with a wooden spoon, then stir in 1 teaspoon of salt, the paprika, and caraway seeds. Pour this sauce over the meat and onions. Add the garlic, green pepper, and tomatoes plus enough water to barely cover the meat. Cover and simmer 10 minutes. Add the potatoes, 1 more teaspoon of salt, and enough water to cover. Simmer 25 minutes or until the potatoes are done. Discard the garlic, degrease the sauce, and add more salt if needed. Serve from the casserole or arrange the meat and potatoes on a platter and pass the sauce separately.

✑ Pork Cutlets with Green Beans
TEMESVÁRI SZELET
(teh-mesh-vah-ree se-let)

Temesvár is a lovely old Hungarian town in Transylvania (the Rumanians call it Timişoara), and this recipe contains one of those startling combinations of ingredients the region is known for. Serve the dish with galuska and a fresh green salad on the side. It would be a pity not to have a decent bottle of white wine with the meal (a Badacsonyi Kéknyelű from the Hungarian side is a good choice). It would be a pity too to skimp on dessert: serve a rakott palacsinta (page 209) or several kinds of rétes (strudel, page 212) for full effect.

1 pound fresh green beans, cut in 1-inch pieces
Salt
¼ pound smoked bacon, diced in ¼-inch pieces (or substitute thick-sliced breakfast bacon)
½ cup finely chopped onions
1 teaspoon paprika
1½ pounds pork cutlets or boned, thinly sliced pork chops
Freshly ground black pepper
Sifted or granular (instant-blending) flour in a shaker
3 tablespoons cooking oil
2 cloves garlic, peeled and stuck on toothpicks
½ medium green pepper, seeded and cut in ½-inch strips
2 small peeled tomatoes, preferably canned
¾ cup sour cream, at room temperature
Vinegar
Galuska (dumplings, page 21)

Parboil the green beans by cooking for 15 minutes, uncovered, in plenty of salted boiling water and then quickly cooling them under the cold tap. In a 3-quart flameproof casserole, fry the pieces of bacon until they start to render fat. Add the onions and sauté until the bacon turns golden and the onions go limp. Sprinkle with 1 teaspoon of salt and the paprika, and stir in ½ cup of water. Meanwhile, pat the cutlets dry. Sprinkle them with salt, pepper, and flour, shaking off any excess, and fry them quickly in oil in a large skillet. As they are done, place them in the casserole with the bacon and onions. Pour in more water so that the sauce barely covers the meat. Drop in the garlic, green pepper strips, and tomatoes. Cover and simmer 30 minutes, turning the meat once. Add the green beans and simmer 10 more minutes. Remove from the heat and let cool. Discard the garlic and skim off as much grease as possible from the surface of the sauce. When it has cooled thoroughly, mix 2 table-spoons of it into the sour cream. Then gradually stir the mixture back into the sauce. Taste the sauce and correct the seasoning. It may call for a few drops of vinegar. Gently bring back to the simmer and serve. Either bring the dish to the table in the casserole or arrange the cutlets on a platter with the green beans and pass the sauce in a gravy boat. Each person should get a helping of galuska, a cutlet, and some beans with sauce spooned over everything.

✍ Pig's Knuckles and Sauerkraut
DISZNÓ CSÜLÖK KÁPOSZTÁVAL
(*dis-noh chū-luk kah-poh-stah-vul*)

Who would ever think of pig's knuckles and sauerkraut as a festive dish? And yet, the day my first son was born in a German hospital, that was what they brought me for dinner as a celebration of all things great and glorious—or so I interpreted it. Right or wrong, pig's knuckles and sauerkraut have never been the same since. This Hungarian version is actually much finer than the German kind and does not have any of that boiled-pork taste that many people object to. Serve it with boiled potatoes and beer.

  6 pig's knuckles, cracked
  3 pounds fresh sauerkraut
  3 tablespoons cooking oil
  1 cup finely chopped onions
  1 teaspoon paprika
  ¼ teaspoon caraway seeds, crushed with the back of a spoon
  2 cloves garlic, peeled and stuck on toothpicks
  1 teaspoon salt
  1 medium green pepper, cored and cut in ½-inch strips

½ cup sour cream, at room temperature
2 tablespoons chopped fresh dill (optional)
Vinegar
Boiled potatoes

Wash the knuckles and set them aside. Rinse the sauerkraut once and taste it. If it is still too briny, rinse a second time. Squeeze the sauerkraut dry. Heat the oil in a heavy-bottomed casserole large enough to hold all the knuckles and sauerkraut (not a cast-iron Dutch oven) and sauté the onions until they wilt. Stir in the paprika and caraway seeds and about ½ cup of water to make a sauce. Put the knuckles in along with the garlic and salt. Pour on enough lukewarm water to cover the knuckles, and slowly bring to the simmer. Cook, partially covered, for 1 hour, skimming off the froth and fat as it forms. Taste the broth and correct the seasoning. Add the sauerkraut and green pepper strips and continue simmering, partially covered, for 1½ hours, or until the meat is tender. (If canned sauerkraut is used, do not add it until later, when the knuckles have cooked for 2 hours; then continue cooking for only 30 minutes more.) Remove from the heat and let cool. Put the knuckles in a side dish. Discard the garlic and skim as much grease as possible off the sauce. Discard the skin, bones, and fat of the knuckles and cut the meat into 1-inch pieces. When the sauce has cooled, mix 2 tablespoons of it in the sour cream, then slowly stir the mixture into the rest of the sauce. Add the chopped dill. Taste and correct the seasoning (more salt may be needed or a few drops of vinegar to sharpen the sauce). Put the meat or knuckles back into the pot and simmer gently for 3 minutes. Serve directly from the casserole or from a deep bowl, with boiled potatoes.

◄§ Jellied Pork
KOCSONYA
(koh-chon-ya)

The pig is surely the most economical farm animal: it eats virtually anything, and when it is butchered and dressed, almost the entire animal can be used for food. What isn't cooked or smoked or seasoned for sausage is thrown into the kocsonya pot to make a light and nourishing dish of jellied meats. It is even, by Hungarian

[83]

standards, nonfattening. Kocsonya connoisseurs rave on and on about the virtues of the dish, recalling in mouth-watering detail the greatest kocsonya they have known. What seems to make it memorable is the range of textures from chewy to very tender meat, all transfixed in a clear, delicately spiced jelly. It is at the most a luncheon dish and is often eaten as a snack or appetizer. Either way, it should be served with sour pickles and bread and a modest white wine or beer. The ingredients can be found or ordered in a pork store or any German or east European butcher shop.

1 pig's ear, tail, and jowl
1 pig's foot, cut in two
1 fresh pig's knuckle, cut in three (a smoked knuckle may also be used)
2 teaspoons salt
6 whole peppercorns
2 cloves garlic
1 medium onion, peeled
1 teaspoon paprika

Wash all the pieces of meat and place them in a large, heavy-bottomed pot (a stock pot if available). Cover with cold water and slowly bring to the gentlest simmer. Cook, partially covered, skimming off the froth as it forms. After 1 hour add the salt, peppercorns, garlic, and onion. The paprika may be added at this point or saved for later. Continue to simmer, partially covered, removing the fat and froth from time to time, for about 1 hour or until the pieces of meat are tender. Place a colander in a large bowl and strain the broth. Let it settle, then skim off every bit of fat. Taste the broth and add more salt if necessary. Cut the ear, tail, and jowl into small pieces. Discard the skin, bones, and fat of the knuckles and cut the meat into bite-size pieces. Discard the foot altogether. Distribute the pieces of meat among individual soup bowls or spread evenly in a large, shallow serving dish. Pour the broth over the meat and sprinkle with paprika if it was not used earlier. Let stand. When the kocsonya begins to jell, cover loosely and refrigerate. Serve cold.

[84]

⊷§ Transylvanian Mixed Grill
ERDÉLYI FATÁNYÉROS
(ehr-day-yi fah-tahn-yay-rohsh)

My husband, who is a Hungarian from Transylvania, can still recall the smoky country taverns where townspeople went to eat erdélyi fatányéros. The charcoal fire was always glowing, and the wooden platters of grilled meats kept coming and coming. No one can hope to re-create that atmosphere in an American dining room, but I have managed to turn out an evocative fatányéros or two on crisp autumn evenings in our Adirondack hideaway.

Erdélyi fatányéros requires a bit more attention than the usual barbecue meals, but it is certainly worth it. In planning one, be sure your grill is large enough to hold three pieces of meat per person: a beefsteak, a pork cutlet, and a veal cutlet. The fourth piece of meat, a coxcomb of smoked bacon, is cooked separately at the end because it generates so much smoke and flames. To duplicate the European balance of flavors, use round steak, ½ to ¾ inch thick, and pork and veal cutlets rather than chops. For the coxcombs, buy a slab of the best-quality smoked bacon you can get. Do not remove the rind. Cut the bacon in slices a good ½ inch thick, then slash the fatty part perpendicular to the rind. The cuts should be ¾ inch apart and come to within ¼ inch of the rind. The slices will fan into shape as they cook. Since the beef, pork, and veal are all very dry cuts of meat, it is a good idea to marinate them for an hour or more in vegetable oil well seasoned with salt and pepper. Blot the pieces of meat with paper towels before grilling, and be sure to cook them high above the embers.

Bearing in mind that the three meats should be finished together, put the pork chops on first, then the beef, and last of all the veal. The exact timing will depend, of course, on the thickness of the meat, the heat of the embers, and the height of the grill. A good rule of thumb is to allow 8 to 10 minutes per side for the pork, 4 to 5 minutes per side for the beef, and 2 to 3 minutes per side for the veal, and as you turn each kind of meat over, put the next one on. When the meats are done, remove the pieces to a warm platter and quickly grill the smoked bacon on both sides. The bacon will glisten and swell before it browns. Take it off the fire just as it starts to brown: if cooked too long, it will turn dry and bitter. Add the coxcombs to the other meats. Arrange the fatányéros on a large platter or individual plates. Even if you don't have wooden platters, keep the ambience as rustic as possible. There is no need for a staggering array of salads and condiments: a tossed salad will suffice. The best thing to drink with a fatányéros is a red country wine like a Hungarian Szekszárdi Vörös. Dessert, obviously, could be very rich indeed. Traditionally, vargabéles, a sort of super-strudel that I have not yet managed to domesticate, followed the fatányéros. A diós torta (page 239) or a datolya torta (page 238) or, for chocolate lovers, Rigó Jancsi (page 236) could be served instead.

Veal
Borjú
(BAWR-YŪ)

$\mathcal{W}$e were in Hungary the year veal reappeared on ordinary restaurant menus, and I remember well the lunchtime scene at the Kárpáthia, a good but not luxurious restaurant in downtown Budapest: it opened at noon, and by ten after, the veal specialty of the day was sold out. Every Hungarian in the house had ordered it. Through the long war and postwar years of privation, the memory of the taste of veal had stayed alive. Hungarians love it, and we managed to sample many superb veal dishes that fall. That made it all the more disappointing to find that they did not always taste quite so good when made with American meat. European veal comes from an animal that is fed, butchered, and dressed differently. American supermarket veal, by comparison, is usually too pink, indicating that it is a bit old and tough. Top-grade veal at the best butcher shops is often so white it is too tender for certain dishes. One pragmatic solution is to buy supermarket veal for stocks and stews, since it can be cooked long enough to flavor the sauce without crumbling. For cutlets and chops, though, it is wiser—and more economical in the long run—to pay premium prices at a butcher shop with a large European and gourmet following. For innards, another reliable source is often a kosher butcher, who either has fresh sweetbreads and brains or can order them. It is a time-consuming way to shop, but the results justify the trouble and expense. A good veal stew with firm pieces of meat in a finely seasoned sauce has no close rival. And a light, crusty bécsi szelet (also known as Wienerschnitzel) ranks very high in the gastronomic order of things.

❧ Veal Paprika Stew
BORJÚ PÖRKÖLT
(bawr-yŭ pur-kult)

The great virtue of pörkölt, particularly veal pörkölt, is its simplicity: pieces of meat are stewed until tender in a light paprika sauce, nothing more. Though it can be served with squiggly noodles or rice, galuska taste infinitely better. A lettuce or cucumber salad on the side is a must. A pleasant white wine, a Debrői Hárslevelű, for example, would be in keeping with the rest of the meal, and just about any dessert would be appropriate: rétes (strudel, page 212), almás pite (page 222), or sponge cake (page 228).

> 2 pounds shoulder of veal
> 1 cup chopped onions
> 3 tablespoons cooking oil or lard
> 1 teaspoon paprika
> 1 teaspoon salt
> 1 small green pepper, cored and cut in ½-inch strips
> 3 small peeled tomatoes, preferably canned
> 1 clove garlic, peeled and stuck on a toothpick (optional)
> Galuska (dumplings, page 21)

Cut the meat in 1-inch cubes and pat dry. Sauté the onions in the oil or lard, using a 3-quart heavy-bottomed flameproof casserole. When the onions start to wilt, push them to one side or remove them to a side dish, and brown the meat lightly on all sides in the same pot. Remove the meat to a side dish. Pour ½ cup of water into the pot and scrape up the pan juices. Stir in the paprika and salt, and put the meat and onions back into the pot. Drop in the green pepper, tomatoes, and optional clove of garlic. Add enough water to barely cover the meat, and simmer, partially covered, for 45 minutes to 1 hour, or until the meat is tender. The pörkölt may be served directly from the cooking pot or from a deep bowl. Serve some galuska on each plate, then a few pieces of meat with lots of sauce spooned over both.

Veal Stew with Paprika and Sour Cream
BORJÚ PAPRIKÁS
(bawr-yū pah-pree-kahsh)

Borjú paprikás is made exactly the same way as borjú pörkölt (preceding recipe), except that half a cup of sour cream is added at the end. To mix in the sour cream without curdling, have it at room temperature and be sure the pörkölt is only lukewarm. Stir 2 tablespoons of sauce into the sour cream and gradually pour that mixture into the pörkölt. Put it back on the heat and let it simmer 2 or 3 minutes. Serve the paprikás with galuska (dumplings, page 21) or rice, and be sure to have a fresh salad on the side. Like the pörkölt, borjú paprikás tastes best with a slightly fruity white wine, like Debrői Hárslevelű or Badacsonyi Szürke Barát. A good dessert to choose would be nut-filled palacsinta (page 207).

✑ Veal Stew with Mushrooms and Sour Cream
BORJÚ TOKÁNY
(bawr-yū to-kahny)

Out of the infinite number of ways to combine veal, mushrooms, and cream, this is one of our favorites. The sautéed parsley cuts right through the blandness, always a risk with a creamy veal stew, and having the meat in narrow strips and the mushrooms in slices gives it a more interesting consistency than the usual stew of pieces of meat in a thick gravy. Borjú tokány should be served with white rice and a green salad to liven things up. A fine dry white wine, say a Leányka, tastes very good indeed. Diós torta (walnut cake, page 239) would make a highly appreciated dessert.

2 pounds shoulder of veal
1 cup chopped onions
About 4 tablespoons cooking oil
1 tablespoon canned tomato purée
½ cup dry white wine
1 teaspoon salt
Pinch of freshly ground black pepper
1 clove of garlic, peeled and stuck on a toothpick
½ pound fresh mushrooms, sliced (about 2½ cups)
1 tablespoon chopped parsley

2 tablespoons butter
1 cup veal stock or water
½ cup sour cream, at room temperature

Cut the veal into strips about 2 inches long, ¼ inch wide, and ¼ inch thick. Sauté the onions in 3 tablespoons of the oil in a 3-quart heavy-bottomed casserole until they turn translucent. Push the onions to one side or put them in a side dish, and start browning the meat lightly on all sides, a handful at a time, in the same pot. Use more oil if necessary. When all the meat is browned, mix the tomato purée in the wine and pour it into the pot, scraping up any bits stuck to the bottom. Stir in the salt and pepper, put the onions and meat back into the pot, and drop in the clove of garlic. Cover and simmer 30 minutes. Meanwhile, sauté the mushrooms, with the parsley, in the butter and 1 tablespoon of oil. Scrape the mushrooms into the tokány and simmer an additional 10 minutes, or until the meat is tender. Remove from heat, discard the garlic, and skim as much grease as possible from the sauce. Gradually stir in the stock or water. Gently simmer for 5 minutes, then taste for seasoning. Let the tokány cool for 10 to 15 minutes. Then mix 2 tablespoons of sauce into the sour cream and slowly stir the mixture back into the tokány. Simmer another 2 or 3 minutes and serve.

◄§ Wienerschnitzel or Breaded Veal Cutlet
BÉCSI SZELET
(bay-chee se-let)

In certain circles, how to cook bécsi szelet is argued even more passionately than how to make a dry Martini. The following recipe is my contribution to the debate. Although there are many "experts" who like a thick, eggy coating, I feel the crust should be thin and light to give the veal a chance to declare itself. Bécsi szelet is traditionally garnished with lemon wedges and served with mashed potatoes. A second hot vegetable, such as peas or green beans, could also be served, and a fresh salad is a must. Bécsi szelet deserves a good white wine: the somewhat fruity ones, like Badacsonyi Szürke Barát and Debrői Hárslevelű, go very well with it. Either an elaborate Dobos torta (page 232) or the simple, beloved madártej (page 201) would be a fitting dessert.

**2 pounds veal cutlets cut from the leg, about ¼ inch thick and
  pounded thin**
3 egg whites
About 1½ cups dry bread crumbs
Salt
Pepper
Sifted or granular (instant-blending) flour in a shaker
1 cup oil

Pat the meat dry, then spread the cutlets out on a plate or sheet
of waxed paper. Add 1 tablespoon of water to the egg whites and
beat very slightly with a fork. Line up the meat, the egg whites, and
another plate or sheet of waxed paper with the bread crumbs on it.
Sprinkle the cutlets evenly with salt, pepper, and flour on both sides,
and shake off any excess. Dip each cutlet in egg white, coating the
entire surface. Lift out and let the excess egg drip off. Then coat
evenly on both sides with bread crumbs. (The breaded cutlets may
be refrigerated until ready to cook.) Heat about ¼ inch of oil in a
large, heavy-bottomed skillet and fry the cutlets 3 minutes on each
side. Regulate the heat so that breading does not burn. Do not crowd
the pieces of meat: either use several pans at once or do the frying
in stages. When the cutlets are done, drain them on paper towels.

⋖§ Veal Cutlets in Paprika and Sour Cream Sauce
PAPRIKÁS SZELET
  (*pah-pree-kahsh se-let*)

This is a light and utterly delicious dish, ideal for a special dinner on a day when the cook is running short of time and energy to
spend in the kitchen. Galuska is the best thing to serve with paprikás szelet; rice is another possibility. Like all dishes made with
sour cream, it really needs a salad, the simpler the better (tossed
greens for example). A Badacsonyi Szürke Barát would go perfectly
with the meal. Dessert might be a sweet női szeszély cake (page
224).

**2 pounds veal cutlets from the leg, thinly sliced and flattened
  (like scaloppine)**
Salt

About 3 tablespoons cooking oil
1 medium onion, finely chopped
1 teaspoon paprika
½ medium green pepper, seeded and cut in ½-inch strips
2 small peeled tomatoes, preferably canned
½ cup sour cream, at room temperature
Galuska (dumplings, page 21) or boiled rice

Sprinkle the cutlets with salt and brown them lightly in 3 table-spoons of oil, using a heavy skillet. Remove them to a side dish. Sauté the chopped onion in the same pan, adding more oil if neces-sary. Stir in the paprika and ½ cup of water. Simmer briefly (2 or 3 minutes), then put the meat back into the pan along with the green pepper and tomatoes. The sauce should barely cover the meat. Simmer for about 15 minutes, turning the meat once. Remove from the heat. When the sauce has cooled, mix 2 tablespoons of it into the sour cream, then pour the mixture slowly into the sauce. Taste for seasoning, and if the sauce seems too thick add some water a spoonful at a time. Put back on the heat and simmer 3 to 5 min-utes. Serve each guest one or two pieces of meat, and some galuska or rice with sauce spooned over both.

⇜§ Kaiser Cutlet, in Lemon and Sour Cream Sauce
CSÁSZÁR SZELET
(chah-sahr se-let)

Whenever someone asks me at five o'clock in the afternoon, "What should I cook for supper tonight?" I suggest császár szelet. In one sense, I am not doing it justice, for this is far too good to end up as a last-minute, last-resort kind of dish. On the other hand, there are moments when even the most imaginative cooks run out of inspiration, and when even the most tireless of them is looking for impressive results from a small investment in time. This is such a dish. Served with rice and a fresh green salad on the side, a bottle of Debrői Hárslevelű to drink with it, and a palacsinta or noodle dessert, it makes a very fine supper indeed.

1 medium-size lemon
Salt

2 pounds veal cutlets, thinly sliced and flattened (like scaloppine)
3 tablespoons oil
Freshly ground black pepper
¼ cup sour cream, at room temperature
Boiled rice

Peel the lemon and cut the skin into julienne strips, the size of a matchstick. Salt the cutlets and brown them lightly in oil in a heavy-bottomed skillet. Remove them to a side dish and pour ½ cup of water into the pan, scraping up the juices. Put the cutlets back in, spread about three-quarters of the lemon strips on top, and grind lots of black pepper over everything. Simmer for about 15 minutes, turning the meat once. Remove from the heat and let cool about 10 minutes. Discard the lemon peel. Mix 2 tablespoons of the pan juices into the sour cream and slowly stir the mixture back into the sauce. Taste for seasoning, and thin the sauce with a spoonful or two of water if necessary. Simmer 2 or 3 minutes. Serve with a few slivers of fresh lemon peel on each cutlet and with the sauce spooned over the meat and rice.

⋑ Veal Chops with Asparagus
BORJÚ KOTLETT KERTÉSZNÉ MÓDRA
(*bawr-yū kot-let kayr-tays-nay mohd-rah*)

Many asparagus recipes do not migrate well to America because the white European asparagus is so much more delicate than our own. This particular recipe, though, does succeed with the lustier American asparagus: the secret ingredient is the sautéed parsley —be careful not to forget it. The dish should be served with rice and a Boston lettuce salad. To my mind, the perfect dessert is fresh strawberries. Their season coincides with that of asparagus, and they seem to belong together. A white wine, a Hungarian Leányka or a German Moselle, would taste delicious with the meal.

1 pound asparagus spears
6 veal chops
Salt
Pepper
2 tablespoons butter

1 tablespoon cooking oil
1 tablespoon chopped parsley
1 tablespoon sifted or granular (instant-blending) flour
¼ cup sour cream

Cook the asparagus for 5 minutes, drain (reserving ½ cup of the liquid), and rinse under cold water. Season the veal chops with salt and pepper and brown them on both sides in hot butter and oil in a heavy-bottomed skillet. Place them in a side dish, and sauté the parsley in the remaining fat. Dilute the asparagus cooking liquid with ½ cup of water, and pour it into the skillet. Scrape up the bits stuck to the bottom of the pan, and let the sauce simmer for 2 to 3 minutes. Put the chops back in, and simmer, covered, for 15 minutes, turning the meat once. Lay the asparagus on top of the chops and simmer another 10 minutes. Remove from the heat. Carefully lift the chops and asparagus out of the pan and put them to one side. Blend the flour in the sour cream, and when the sauce has cooled to tepid spoon some of it into the sour cream. Then slowly stir the sour-cream mixture into the sauce. Put the meat and asparagus back in, and simmer gently, uncovered, for 5 minutes. Arrange the chops and asparagus on a serving platter, pour a little sauce over them, and serve, passing the rest of the sauce in a gravy boat.

✎§ Chopped Veal
BORJÚ FASIRT
(*bawr-yū fah-sheert*)

Some people rave about veal loaf and veal patties, but they have always struck me as a ho-hum kind of dish. The point of the exercise is to create something with a subtle, delicate taste; the risk is that the flavor will vanish into thin air. My own borjú fasirt has always been successful, but if the truth be told, I would rather make a meat loaf with beef (and pork and veal) or exchange my fakanál (wooden spoon) for a *toque blanche* and make a French liver pâté. For those who disagree, veal loaf, patties, or balls can be made by following the recipes for beef fasírozott (page 127), using 1¾ to 2 pounds of shoulder of veal ground together with ¼ pound of fat pork. A veal loaf might have pieces of ham or leftover chicken mixed in it for a change from hard-boiled eggs. It does seem to taste better cold, and I would build a meal like this around it: karfiol krém leves (cream of cauliflower soup, page 12), veal loaf with rakott krumpli (page 176), and tomato salad. Nothing overpowering for dessert, maybe apple or cherry rétes (strudel, page 212). A Rizling would be the right wine to drink.

⇜§ Veal Kidneys in Mustard Sauce
VESEPECSENYE
(ve-she-pe-chen-ye)

Over the years, my husband converted me to kidneys. It started with cooking them for him and something else for myself, but when I then had to cook a third meal for the children, I gave in. Now I have to admit they are delicious. The following recipe offers two options: without the sour cream, it is a light but very satisfying dish; with the sour cream, it is quite substantial. I serve it with rice and a green salad, and if the fancy strikes us, we have a dry red wine, like the Hungarian Szekszárdi Vörös, to drink with it. Most of the time, we stick to fresh fruit for dessert, but there is no logical reason not to have something more substantial, like palacsinta, to end the meal.

3 or 4 veal kidneys
¼ cup (½ stick) butter
1 tablespoon cooking oil
1 tablespoon minced onions
1½ tablespoons chopped parsley
¼ teaspoon dried marjoram
1 tablespoon lemon juice
1 tablespoon Dijon or Düsseldorf mustard
Salt
Freshly ground black pepper
½ cup sour cream, at room temperature (optional)

Clean the kidneys by removing all the fat and filament. Do not wash them. Heat the butter and oil in a large, heavy-bottomed skillet and brown the whole kidneys on all sides. On very low heat, cook the kidneys, uncovered, for 15 minutes, turning often. Transfer them to a side dish and keep them warm. Sauté the onions and parsley in the pan. When the onions wilt, add the marjoram, dilute the lemon juice with ½ cup of water and pour it into the pan, scraping up the juices. Simmer for 3 minutes, take the skillet off the heat, and stir in the mustard. Add salt and pepper to taste. Starting at the short end, slice the kidneys ¼ inch thick and put them in the pan, spooning sauce over them. If you wish to use sour cream, mix some sauce into it, then slowly stir the mixture into the pan. Warm the kidneys thoroughly over very low heat and serve.

✌§ Sweetbreads and Brains
BORJÚ MIRIGY ÉS BORJÚ VELŐ
(*bawr-yū mi-rij aysh bawr-yū ve-lu*)

Sweetbreads and brains are among the most delicate and perishable of meats, and they are increasingly hard to find. Eventually, they will probably disappear entirely, like lungs, which were banned from sale by the U.S. Department of Agriculture in the summer of 1971. Big-city Italian, Greek, and kosher butcher shops still have brains and sweetbreads occasionally or will order them for you. The logistical problem is such, however, that I for one now buy them when I see them, take them home, clean and blanch them, and fit them into the menu the next day. Both sweetbreads and brains seem to go best with rice and a tossed green salad. A good wine to drink with either would be a Hungarian Rizling.

Count three people to the pound (or two people to the piece) when buying sweetbreads or brains. To clean them, rinse them off, then place them in a large bowl of cold water under the tap. Let the cold water trickle into the bowl for 1½ to 2 hours. Every once in a while, peel off as much of the filament (the membrane that covers them) as you can without tearing the flesh. Then soak them in cold vinegar water (1 tablespoon vinegar per quart of water) for another 1½ to 2 hours, continuing to pull off the filament. Cut the lobes of the sweetbread away from the tube and discard it; cut away the white bits at the base of the brain and discard them. To blanch the sweetbreads or brains, place them in an enameled or stainless steel saucepan and cover with cold water. Add a teaspoon of salt and a tablespoon of lemon juice and slowly bring to the barest simmer. Keep the water just below the simmer for 15 to 20 minutes, then drain and cool the meat under cold water. Refrigerate until ready to use.

✏️ Breaded Brains or Sweetbreads

RÁNTOTT BORJÚ VELŐ / RÁNTOTT BORJÚ MIRIGY
(*rahn-tot bawr-yŭ ve-lu/rahn-tot bawr-yŭ mi-rij*)

One simple but very successful way to finish cooking the blanched brains or sweetbreads is to bread them and fry them in hot oil. Since they are already cooked, they will warm through sufficiently in the time it takes the coating to brown.

2 pounds brains or sweetbreads
Salt
Pepper
Sifted or granular (instant-blending) flour in a shaker
2 eggs
1½ cups bread crumbs
1 cup cooking oil
Boiled rice

Prepare brains or sweetbreads and blanch according to preceding directions. Cut the brains in half, or the sweetbreads in ½-inch slices, sprinkle with salt and pepper and flour, and shake off the excess. Beat the eggs lightly with a fork. Dip the pieces of brains or sweetbreads in the eggs, then roll in bread crumbs. Heat the oil in a skillet and quickly brown the pieces on all sides. Serve hot with rice.

✏️ Brains with Eggs

TOJÁSOS BORJÚ VELŐ
(*toi-ahsh-osh bawr-yŭ ve-lu*)

Tojásos velő is a light, delicate dish that is saved from excessive subtlety by onions and parsley. Serve it with fresh bread and salad and, if you wish, an unpretentious white wine.

3 brains (about 2 pounds)
1 small onion, minced
2 tablespoons butter
1 tablespoon oil
1 tablespoon chopped parsley
½ teaspoon salt
Pinch of freshly ground pepper
Pinch of dried marjoram
8 to 10 eggs
Paprika

Prepare and blanch the brains according to directions on page 98. Sauté the minced onion in the butter and oil until the pieces start to wilt. Add the parsley and brains, cut in ½ inch dice, and sprinkle with the salt, pepper, and marjoram. Sauté for 5 or 6 minutes. Beat the eggs, pour them over the brains, and cook like scrambled eggs. Sprinkle with paprika and serve immediately.

Beef
Marha

(MAHR-HA)

Beef falls way behind pork and veal in popularity among Hungarians. For the most part, they do not care for bloody meats or the sweet aftertaste of prime-grade American beef. For Americans, on the other hand, beef is what they mean by meat, and it is always available in a wide range of cuts and quality, unlike pork and veal. The secret of making good Hungarian dishes with American beef is to use the leaner, though not necessarily cheaper, cuts. They survive the stewing or braising process with both taste and texture intact. Keeping that basic fact in mind, you can serve a Hungarian pot roast or stew without hesitation: it will be a sure winner.

ৰ্ছ Goulash
BOGRÁCS GULYÁS
(boh-grahch gū-yahsh)

True Hungarian goulash is a spicy, rather thin stew to which potatoes or other vegetables are added shortly before serving. Traditionally, it was cooked in a bogrács, or cauldron, over an open fire. In a modern kitchen it should be cooked slowly in a heavy pot on a low, steady source of heat. It cannot be rushed, but the results are worth it. A good goulash is a meal in itself, needing nothing more than fresh bread to soak up the sauce. The inspired cook can invent scores of variations on the basic gulyás recipe, despite conditions of life in the supermarket era. Some suggestions and guidelines follow the main recipe.

Bogrács gulyás always tastes best with a dry white wine—a

Badacsonyi Kéknyelű or a Leányka. A fruitier white wine, like the Hungarian Badacsonyi Szürke Barát, goes very well with the gulyás variations. One of the lighter cakes like almás pite (page 222) or női szeszély (page 224) would be the best choice for dessert after any kind of gulyás.

1 large onion, finely chopped
About 3 tablespoons cooking oil or lard
1½ pounds lean stewing beef, cut in 1-inch cubes
1 teaspoon paprika
¼ teaspoon caraway seeds, mashed with the back of a spoon
Pinch of marjoram
Salt
2 cloves garlic, peeled and stuck on toothpicks
4 cups beef stock or canned beef broth
1 medium green pepper, cored and cut in ½-inch strips
3 small peeled tomatoes, preferably canned
2 pounds (about 8 or 9 medium) potatoes
Csipetke (pinched noodles, page 22) (optional)

Using a Dutch oven or a heavy casserole with a cover, sauté the onion in 3 tablespoons of oil or lard until it wilts. Remove to a side dish. Pat the meat dry and brown it, using more oil or lard if necessary. Put the meat in the side dish. Pour ½ cup of water into the pot, scrape up the juices and stir in the paprika, caraway seeds, marjoram, and 1 teaspoon of salt. Add the garlic. Put the beef and onions back in the pot, and add enough stock to cover the meat by 2 inches. Simmer for 1 hour, covered, adding more stock as necessary to keep the meat well covered with sauce. Mix in the green pepper strips and tomatoes and continue simmering. Peel the potatoes and cut them in ½-inch dice; keep them in cold water until ready to use. When the gulyás has been simmering for 1½ hours, stir in the potatoes and 1 teaspoon salt and enough water to cover them. Simmer another 25 minutes, partially covered, or until the potatoes are done. Ideally, gulyás has the consistency of a good Manhattan clam chowder, though it can also be somewhat thinner. If it is too thick, add some hot water, a little at a time. Discard the garlic, degrease and taste the sauce. It may need more salt. Stir in the csipetke and serve. Gulyás is usually brought to the table in the cooking pot or a soup tureen and ladled out into flat soup bowls.

Goulash with Cabbage
KOLOZSVÁRI GULYÁS
(koh-lohzh-vah-ree gū-yahsh)

One of the best ways to embellish a simple bogrács gulyás
(page 103) is with cabbage. Stir in 1 to 1½ pounds of cleaned,
shredded cabbage (about half a medium-size head) about 10 minutes
after adding the potatoes to the gulyás. Omit the csipetke.

Goulash with Savoy Cabbage
SZERB GULYÁS
(sayrb gū-yahsh)

For a unique taste sensation, try opposing the nutty mellowness
of Savoy cabbage and the spicy tang of gulyás. Clean and shred a
small head of Savoy cabbage (about 1½ to 2 pounds) and stir it into
the bogrács gulyás (page 103) about 10 or 15 minutes after the potatoes. Omit the csipetke.

Goulash with Vegetables
SZEGEDI GULYÁS
(seh-geh-dee gū-yahsh)

Vegetables other than cabbage can be added to gulyás too.
About 2 cups of partially cooked carrots (in ½-inch slices), kohlrabi
(in ½-inch dice), and green beans (in 1-inch pieces) should be
stirred into the bogrács gulyás (page 103) after the potatoes have
cooked 20 minutes. Add the csipetke as well.

◄§ Goulash with Sauerkraut
CSÁNGÓ GULYÁS
(chahn-goh gū-yahsh)

The Csángós are one of the "lost tribes" of Hungary, a group
of Szeklers who settled on the far side of the Carpathian Mountains
and were thus cut off from Hungarian influence. This dish which
bears their name is, in fact, a Székely gulyás made with beef. It has
a lighter, more subtle flavor than the pork version, and for that
reason might be more palatable to newcomers to Hungarian cuisine. Our family, I might note, prefers the uncompromised zing of

Székely gulyás (with pork). Both versions are served with boiled potatoes and seem to taste best with a Badacsonyi Kéknyelű. Fresh fruit or an aranygaluska coffeecake (page 218) would balance out the meal.

1 pound sauerkraut, preferably fresh or in a plastic package
   (or if not available, canned sauerkraut)
1 cup minced onions
About 3 tablespoons cooking oil or lard
1½ pounds lean stewing beef (such as top round), cut in 1-inch
   cubes
Beef stock or canned beef broth
1 teaspoon salt
1 teaspoon paprika
¼ teaspoon crushed caraway seeds
2 cloves garlic, peeled and stuck on toothpicks
½ green pepper, seeded and cut in ½-inch strips
½ cup sour cream, at room temperature
Boiled potatoes

Rinse the sauerkraut and drain it. If it still tastes briny, rinse a second time. Squeeze dry, and set it aside. In a large frying pan, cook the onions in 3 tablespoons of oil until they turn translucent. Pat the meat dry and brown it on all sides, a bit at a time so that the pan is not crowded, adding more oil if necessary. Place the meat in a 3-quart heavy-bottomed, covered, flameproof casserole (not an unlined cast-iron pot). When all the meat has been browned, pour ½ cup stock into the pan and scrape up the juices. Stir in salt, paprika, and caraway seeds. Simmer for 2 minutes, then pour over the meat in the casserole. Add the garlic and enough stock to cover the meat by 2 inches. Cover and simmer gently, adding more stock if necessary to keep meat well covered with sauce. After 1 hour (1½ hours if canned sauerkraut is used) add the sauerkraut and green pepper strips, by spreading them over the meat. Cover and simmer until the meat is tender, adding more stock if needed to keep the sauerkraut covered with sauce. Total cooking time: about 2 hours. When done, remove the pot from the heat, uncover, and let cool. Discard the garlic. Mix 2 tablespoons of sauce into the sour cream, then gradually stir the mixture into the stew. Correct the seasoning and slowly bring back to the simmer. Serve directly from the casserole or from a large bowl with boiled potatoes.

◄§ Beef Paprika Stew
MARHAPÖRKÖLT
(*mahr-ha-pur-kult*)

Marhapörkölt is what most people think of as goulash—a thick, hearty beef stew. With heaps of galuska, those tiny egg and flour dumplings the Germans call *Spätzle*, or broad egg noodles and a lettuce or cucumber salad, it makes a substantial meal. Beer tastes even better than wine with it. As with so many of the Hungarian stews, picking a dessert is not easy: rétes (strudel, page 212) is always applauded, of course, but fresh fruit—say, grapes and pears, since marhapörkölt is a cold-weather dish—would be my own first choice.

> 1 cup chopped onions
> About 3 tablespoons cooking oil or lard
> 2 pounds lean stewing beef (such as top round), cut in 1-inch cubes
> Beef stock or canned beef broth
> 1½ teaspoons salt
> 1½ teaspoons paprika
> ¼ teaspoon caraway seeds, crushed with the back of a spoon
> ⅛ teaspoon marjoram
> 1 medium pepper, seeded and cut in ½-inch strips
> 3 small peeled tomatoes, preferably canned
> Galuska (dumplings, page 21)

Fry the onions in 3 tablespoons of oil or lard in a 2- or 3-quart flameproof casserole until they turn transparent. Put them in a side dish or simply push them to one side. Pat the meat dry and brown it a few pieces at a time in the same pan, adding more oil if necessary. Remove the meat to a side dish. When all the meat has been browned, pour ½ cup of stock into the pot and scrape up any bits stuck to the bottom. Stir in the salt, paprika, caraway seeds, and marjoram. Cover and simmer 2 minutes. Put the beef and onions back in the pot. Add enough warm stock to barely cover the meat. Bring slowly to a simmer, cover, and cook for 1 hour, stirring from time to time and adding more stock as needed to keep the meat barely covered. Add the green pepper strips and tomatoes (just lay them on top of the meat), cover again, and continue simmering for 1 more hour. Stir now and then, and add more stock if the sauce evaporates. When the meat is tender, remove the casserole from the heat. Tip the pot and skim off as much fat as possible. Taste the sauce and correct the seasoning. Reheat and serve directly from the cooking pot or from a deep bowl. The galuska dumplings are served from another bowl, not mixed into the pörkölt.

⋖ঌ Seven Chieftains Tokány
HÉT VEZÉR TOKÁNY
(hayt ve-zayr to-kahny)

Of all the Hungarian stews, this is surely the most spectacular. It has everything—three kinds of meat, bacon, green peppers, tomatoes, sour cream—each element bringing out the noble qualities of the others while retaining its own identity. According to legend, each of the seven tribes of Hungary contributed one of the ingredients. True or not, hét vezér tokány, served with galuska and a crisp green salad, is a dish fit for kings—or nomadic tribal chieftains at the very least. A Leányka wine can give the meal a properly regal touch. One of the fancier cakes, a Dobos torta (page 232) or a diós (walnut) torta (page 239), might be served as dessert.

> ¼ pound smoked bacon (slab bacon is preferable, but
>   thick-sliced breakfast bacon may be used)
> 1 pound lean beef, preferably top round or flank steak
> ¾ pound shoulder of pork
> ¾ pound shoulder of veal
> 1 cup finely chopped onions
> Additional bacon fat or cooking oil
> 1½ teaspoons paprika
> 1½ teaspoons salt
> ¼ teaspoon marjoram
> ¼ teaspoon caraway seeds, crushed with the back of a spoon
> About ¾ cup cooking oil
> 1 medium green pepper, cored and cut in ½-inch strips
> 3 medium peeled tomatoes, preferably canned
> 1 cup beef stock, canned beef broth, or water

½ cup sour cream, at room temperature
Galuska (dumplings, page 21)

Cut the bacon, beef, pork, and veal into strips about 2 inches by ¼ inch by ¼ inch, making four separate piles. In a 3-quart heavy-bottomed casserole, fry the bacon until golden but not crisp. Using a slotted spoon, transfer the bacon to a side dish. Fry the onions in the same pan until they wilt, adding more fat or oil if needed. Stir in the paprika, salt, marjoram, caraway seeds, and ½ cup of water. Cover and simmer 2 minutes. Heat ¼ cup of cooking oil in a heavy skillet and start browning the beef strips a handful at a time. More oil may be needed to brown them all. Scrape the meat and juices into the casserole, cover, and simmer, stirring from time to time. Add more water as necessary to keep the sauce from cooking away. Next, brown the pork strips in the skillet, using another ¼ cup of oil. When the beef has cooked 1 hour, mix in the browned pork and lay the green pepper strips and tomatoes on top. Cover and continue simmering. Then brown the veal strips in the skillet, using the last ¼ cup of oil, and 30 minutes after adding the pork, mix the browned veal into the stew. Cover and simmer another 30 minutes. Taste a piece of each kind of meat to see if it is tender. If not, cook another 10 minutes or until the meat is done. Remove from the heat and let stand for 5 minutes. Tilt the pot and skim off as much grease as possible. Slowly pour in the beef stock or water and simmer for 5 minutes. Stir in the bacon strips and let the tokány stand until lukewarm. Beat the sour cream lightly with a fork, mix 2 tablespoons of sauce into the sour cream, then stir it into the stew. Taste and add more salt if the sauce seems flat. Just before serving, slowly reheat the tokány and let it simmer 2 or 3 minutes. The tokány may be brought to the table in the cooking pot or a covered bowl. To serve, place a generous amount of galuska on each dinner plate and spoon the tokány over them.

⊷§ Beef Stew with Pepper
BORSÓS TOKÁNY
(bor-shohsh to-kahny)

Borsós tokány is the simplest of dishes: thin strips of beef cooked in a thick, peppery sauce. To bring out its Oriental overtones, serve it with white rice. Tarhonya, another traditional garnish, is also very good, though a bit heavier. A green salad or cucumber salad is needed to round out the main course. Egri Bikavér, a rather mellow red wine, seems to go best with this particular tokány. For dessert, a fruit-filled rétes (strudel, page 212) or palacsinta with nuts (page 207) would be just right.

> About 6 tablespoons lard or cooking oil
> 1 cup finely chopped onions
> 2 pounds lean beef (such as top round or flank steak), cut in
>   strips 2 by ¼ by ¼ inch
> 1 tablespoon canned tomato purée
> 1½ teaspoons salt
> ¼ teaspoon marjoram
> ¼ teaspoon freshly ground black pepper
> 1 clove garlic, peeled and stuck on a toothpick
> ¾ cup beef stock, canned beef broth, or water
> Boiled rice or tarhonya (egg barley, page 27)

Heat 3 tablespoons of lard or oil in a 2-quart flameproof casserole, and sauté the onions in it until they wilt. Remove from the heat. Heat the remaining lard or oil in a heavy skillet and start browning the beef strips a handful at a time, using more lard or oil if necessary, and put them in the casserole with the onions. When all the meat is browned, stir the tomato purée into ½ cup of water and pour it into the skillet, scraping up the pan juices. Stir in the salt, marjoram, and pepper, and pour this sauce over the beef and onions. Add the garlic, cover, and simmer until the meat is tender, about 1½ to 2 hours. During the cooking, stir occasionally and add water as needed to keep the sauce from evaporating. When the meat is done, remove the casserole from the heat and let it stand for 5 minutes. Discard the garlic and tilt the pot to skim off as much grease as possible. Then gradually stir in the stock or water to make a thick, gravy-like sauce. Simmer for 5 minutes. Taste for seasoning and texture. If it is too thin, simmer 2 or 3 minutes more; if it seems too thick, add more stock or water, a tablespoonful at a time. Serve the tokány directly from the cooking pot or from a covered tureen. Give each person a helping of rice or tarhonya, and then spoon the tokány over it.

✑§ Beef Stew with Onions
HAGYMÁS TOKÁNY
(hudj-mahsh to-kahny)

Hagymás tokány gets its unique taste from the uncommon trio of marjoram, onions, and sour cream. It is a rich but delicately spiced dish that should be served with white rice and a tossed salad after the main course. A dry red Szekszárdi Vörös or a faintly fruity white Badacsonyi Szürke Barát wine would go with the meal. And, though hearty Magyar trenchermen could probably handle a tray of rétes (strudel) for dessert, almás (page 222) or túrós pite (page 224) or fresh fruits in season might be a wiser choice for American palates.

> 1 pound onions, finely chopped (about 4 cups)
> 6 tablespoons lard or cooking oil
> 2 pounds lean stewing beef (top round, flank steak, or top of the rib), cut in strips 2 by ¼ by ¼ inch
> 1 teaspoon salt
> ¼ teaspoon marjoram
> Freshly ground black pepper
> 1 cup beef stock, canned beef broth, or water
> ½ cup sour cream, at room temperature
> Boiled rice

In a 3-quart heavy-bottomed casserole with a cover, fry the onions in 3 tablespoons of the lard or oil until they wilt. Remove from heat. Heat 3 tablespoons of lard or oil in a heavy skillet and brown the meat strips a handful at a time. Add the meat to the onions. When all the meat has been browned, pour ½ cup of water into the skillet, scrape up the pan juices, and stir in the salt, marjoram, and pepper. Pour this sauce over the meat and onions, cover the casserole, and bring to a simmer. Continue to simmer for 1½ to 2 hours, or until the meat is tender. Stir occasionally, and add more water as necessary to keep the sauce from burning. Remove from heat and let stand 5 minutes. Then skim off as much grease as possible. Slowly stir in the beef stock, broth, or water and simmer 5 minutes. Remove from heat, and let cool. Lightly beat the sour cream with a fork, stir in 2 tablespoons of sauce, then gradually stir the sour-cream mixture into the stew. Taste for seasoning and add more salt and pepper if need be. Bring gently back to the simmer without boiling. Serve directly from the cooking pot or from a covered soup tureen, spooning a little tokány over each portion of white rice and the rest alongside.

✑ Beef Stew with Kidneys
HERÁNY TOKÁNY
(*heh-rahny to-kahny*)

The kidney expert in our family sampled this dish in reverential silence, and even I, though not a fancier myself, had to admit it was quite good. The children aged two and five, who can deliver an uninhibited "yuck!" if so moved, came back for seconds. In conclusion: this is a tokány worth trying. Serve it with tiny galuska dumplings or mashed potatoes and a tossed green salad on the side. A rich red wine like an Egri Bikavér would go best with this dish.

2 veal kidneys or 1 beef kidney
1 pound lean beef, preferably top round or flank steak
½ pound shoulder of pork
1 medium onion
½ cup cooking oil
1 teaspoon paprika
1 teaspoon salt
¼ teaspoon marjoram
1 cup beef stock, canned beef broth, or water
2 cloves garlic, peeled and stuck on toothpicks
¼ pound of mushrooms
3 tablespoons butter
½ cup sour cream, at room temperature
Galuska (dumplings, page 21) or mashed potatoes

Clean the kidney by discarding the fat and peeling off the filament if it was left on. Do not wash it. Cut the veal kidneys into ¼-inch slices, or the beef kidney into ½-inch cubes, and set aside. Cut the beef and pork into strips about 2 inches by ¼ inch by ¼ inch, keeping the two separate. Chop the onion and sauté it in ¼ cup of oil in a heavy skillet. When it turns translucent, push to one side and brown the beef a handful at a time. Transfer it to a 2- or 3-quart flameproof casserole or heavy pot, and sprinkle with the paprika, salt, and marjoram. Pour ½ cup of stock or water into the skillet, scrape up the juices, and pour over the beef. Stir thoroughly, drop in the garlic, cover and simmer gently. Wash and dry the skillet, then heat another ¼ cup of oil in it and brown the pork a handful at a time. After the beef has cooked for ½ hour, stir in the pork and the rest of the beef stock and continue simmering for 40 minutes. Lay the veal kidney pieces on top of the meat, and simmer, covered, for 10 minutes. (If beef kidney is used, add it after the pork has cooked 20 minutes.) Slice the mushrooms, brown them in butter, and put them in when the pork has cooked 50 minutes. Simmer another 10 minutes, then taste a piece of each meat for tenderness. If necessary, cook a few minutes longer. Remove from heat, discard the garlic, and skim off as much fat as possible. When the tokány is lukewarm, stir 2 tablespoons of it into the sour cream, then slowly stir the mixture into the stew. Taste for seasoning, then slowly bring the tokány back to the simmer and cook for 3 to 5 minutes. Serve it directly from the cooking pot or from a bowl, putting some galuska or mashed potatoes on each plate, then some tokány with a spoonful of sauce over everything.

Transylvanian Beef Stew
ERDÉLYI TOKÁNY
(*ehr-day-yi to-kahny*)

Erdélyi tokány never fails to please our guests, no matter which bank of the Tisza they were born on. To do full justice to its smoky aromatic flavor, we serve it with puliszka (yellow corn meal mush). By comparison, mashed potatoes are a poor second choice, because they just coast along without adding anything of their own to the meal. In any event, a mixed green salad should be served with the main course. Szekszárdi Vörös, a light red wine, goes best with erdélyi tokány. And the perfect dessert, in my opinion, is meggyes rétes (sour-cherry strudel, page 212).

> ¼ pound smoked bacon, preferably slab bacon, but
>   thick-sliced breakfast bacon may be used
> 2 pounds lean beef (such as top round or flank steak)
> 1 cup finely chopped onions

Additional bacon fat or lard
¼ cup lard or cooking oil
1 tablespoon canned tomato purée
½ cup dry white wine
1½ teaspoons salt
¼ teaspoon marjoram
Pinch of freshly ground black pepper
1 clove garlic, peeled and stuck on a toothpick
1 cup beef stock, canned beef broth, or water
Puliszka (page 28) or mashed potatoes

Cut the bacon and beef in strips 2 inches by ¼ inch by ¼ inch. Fry the bacon in a skillet until golden but not crisp. Using a slotted spoon, transfer the bacon to a side dish. Fry the onions in the same pan until they turn translucent, adding more fat or lard if necessary. Scrape them into a 2-quart, heavy-bottomed, flameproof casserole. Heat ¼ cup of lard or oil in the skillet. Pat the meat dry and start browning it, a handful at a time, in the skillet. Transfer it to the casserole, and when all the meat is browned, stir the tomato purée into the wine and pour it into the pan to scrape up the juices. Add the salt, marjoram, and pepper and simmer for 2 minutes. The sauce will be quite thick. Pour it over the beef and onions in the casserole and add the clove of garlic. Cover and simmer, stirring from time to time and adding more water if needed to keep the sauce from burning, until the meat is tender—about 1½ to 2 hours. Remove from heat, discard the garlic, and skim as much grease as possible from the sauce. Gradually stir in the beef stock, then simmer for 5 minutes and taste for seasonings. Tokány is supposed to have a thick gravy-like sauce: if it is too watery, simmer it another 2 or 3 minutes; if it seems too thick, add a little warm water, a tablespoonful at a time. Stir in the bacon. Just before serving, reheat the tokány and let it simmer for 2 or 3 minutes. Tokány can be served from the cooking pot or from a covered bowl. Give each person a generous helping of puliszka or mashed potatoes and spoon a little sauce and meat over it, putting the rest of the helping alongside.

Beef Stew with Mushrooms
GOMBÁS TOKÁNY
(gohm-bahsh to-kahny)

To make a tokány with mushrooms, follow the preceding recipe for erdélyi tokány. Leave out the bacon and fry the onions in an additional ¼ cup lard or cooking oil. Just before serving, stir in ½ pound of sliced fresh mushrooms that have been quickly sautéed in 3 tablespoons of butter.

Butcher's Stew
HENTES TOKÁNY
(hen-tesh to-kahny)

Hentes tokány is an erdélyi tokány (page 113) with frankfurter slices. It may sound weird, but it tastes delicious. As always, it is best to use the kind of loose frankfurters (not skinless) sold in butcher shops or kosher frankfurters, which seem to be a bit spicier than the ordinary kind. Cut 3 or 4 frankfurters in ½-inch slices, and add them to the tokány with the beef stock at the end. That way, they will cook long enough, about 8 to 10 minutes, but still be firm. Serve hentes tokány with puliszka (page 28) or mashed potatoes, just like erdélyi tokány.

✎§ Heart and Kidney Stew
VESE PÖRKÖLT
(ve-sheh pur-kult)

This is one of the classics of the Hungarian repertoire, a spicy, hearty stew that sticks to your ribs. It really is good. It can be served with galuska or mashed potatoes or tarhonya, and a green salad or cucumber salad on the side. An Egri Bikavér would be the right wine to drink with it. Since the dish is so filling, dessert should be light; my own choice would be boszorkányhab (page 200) or a bowl of fruit.

1 beef heart
1 beef kidney
¼ cup cooking oil or lard
1 medium onion

1 teaspoon paprika
1 teaspoon salt
Pinch of caraway seeds, crushed with the back of a spoon
½ medium green pepper, cut in strips
2 small, peeled tomatoes, preferably canned
1 clove garlic, peeled and stuck on a toothpick
1½ cups beef stock, canned beef broth, or water
Galuska (dumplings, page 21), or mashed potatoes, or
    tarhonya (egg barley, page 27)

Clean the heart and kidney, removing the fat, filament, and tubes, and cut them into 1-inch cubes. Heat the oil in a large, heavy-bottomed frying pan. Chop the onion and sauté it in the oil until it wilts. Transfer the onion to a 2- or 3-quart flameproof casserole, and brown the pieces of meat lightly on all sides, using more oil if necessary. Place them in the casserole with the onions, and sprinkle with paprika, salt, and caraway seeds. Lay the pepper strips, tomatoes, and garlic on top. Use ½ cup of stock or water to rinse out the frying pan, scraping up any bits stuck to the bottom, and pour this sauce over the meat and vegetables. Add enough stock or water to barely cover the meat. Bring to a simmer, and cook, covered, for 45 minutes, or until the meat is tender. Serve directly from the pot or from a bowl, spooning lots of sauce over each portion of galuska, potatoes, or tarhonya.

✑ Pot Roast
DINSZTELT MARHAHÚS
(deen-stelt mahr-hah-húsh)

It is one of the ironies of modern life that so many good cooks either sail along throwing slabs of bloody beef on the fire or slave for hours transforming butchers' scraps into a *ragoût de Saispasquoi* while the worthy pot roast lies neglected. Yet it is the ideal dish for family and friends (though not, perhaps, the boss's wife), since it can be made at any time and reheated—in fact, it tastes better that way. Dinsztelt marhahús is the universal Middle European pot roast; vadas hús, in which the meat is marinated and cooked like big game, gives it a unique trans-Danubian twist. Potato dumplings always go with pot roast, as do flat egg noodles. A mixed green salad should be served as well, with a pleasant dry wine, a red Szekszárdi Vörös or a white Badacsonyi Kéknyelű, to drink. Dessert might be an almás (page 222) or a túrós pite (page 224).

4 pounds beef for potting, preferably rump roast or brisket
6 tablespoons cooking oil
Salt
1 cup carrots, sliced ¼ inch thick
1 cup onions, sliced ¼ inch thick
2 tablespoons flour
¾ cup (one 6-ounce can) mixed vegetable juice (if not available, use tomato juice)
1¼ cups beef stock or canned beef broth
2 cloves garlic
12 peppercorns
1 bay leaf
Pinch of thyme
Potato dumplings (page 26) or egg noodles or mashed potatoes

Brown the beef on all sides in 3 tablespoons of hot oil in a heavy skillet. Salt the meat liberally. In a Dutch oven or casserole large enough to hold the piece of meat comfortably, heat the rest of the oil and cook the carrot and onion slices until the onions start to wilt. Sprinkle on the flour, and cook, stirring constantly, until the flour begins to brown. Mix together the juice and stock and pour slowly into the pot, scraping up any bits stuck to the bottom. Simmer for 2 minutes, then stir in the garlic, peppercorns, bay leaf, and thyme. Place the browned meat in the sauce, cover, and simmer very slowly. Add more stock as the braising juices evaporate, and turn the meat once or twice so that it cooks evenly. Take the meat out of the sauce when it is tender enough to be pierced with a table fork: this should take 3 hours, more or less, depending on the cut and quality of the beef. Strain the sauce and let it settle, then skim off as much fat as possible from the surface. Taste and correct the seasoning. Put the roast back in the sauce and reheat before serving. Slice the meat and arrange it on a platter, and pour the sauce into a gravy boat. Serve with plenty of dumplings, egg noodles, or mashed potatoes.

✑ Hunter-Style Pot Roast
VADAS HÚS
(va-dahsh hūsh)

If one day somebody brings home a haunch of wild boar or a
leg of venison, you can follow this recipe to cook it, for that was its
original intent. Just substitute the game meat for the beef, lard it
with strips of fat bacon, and proceed. To prepare for that eventu-
ality, keep practicing with beef for a truly sensational pot roast.
Serve it with potato dumplings or wide egg noodles and a mixed
green salad. Either white or red wine goes with this dish: our choice
would be a red Nemes Kadar or a white Badacsonyi Szürke Barát.
A light sweet dessert should be served, ízes tekercs (jelly roll,
page 230) perhaps.

> 3 tablespoons vinegar
> 1 cup cooking oil
> 12 peppercorns
> 1 bay leaf
> Pinch of thyme
> Peel of 1 lemon, cut in ½-inch strips
> 2 to 3 tablespoons lemon juice
> 1 carrot, cut in ½-inch pieces
> 1 medium onion, sliced ¼ inch thick
> 3 sprigs parsley
> 2 cloves garlic, peeled
> 3 strips bacon rind, ¼ by 2 inches (optional)
> 4 pounds beef for potting, preferably rump roast
> ¼ cup diced bacon (smoked slab bacon is preferable, but
>   thick-sliced breakfast bacon may be used instead)
> 3 tablespoons cooking oil
> Salt
> About 4 cups beef stock or canned beef broth
> 1 tablespoon lemon juice
> 2 teaspoons sugar
> 1 tablespoon Dijon mustard, or 1 teaspoon dry mustard
> 1 cup sour cream, at room temperature
> 1 teaspoon capers (optional)
> Potato dumplings (page 26) or wide egg noodles

Place the first twelve ingredients in an enameled saucepan and simmer for 20 minutes to make a marinade. Tie the meat securely and place it in a glass or porcelain dish. When the marinade has cooled completely, pour it over the meat. Leave it in the marinade for anywhere from 6 hours to 3 days, turning once in the morning and once at night. Refrigeration is not necessary. Just before cooking, take the piece of beef out of the marinade, drain it on a rack for 20 minutes, and dry it thoroughly. Fry the bacon bits in a large enameled flameproof casserole (not an unlined cast-iron Dutch oven), and when they start to render fat, add the cooking oil. Brown the meat carefully on all sides and salt it liberally. Boil down the marinade, reducing it by half, and pour it over the meat. Add enough beef stock to come three-quarters of the way up the meat. Cover and simmer gently until the meat is done, at least 3 hours for a 4-pound piece of meat. (Cooking time varies greatly according to the cut and quality of the meat.) Add more stock from time to time if the braising juices evaporate, and turn the meat at least once so that it cooks evenly. When the meat is done, place it in a side dish and keep it warm. Strain the sauce, let it settle, and skim off as much fat as possible. Blend the lemon juice, sugar, and mustard together, and add them to the sauce. Simmer for 10 to 15 minutes. The sauce should be rather thick: if it seems too watery, raise the heat and boil off some liquid. Then let the sauce cool thoroughly. Stir 2 tablespoons of sauce into the sour cream before pouring the cream into the sauce. Add the capers if you wish to use them, and taste for seasoning. Put the meat back in the pot, and just before serving, bring everything back to the simmer. Arrange slices of meat on a platter with the dumplings or noodles, and pass the sauce in a gravy boat.

⊸§ Mock Hunter-Style Pot Roast
HAMIS VADAS HÚS
(ha-mish va-dahsh hūsh)

The one drawback to vadas hús is that it has to be thought of and started days ahead. It can be faked, though, by adding some of the marinade ingredients to an ordinary pot roast, and the results, while less stunning than a true vadas hús, are quite impressive. Serve hamis vadas hús with noodles or potato dumplings and a green salad. Nemes Kadar wine is particularly good with the dish, and almás pite (page 222) is the kind of light dessert the meal needs.

¼ cup diced bacon (smoked slab bacon is preferable, but
    thick-sliced breakfast bacon may be used instead)
2 carrots, sliced ½ inch thick
1 medium onion, thinly sliced
2 tablespoons flour
1 tablespoon vinegar
2 cups beef stock, canned beef broth, or water
4 pounds beef for potting, preferably rump roast
3 tablespoons cooking oil
Salt
Peel of 1 lemon, cut in ½-inch strips
Slivers of bacon rind, if smoked slab bacon was used
2 cloves garlic
12 peppercorns
1 bay leaf
Pinch of thyme
1 tablespoon lemon juice
2 teaspoons sugar
1 tablespoon Dijon mustard, or 1 teaspoon dry mustard
1 cup sour cream, at room temperature
1 teaspoon capers (optional)
Potato dumplings (page 26) or noodles

Fry the bacon bits in a flameproof enameled casserole (not an unlined cast-iron pot) that will be large enough to hold the piece of meat. When the bacon starts to render fat, add the carrots and onions and cook them, stirring occasionally, until the onions wilt. Sprinkle with flour and brown it. Mix the vinegar in the stock and pour it on, scraping up any pieces of food stuck to the bottom of the pot. Brown the beef on all sides in hot oil in a large, heavy frying pan. Salt it liberally, place it in the casserole, and spread the lemon peel, bacon rind if you have it, garlic, peppercorns, bay leaf, and thyme around it. Cover and simmer until the meat is done (when it is tender enough to be pierced easily with a table fork). Cooking time will vary with the cut and the quality of the meat; count on a minimum of 3 hours for a 4-pound piece of beef. While the roast is cooking, be sure to add stock or water if the braising juices evaporate and to turn the meat at least once so that it cooks evenly. When the meat is done, place it in a side dish. Strain the sauce, let it settle, and skim off as much fat as possible. Blend the lemon juice, sugar, and mustard together and add them to the sauce. Simmer for 10 to 15 minutes, stirring from time to time. The sauce should be rather thick: if it seems too soupy, raise the heat and boil off some liquid. Then let the sauce cool thoroughly. Stir 2 tablespoons of lukewarm sauce into the sour cream, and slowly pour the mixture into the sauce. Add the capers if you wish, and taste the sauce for seasoning. Before serving, return the meat to the pot and slowly bring everything back to the simmer. Arrange slices of meat on a platter with the dumplings or noodles, and pass the sauce in a gravy boat.

ᴥᶳ Giant Beef Roll
STEFÁNIA TEKERCS
(shte-fah-nee-a te-kayrch)

It may be that pot roast is not fancy enough for the boss's wife —Stefánia tekercs certainly is. Rolled beef is prepared like pot roast and served with that marvelous sauce. The surprise comes when the meat is sliced and the hard-boiled eggs make their appearance. Egg noodles or mashed potatoes seem to go best with this dish, and the thing to drink would be a dry red wine like the Hungarian Szekszárdi Vörös or a French St.-Émilion. To complete the meal, a fresh green salad is needed. Either something rich like a fancy torta or something elegantly simple like a madártej (floating island, page 201) could be served for dessert, depending on the occasion.

2½- to 3-pound piece of top round about 6 inches wide and at least 1½ inches thick
Salt
Freshly ground black pepper
Marjoram
Strong Dijon or Düsseldorf mustard
3 hard-boiled eggs, cooled and shelled
½ pound of smoked bacon, sliced (slab bacon is preferable, but thick-sliced breakfast bacon can be used)
6 tablespoons cooking oil

[121]

1 cup sliced carrots
1 cup sliced onions
2 tablespoons flour
About 2 cups beef stock or canned beef broth
2 cloves garlic
12 peppercorns
1 bay leaf
Pinch of thyme
Egg noodles or mashed potatoes

Place the meat on a flat surface and cut it horizontally almost all the way through the middle—as if you were cutting a roll for a hero sandwich: starting at one long side, slice it parallel to the table to within ½ inch of the other long side. Open the meat out and pound the seam flat if necessary. Sprinkle the meat liberally with salt, pepper, and marjoram and spread it with mustard. Place the eggs close together in a row parallel to the seam about 1½ to 2 inches in from the edge. Then roll the meat lengthwise as tightly as you can. Lay the slices of bacon on the meat, covering the seams and the ends, and tie the roll securely. Heat 3 tablespoons of oil in a heavy skillet and brown the meat lightly on all sides, handling it very carefully. In a Dutch oven or casserole large enough to hold the piece of meat comfortably, heat the rest of the oil and cook the carrot and onion slices until the onions start to wilt. Sprinkle with flour and continue to cook, stirring constantly, until the flour begins to brown. Pour ½ cup of stock into the pot, and scrape up any bits stuck to the bottom. Simmer for 2 minutes, then add the garlic, peppercorns, bay leaf, and thyme. Place the beef roll in the casserole and add enough stock to come halfway up the meat. Cover and simmer very slowly until the meat is tender when pierced with a knife, at least 2 hours. During the cooking, be sure to add more stock as the braising juices evaporate and to turn the meat carefully once or twice so that it cooks evenly. When the meat is done, take it out of the sauce and keep it warm. Strain the sauce and let it settle, then skim off as much fat as possible from the surface. Taste and correct the seasoning. Put the meat back in the sauce. Reheat just before serving. Remove and discard the string and bacon. Slice the meat and arrange it on a platter. Pour the sauce into a gravy boat, and serve with plenty of noodles or mashed potatoes.

✑§ Stuffed Beef Rolls
MARHATEKERCS
(*mahr-hah-te-kayrch*)

Every culture has its beef rolls—marhatekercs, rouladen, paupiettes, brasciole—for this is one of the universal ways of transforming mundane ingredients into a sublime dish. The rolls can be made in advance and reheated, though in that case it would be better not to add the sour cream to the sauce until just before serving. The last time we had marhatekercs, there were two pieces left over, so we ate them cold the next day. They were very good that way too. Rice or noodles can be served with the meat, but for a more distinctly Hungarian touch, try tarhonya. Salad is a must. For wine, pick a light red one: a Szekszárdi Vörös. This is a meal that can take a homemade cake or pastry for dessert, like almás pite (page 222) or női szeszély (page 224).

> 5 tablespoons lard or cooking oil
> 1 small onion, finely chopped
> 1 pound ground pork
> 1 egg yolk
> Salt
> ½ teaspoon dried marjoram
> Pinch of freshly ground black pepper
> About ½ cup sour cream
> About ¼ cup dry bread crumbs
> 2 to 2½ pounds top round, cut in ¼-inch slices and flattened
> 2 cups of beef stock or canned beef broth
> 1 teaspoon paprika
> ¼ teaspoon caraway seeds, crushed with the back of a spoon
> 2 cloves garlic, peeled and stuck on toothpicks
> Tarhonya (egg barley, page 27)

To make the filling, heat 2 tablespoons of lard in a skillet and fry the onion in it. When the onion pieces start to wilt, add the ground pork and brown it all over. Scrape it all into a bowl, let it cool for 10 minutes, then add the egg yolk, ½ teaspoon of salt, the marjoram, and pepper. Stir in 1 to 2 tablespoons of sour cream and add as much bread crumbs as needed to make the mixture stick together. It should be moist but not wet. Cut the beef into pieces about 3 to 4 inches in diameter, and divide the stuffing evenly among them, spooning some on the lower half of every piece. Roll up each piece and tie it with string. Heat the remaining lard or oil in a clean skillet, and brown the rolls lightly on all sides. Transfer them to a large, heavy-bottomed casserole. Pour ½ cup of beef stock into the pan and scrape up the juices. Stir in the paprika and ½ teaspoon of salt, and pour the sauce over the beef rolls. Add the rest of the stock and as much water as needed to barely cover them. Sprinkle with caraway seeds, drop in the cloves of garlic, and bring to a simmer. Continue to simmer, covered, for about 1 hour, basting the rolls from time to time. Rearrange them at least once so that they cook evenly. Remove the rolls to a side dish and remove the strings. Discard the garlic. Taste the sauce; if it is too thin, boil it down to concentrate it. Let it cool to tepid. Blend some of the meat sauce in the remaining sour cream and stir it in slowly, using only as much as needed to make a thick but not milky sauce. Bring the sauce back to the simmer and correct the seasoning. Put the rolls back into the sauce, and set the casserole aside until about 15 minutes before serving. Then bring it back to a simmer and let it cook gently for 3 to 5 minutes. Serve directly from the casserole, along with tarhonya.

◄§ Braised Steak
ROSTÉLYOS
(rosh-tay-yohsh)

In Hungary, as elsewhere in Europe, braised or potted steak appears quite often on the menu of simple restaurants and on the table at home. Rostélyos can be good, but it seldom goes beyond its basic function, namely to make tough beef edible. In my experience, American steak is seldom tough enough to justify a rostélyos, and I have come to regard it as a waste of time and effort that could have gone into a great stew. That is one cook's opinion. For the contrary-minded, here is a basic recipe for rostélyos, followed by three classic variations. If possible, use top round or some other lean steak; under no circumstances use chuck or what is called California steak in some parts of the country—it is far too fatty and gives an unpleasant taste to the sauce. Szekszárdi Vörös is the wine to serve with rostélyos. Dessert might be stuffed palacsinta or diós tészta (noodles with nuts, page 206).

3 tablespoons lard or cooking oil
2 to 2½ pounds top round steak, cut in 6 individual portions
½ cup minced onions
About 2 cups beef stock or canned beef broth
1½ teaspoons paprika
Salt
Pinch of caraway seeds, crushed with a spoon
Pinch of marjoram
1 clove garlic, peeled and stuck on a toothpick
½ medium green pepper, seeded and cut in ½-inch strips
2 small peeled tomatoes, preferably canned
About 1½ pounds (6 medium) potatoes

Heat the lard or oil in a large, heavy-bottomed skillet. Pat the pieces of meat dry, and brown them lightly on both sides. Remove to a side dish and keep warm. Sauté the onions in the browning fat until they turn translucent, then pour in ½ cup of stock and scrape up all the juices. Stir in the paprika, salt, caraway seeds, marjoram, and garlic. Return the steaks to the skillet, lay the green pepper and tomatoes on top, and add enough stock to barely cover the meat. Simmer, covered, for 30 minutes. Meanwhile, peel the potatoes and slice them into half-moons. (To make half-moons, cut the potato in half lengthwise, lay it flat, and slice it ¼ inch thick the long way.) Let them stand in a bowl of cold water until ready to use. Place the potatoes on top of the meat, and add ½ teaspoon salt and enough stock or water to cover them. Cover and simmer another 30 minutes or until the potatoes are done. Discard the garlic, degrease the sauce, taste and serve at once.

Braised Steak with Galuska
HORTOBÁGYI ROSTÉLYOS
(hor-toh-bahd-yee rosh-tay-yohsh)

Hortobágyi rostélyos is made the same way as ordinary rostélyos, but it is garnished with galuska (page 21), and that fact alone makes an amazing difference. Follow the preceding basic rostélyos recipe, omitting the potatoes, and cook enough galuska for six. Put a few dumplings on each steak and serve the rest in a bowl.

Braised Steak with Bacon
BÁCSKAI ROSTÉLYOS
(*bahch-koi rosh-tay-yohsh*)

This is a smoky rostélyos, and it seems to go best with tar-honya (egg barley, page 27) or plain boiled potatoes. To make bácskai rostélyos, start as in the master rostélyos recipe (page 124), browning the steaks and making the sauce. While it is simmering, fry ¼ pound of smoked slab bacon cut in strips 1 inch long by ¼ inch thick. When the bacon starts to render fat, add the green pepper strips and the tomatoes cut in quarters. Sprinkle with ½ teaspoon of salt, cover, and simmer 10 minutes. Add to the meat and continue cooking until it is done. Omit the potato half-moons, and serve with tarhonya or boiled potatoes instead.

Braised Steak with Vegetables
ESZTERHÁZY ROSTÉLYOS
(*es-ter-hah-zee rosh-tay-yohsh*)

So many culinary bastards have assumed the Eszterházy name that it is hard to guess by now what went on in the kitchens of the original Eszterházys. For their version of rostélyos (page 124), the significant characteristic—the family nose, so to speak—is the garnish of julienned vegetables.

Brown the steaks in lard or oil and put them to one side. Sauté ½ cup of chopped onions in the browning fat until they wilt, then pour in ½ cup of beef stock to scrape up the juices. Salt and pepper the steaks and put them back in the skillet. Add enough stock to nearly cover them. Drop a clove of garlic in, plus a zest of lemon rind (a piece of peel about 3 inches by ½ inch) and 2 or 3 slivers of bacon rind. Put the lid on and simmer for 1 hour, turning the meat at least once and adding more stock as necessary to keep the sauce from evaporating. Meanwhile, peel 1 carrot and 1 parsnip or small kohlrabi and cut them into julienne strips, about the size of a matchstick. Drop them into boiling salted water and let them cook for 5 minutes. Drain and cool instantly under running cold water. When the meat is done, transfer it to a serving platter, and taste and correct the seasoning of the sauce. Pour a little sauce over the steaks, and garnish each one with the vegetable strips. Serve with mashed potatoes, and pass the rest of the sauce in a gravy boat.

[126]

⋙ Meatballs

FASÍROZOTT

(fah-shee-ro-zot)

Sometimes it seems everyone likes meatballs except me. But if I have to have them, this is the way I like them to be. Not too hard, not too soft, bathed in a sour cream gravy, and served with lots of noodles and salad.

1 pound chopped beef
½ pound chopped pork
1 dry bread slice
1 small onion, finely chopped
6 tablespoons lard or cooking oil
1 teaspoon salt
Pinch of black pepper
½ teaspoon marjoram
1 egg
½ teaspoon paprika
1 cup beef broth or water
2 to 4 tablespoons sour cream

Mix the beef and pork together in a large bowl. Soak the slice of bread in water, squeeze it out, and shred it. Work the bits of bread into the meat. Fry the onion in 2 tablespoons of lard or oil until the pieces turn translucent. Scrape the onion and fat into the bowl, and mix well into the meat, then add the salt, pepper, marjoram, and egg, and knead thoroughly by hand. Dust your hands with flour and form meatballs. Heat the rest of the lard or oil in a large skillet and brown the balls lightly on all sides. Cover and cook for 20 minutes, turning once. To make a gravy, remove the meatballs to a side dish and keep them warm. Pour off some of the fat, leaving about 2 or 3 tablespoons in the pan. Briefly sauté the paprika in the fat, then stir in 1 cup of broth or water, scraping up the bits of meat. After simmering the sauce for 2 minutes, let it cool. Mix some of the sauce in the sour cream before stirring the sour cream into the pan. Use only 2 tablespoons of sour cream at first, and taste the gravy for consistency and seasoning: add more sour cream and more salt if needed. Bring back to a simmer, pour over the meatballs, and serve.

⊸§ Meat Loaf
TÖLTÖTT FASÍROZOTT
(*tul-tot fah-shee-ro-zot*)

In a rather cinematic flash-forward, I can see the Hungarians shaking their heads and hear them tut-tutting over this recipe. And that is because every mother made it differently, and probably made it differently each time. The one heresy I do acknowledge is the use of rice and vegetable juice instead of the classic hard roll soaked in milk, which we have found makes the meat loaf too pasty and bland. Instead of hard-boiled eggs, it could have a smoked sausage buried in it for a change of pace. Just about any vegetable goes with meat loaf: in our family we like it with mashed potatoes or rakott krumpli (page 176), a vegetable, and salad.

5 eggs
¼ cup diced bacon
½ cup chopped onions
1 tablespoon chopped fresh parsley
1 pound ground beef
1 pound ground pork (or ½ pound ground pork plus ½ pound ground veal)
2 tablespoons rice, instant or regular
1½ teaspoons salt
¼ teaspoon freshly ground black pepper
½ teaspoon marjoram
¾ cup (6-ounce can) mixed vegetable juice or tomato juice

Put 3 of the eggs in an enameled or stainless steel saucepan, cover with cold water, and bring to a boil. Cook for 6 to 8 minutes, no longer, cool quickly under running cold water, and shell. Fry the bacon in a skillet until it has rendered fat, stir in the onions and parsley, and sauté, stirring occasionally, until the onions wilt and the bacon turns golden. Mix the two meats together in a large bowl and scrape in the bacon and onion mixture with all its fat. Add the instant rice (or half-cooked regular rice), the salt, pepper, and marjoram, the juice, and the remaining two eggs. Using your hands, knead it all thoroughly together. Pack a third of the meat into the bottom of a loaf pan measuring 9 inches by 5 inches by 3 inches.

Lay the shelled hard-boiled eggs lengthwise down the middle and cover with the rest of the meat. (Or form a rye-bread-shaped loaf with your hands and bake it in a roasting pan.) Score the top of the loaf in a diamond pattern, place in a preheated 350° degree oven, and bake for 1 hour or until the meat shrinks away from the sides of the pan. When the meat loaf is done, pour off all the fat and either place the loaf on a serving platter or serve it directly from the pan. It tastes good either hot or cold.

Lamb
Bárány

(BAH-RAHNY)

Lamb does not rank high in the Hungarian culinary hierarchy. Urban Hungarians, in fact, seldom eat it except for the Paschal lamb. But there are some excellent ways to prepare lamb with a Magyar twist that come from those regions of the country where sheep are raised. Since Americans do like lamb, I have culled a few of those recipes from old Hungarian cookbooks, tried them out on family and friends, and narrowed the list down to one superb stew and three new ways to prepare leg of lamb.

◄§ Lamb Goulash
PALÓC GULYÁS
(*pah-lohts gū-yahsh*)

For years I have sought to tame the lamb stew, with little success. I have tried the most sophisticated French elaborations; I have added potpourris of spices and painstakingly removed every speck of fat. Still no luck. So it was with some trepidation that I embarked on the Hungarian experiments. Fortunately, I hit the jackpot first time around with this lamb goulash. The spicy sweet-sour sauce eliminates all the gamy aftertaste of stewed lamb, and although potatoes and green beans are the most conventional complement to lamb, in this dish they manage to appear quite exotic. Stew can be a humble meal, but with a light, dry red wine like a Hungarian Szekszárdi Vörös to drink, this one is positively festive. To my way of thinking, the best dessert to serve with paV́ gulyás is fresh fruits and nuts. If the occasion demands something more elaborate, how-

ever, it should be kept very light, like ízes tekercs (jelly roll, page
230) or aranygaluska (yeast cake, page 218).

> 3½ pounds lamb for stewing (shoulder and breast), cut in
>   2-inch pieces
> 6 tablespoons cooking oil or lard
> 1 tablespoon sugar
> 2 medium onions, finely chopped
> About 3 cups beef stock or canned beef broth
> 1 tablespoon vinegar
> 2 teaspoons salt
> 1 teaspoon paprika
> ¼ teaspoon caraway seeds, crushed with the back of a spoon
> ⅛ teaspoon dried marjoram
> 3 cloves garlic, peeled and stuck on toothpicks
> 1 medium green pepper, cored and cut in ½-inch strips
> 3 small peeled tomatoes, preferably canned
> 2 pounds potatoes, peeled and cut in ½-inch dice (about 5 cups)
> 1 pound cooked green beans, cut in 1-inch pieces
> ½ cup sour cream

Brown the lamb in 3 tablespoons of oil or lard in a large heavy
skillet. Sprinkle the pieces of meat with sugar, and toss in the pan
until the sugar browns. Heat the remaining oil or lard in a flameproof casserole large enough to hold all the meat comfortably, and
fry the chopped onions in it until they wilt. Transfer the meat to the
casserole, pour the fat out of the skillet, and deglaze it with about
½ cup of beef stock. Stir in the vinegar, 1 teaspoon of salt, and the
paprika, caraway seeds, and marjoram, and pour this sauce over the
meat. Add more stock until the meat is barely covered. Drop in the
garlic, green pepper, and tomatoes, cover, and simmer. After 1 hour,
place a colander in a large bowl and strain the gulyás. Discard the
garlic and all the lamb fat and bones. Remove as much grease as
possible from the sauce, and put the pieces of meat back in. Mash
the green pepper and the tomatoes through the colander and add
that pulp to the gulyás. Add the diced potatoes and 1 teaspoon of
salt, and simmer for 20 minutes. Stir in the green beans and simmer
for 10 minutes more. Remove from the heat and skim off as much
fat as possible from the sauce. When it is cool enough to put your

finger in, mix 2 tablespoons of sauce into the sour cream, then slowly add that mixture to the gulyás. Taste for seasoning: more salt and vinegar may be needed. Just before serving, bring back to a simmer. Transfer the stew to a soup tureen or deep bowl, or take the cooking pot directly to the table.

✒️ Roast Leg of Lamb/Leg of Mutton
SÜLT BÁRÁNYCOMB/BIRKACOMB
(shült bah-rahny-tsohmb/beer-ka-tsohmb)

The best place to buy lamb is from a Greek or Italian butcher, if you're lucky enough to have one around. If not, supermarket lamb is generally of good quality. Always make sure lamb is fresh. Smell the shank end: high lamb has an unpleasant aroma, and it starts around the bone. Allow a whole leg of lamb to serve six or more people, half a leg or a boned and rolled shoulder to serve four to six.

To prepare lamb for cooking, trim off most of the fat and the purple USDA stamps. Make slits in the meat with the tip of a paring knife and insert slivers of garlic (up to three cloves for a whole leg), and sprinkle liberally with salt and pepper. Wrap the meat loosely in waxed paper and keep it in the refrigerator until ready to roast. Then oil a roasting pan with 2 tablespoons of cooking oil, put the meat in, fat side up, and roast in a preheated hot oven (450°) for 15 minutes. Turn the heat down to 350° and roast until done (turn the pan around occasionally if the oven heats unevenly), counting 15 to 20 minutes per pound for unboned meat. If the meat is boned, allow 30 to 35 minutes per pound. At these cooking times, the lamb will be medium well done, with some parts still rather rare. When the meat is done, take it out of the pan and let it stand for about 20 minutes. Since lamb cools so fast, it is advisable to carve it only at the very last minute and, if possible, to keep the meat warm at the table on a hot tray or some other device. Up to this point the leg of lamb is culturally neutral; to Magyarize it, try one of the following recipes.

✑ Leg of Lamb Baker's Wife Style
BÁRÁNYCOMB PÉKNÉ MÓDRA
(bah-rahny-tsohmb payk-nay mohd-rah)

This is a welcome variation on the theme of lamb with oven-browned potatoes, which are all too often a dismal flop. The potato slices have plenty of time to cook through and brown, and they give the lamb a happy new aspect. The meal definitely needs a green salad, and, perhaps, another hot vegetable like green beans or grilled tomatoes. Any of the Hungarian red wines would go with the lamb; we prefer a Szekszárdi Vörös. This is one of those rare meals at which any dessert could be served, and since the main course requires little advance preparation, it would be a good occasion for a palacsinta extravaganza.

1 lamb roast
Potatoes (allow 2 medium potatoes per person)
2 tablespoons butter
Salt

Cook the roast as directed in the preceding master recipe. While the meat is cooking, peel and slice the potatoes as thinly as possible (use a potato peeler or cucumber slicer if available). Leave the potato slices in cold water until ready to use. About 1 hour before the end of the meat's cooking time, drain and dry the potato slices and spread them evenly around the roast in a layer two to three slices thick. A large whole leg of lamb may not leave enough room in the pan for all the potatoes. In that case, pour the pan fat and juices into a shallow baking dish and spread the potatoes in that. Dot with butter and salt liberally. Put everything back in the oven. After 30 minutes, turn the potatoes over, then put them back in the oven for another 30 minutes. When the meat is done, remove it from the pan and let it cool for 20 minutes. Since potatoes cooked in the pan this way absorb most of the juices, it is possible to make only a bit of sauce. Remove the potatoes to a side dish and place the pan on the heat. Pour in ½ cup of hot water, scrape up the remaining juices, and boil rapidly for 1 minute. Slice the meat in the kitchen and arrange it on a platter with the potatoes, or carve it at the table and serve the potatoes separately. Pass the sauce in a small gravy boat.

ᷔᷓ Leg of Lamb with Dill
BIRKACOMB KAPORMÁRTÁSSAL
(*beer-ka-tsohmb kah-pawr-mahr-tah-shahl*)

The dill/sour cream combination is one of the minor triumphs of Hungarian cookery, and it does something extraordinary for lamb. The dish turns out to be quite rich, so it is wise to keep the rest of the meal simple: boiled potatoes and green beans with the meat and a green salad on the side. Red wine is the conventional choice for lamb, but because of the sour cream sauce, a dry white wine goes almost as well. We often have cheese and fruit—a distinctly non-Hungarian dessert—after lamb, but I have never seen anyone refuse a portion of apple or cherry rétes (strudel, page 212) or a rakott palacsinta (page 209) when it was offered around.

1 lamb roast
2 medium onions, thinly sliced
½ cup sour cream
1 tablespoon chopped fresh dill

Roast the lamb as directed in the master recipe (page 135). About 30 minutes before the end of the meat's cooking time, spread the onion slices in the bottom of the roasting pan. When the meat is done, remove it from the pan and let it stand in a warm place. Pour off all but about 2 tablespoons of fat, and discard any burned pieces of onion. With the roasting pan on the heat, pour in 1 cup of hot water and scrape up the bits stuck to the bottom of the pan. Boil for 2 minutes, then let cool. When the sauce is lukewarm, blend 2 tablespoons of it into the sour cream, then stir that mixture slowly into the sauce. Stir in the chopped dill, and taste the sauce for seasoning: it may need more salt to bring out the flavor. Simmer gently for 2 to 3 minutes. Slice the meat and arrange it on a platter, or carve it at the table. Pass the sauce in a gravy boat or deep bowl.

ᷔᷓ Leg of Lamb Prepared like Game
BIRKAHÚS VADASAN
(*beer-ka-hūsh vah-dah-shahn*)

This dish is, essentially, lamb dressed like venison, and while it wouldn't fool a hunter, it certainly has kept some people I know guessing. To set the stage properly, I like to serve it with braised red cabbage (page 155) and potato dumplings (page 26) and a strong red wine. Though a bit heavy for a simple roast lamb, Egri Bikavér goes very well with this dish. A good choice for dessert would be madártej (floating island, page 201) or a rum-flavored boszorkányhab made with apples (page 200).

3 tablespoons vinegar
1 cup cooking oil
12 peppercorns
1 bay leaf
¼ teaspoon dried thyme
Peel of 1 lemon, cut in ½-inch strips
2 to 3 tablespoons lemon juice
1 carrot, cut in ½-inch pieces
1 medium onion, sliced ¼ inch thick
3 sprigs parsley
2 cloves garlic, peeled
3 strips bacon rind, ¼ by 2 inches (optional)
1 leg of lamb
3 tablespoons lard
Salt
2 tablespoons flour
½ cup sour cream

Place the first twelve ingredients in an enameled saucepan and simmer for 20 minutes. Trim the excess fat off the lamb, cut away the meat-inspection stamps, and place it in a glass or porcelain dish. When the marinade has cooled completely, pour it over the lamb. Leave it in the marinade for at least 2 days, turning once in the morning and once at night. Refrigeration is not necessary. Just before cooking, take the lamb out of the marinade, let it drain on a rack for 30 minutes, then dry it thoroughly. Heat the lard in a large flameproof casserole and brown the lamb on all sides. Salt it liberally. Strain the marinade, mix it with an equal amount of water, and pour it over the meat. Cover the casserole and place in a preheated 375° oven. Allowing 15 minutes per pound cooking time, roast until done, basting often. Transfer the meat to a platter, pour out the pan gravy, let it cool, and skim off the fat. To make a sauce, blend the flour into the sour cream and gradually add the pan juices. After adding 1 cup, taste for seasoning, and pour the mixture back into the casserole. Simmer very gently for 10 minutes, thinning out the sauce with more pan juices or water as necessary. Taste again for seasoning. Keep the sauce hot while carving the meat, then pour it into a sauceboat and serve.

Vegetables
Zöldségek

(ZULD-SHAY-GEK)

*T*oward the end of the summer when so many good vegetables come into season, it is hard to find the appetite to eat much else. My friend Joan Trombly sometimes brings us presents from her garden, and they have come to be known in our house as "Joanie's tomatoes" and "Joanie's cucumbers," as if they were a breed apart from the kind we buy in the store. Unfortunately, though vegetables are available all year round nowadays, they are seldom very fresh and never as good as garden vegetables. They even take longer to cook. Still, they are infinitely better than anything canned or frozen, and they can easily be transformed into delicious Hungarian dishes. Most are merely side dishes, but some would make a substantial meal in themselves, like lucskos káposzta. Many others could serve as a simple lunch or supper main course (töltött paprika or sonkás karfioltorta, for example). Hungarians are also very fond of fresh vegetables served in their own thickened broth. Besides being delicious, this is probably the most nourishing way to eat cooked vegetables, since all the vitamins stay in the dish. The broth should be thickened with roux (rántás), a mixture of fat and flour that has been briefly cooked together. Sometimes onions or parsley or paprika is added to the roux for extra flavor. All of the recipes have been acclaimed by family and friends who would, they assure me, repeat the entire repertoire with enthusiasm.

ASPARAGUS
SPÁRGA
(*shpahr-ga*)

The white European asparagus is a delicate creature which comes into season in May. What a month for gourmets and *Feinschmeckers!* Even the humblest restaurant features some asparagus specialty, and the best chefs turn their attention to this, the palest and most fragile of vegetables. Its American cousin is a far lustier character, and some of the classic asparagus dishes turn out to be somewhat disappointing when it is used. Still, dark green asparagus is better than none at all, and when it is fresh I find it very tempting to cook it every way I know how before time runs out. After serving asparagus merely buttered once or twice, we move on to various sour cream and bread crumb embellishments. Though Europeans prefer asparagus as a separate vegetable course, most Americans think of it as a vegetable side dish. In either case, asparagus goes best with the lighter meats—chicken, veal, lamb, and ham.

◄§ Boiled Asparagus

When buying asparagus, pick stalks that look firm and have closed heads. Allow 1 pound for every two to three persons. Clean the asparagus by cutting off the tough bottoms and trimming the scales with a paring knife. If you like, tie the cleaned asparagus into small bundles for easier handling. Plunge the asparagus into plenty of boiling salted water, and boil for 10 to 15 minutes. When the asparagus is done (try piercing the thickest ends with a paring knife), drain it carefully and place on paper towels to absorb the last of the moisture.

◄§ Asparagus with Bread Crumbs and Mimosa
SPÁRGA VAJAS MORZSÁVAL
(*shpahr-ga voi-yash mor-zhah-vul*)

2 to 3 pounds asparagus
2 tablespoons butter
½ cup dry bread crumbs
1 hard-boiled egg yolk

[144]

Prepare the asparagus according to preceding directions. Melt the butter in a small pan, then sauté the bread crumbs in it, stirring constantly so they do not burn. When they are browned, spread them over the asparagus, then sprinkle the crumbled egg yolk on top.

⊸§ Asparagus with Sour Cream
TEJFÖLÖS SPÁRGA
(*tay-fu-losh shpahr-ga*)

2 to 3 pounds asparagus
2 tablespoons butter
1 tablespoon chopped parsley
2 heaping tablespoons flour
¼ cup sour cream, at room temperature

Prepare the asparagus according to the directions on page 144, but cook for only 5 minutes. Reserve ½ cup of the asparagus cooking liquid. Melt the butter in a heavy-bottomed saucepan, add the parsley, stir in the flour, and cook for 2 or 3 minutes. Gradually stir in the ½ cup of asparagus broth and 1½ cups of water. Put the asparagus in the roux and let it cook for 10 minutes. When the asparagus is done, remove it from the sauce. Let the sauce cool. When it is lukewarm, mix some of it into the sour cream. Slowly pour the cream into the sauce, taste it (it may need salt), and bring back to a simmer. Pour over the asparagus and serve immediately.

⊸§ Baked Asparagus
SPÁRGA PUDDING
(*shpahr-ga pud-ding*)

Vegetable "puddings" and timbales can be very elaborate; this one is simple, and I think more appropriate to asparagus. Since the custard has a sour-cream base, be sure the oven stays at 300° to 325°; if it gets any hotter the sauce will curdle, and though it is still edible, the texture and appearance are not as appetizing.

2 to 3 pounds asparagus
Butter

Dry bread crumbs
2 cups sour cream
2 egg yolks
2 tablespoons flour
1½ teaspoons salt
1 teaspoon sugar

Prepare the asparagus according to the directions on page 144, cooking for only 10 minutes. Drain and dry thoroughly. Preheat the oven to 300° or 325°. Grease a flat baking dish with butter, sprinkle with bread crumbs, shaking out the excess, and arrange the asparagus in the dish. Thoroughly blend together the sour cream, egg yolks, and flour, and season with salt and sugar. Pour the sauce over the asparagus, spreading it out to cover all the pieces, sprinkle with bread crumbs, and dot with butter. Place in the preheated oven and bake for 25 to 30 minutes, or until the top is golden brown. Serve immediately.

DRIED BEANS
FEHÉR BAB
(feh-hayr bab)

Cooked this way, in the Continental fashion with a Hungarian stroke of genius at the end, beans are good and good for you. Be sure to add the vinegar: it perks up the flavor and aids digestion as well. Bean fanciers will, as everyone knows, eat beans with anything, but they seem particularly apt with ham and pork.

✐ Hungarian White Beans
FEHÉR BAB FŐZELÉK
(feh-hayr bab fu-ze-layk)

1 pound navy or pea beans
1 teaspoon salt
1 bay leaf
1 carrot
1 leek (if not available, use an onion)
1 clove garlic, peeled and stuck on a toothpick

½-pound piece of smoked bacon or a smoked pig's knuckle or
    ham hock (optional)
2 tablespoons butter
¼ cup chopped onions
1 teaspoon paprika
2 tablespoons chopped parsley
2 heaping tablespoons flour
¼ to ½ cup sour cream, at room temperature
1 tablespoon vinegar

Wash the beans and soak them overnight in cold water. Or boil five minutes, cover and soak one hour. Drain and rinse the beans and put them in a clean pot. Add the salt, bay leaf, carrot, leek, garlic, and piece of smoked meat. Pour on enough water to barely cover the beans and meat, and bring to a simmer. Cook slowly, partially covered, for 2½ to 3 hours, or until the beans are tender, adding more boiling water as necessary to keep them covered. When they are done, discard the carrot, leek, and garlic, put the meat in a side dish, and drain off the cooking liquid to use in the roux. Melt the butter in a heavy-bottomed saucepan over low heat. Sauté the onions until they wilt, add the paprika and parsley, and stir in the flour. Cook for 2 or 3 minutes, then gradually stir in 2 cups of the bean cooking liquid. Pour the roux into the beans, blend, and simmer another 10 minutes. If the sauce is too thick, add more of the bean cooking liquid. Let the beans cool. Stir some of the beans into the sour cream, then slowly pour it all back into the bean pot. Mix in the vinegar, and taste for seasoning (more salt may be needed). Cut the meat into bite-sized pieces, add it to the beans, and serve.

BRUSSELS SPROUTS
KELBIMBÓ
(kel-bim-boh)

Vivid memories of mushy Brussels sprouts kept us away from this superb vegetable until recent years. What a waste! Their sweet, nutty flavor complements beef, pork, smoked ham, or poultry like no other cooked vegetable. To keep the crunch in, cook Brussels sprouts the French way—parboil them for 10 minutes in lots of salted boiling water, then braise them with butter in a covered saucepan on top of the stove for 10 minutes or in a covered casserole in a 350° oven for 20 minutes. Or bake them with bacon and sour cream as in the following recipe for kelbimbó kontinentál.

⋰§ Baked Brussels Sprouts
KELBIMBÓ KONTINENTÁL
(kel-bim-boh kon-tee-nen-tahl)

3 pints fresh Brussels sprouts
Salt
½ cup diced bacon (smoked slab bacon is preferable, but
    thick-sliced breakfast bacon may be used)
1 small onion, finely chopped
Pinch of freshly ground black pepper
1½ cups sour cream
4 tablespoons bread crumbs
2 tablespoons butter

Wash and trim the Brussels sprouts and drop them into a large pot of boiling salted water. Boil, uncovered, for 10 minutes, then drain and rinse with cold water. Fry the bacon bits in a 3-quart saucepan until they render fat. Add the chopped onion and sauté it until it turns translucent. Pour in ¼ cup of warm water, scrape up any bits stuck to the bottom. Season with pepper and ½ teaspoon of salt, and simmer for 1 minute. Remove the pan from the heat. When the sauce is cool enough to put a finger in, add the sour cream and blend thoroughly. Add the Brussels sprouts and turn carefully to coat every piece. Turn into a greased 3-quart ovenproof casserole, sprinkle with bread crumbs, and dot with butter. Bake in a preheated 325° oven for 20 minutes or until golden brown on top.

CABBAGE
KÁPOSZTA
(kah-poh-sta)

One crisp fall day I took a bus from my home in the northern outskirts of New York City to midtown Manhattan. As we rode through Harlem, I noticed dozens of huge green cabbages displayed on every sidewalk vegetable stand we passed. Then we went through Yorkville, which still has some German and eastern European enclaves: more magnificent heads of the stuff. Then we got to the East Seventies and Sixties: the cabbages had entirely disappeared, and in their place were the hothouse artichokes and tropical avocados that sustain life in the fashionable neighborhoods of New York. What a loss! Cabbage is full of vitamins and scant of calories, and it is one of the most versatile vegetables around. The only way to spoil it is by overcooking. Out of the vast Hungarian repertoire, I have picked two classic main-course dishes and three side dishes that in my experience have the greatest appeal to Magyars and non-Magyars alike. Any one of them is worth a bus or taxi ride across town to buy a cabbage. A good head of cabbage is firm and heavy for its size, with fresh-looking outer leaves. It will keep four days to a week in the refrigerator.

⋞⟆ Stuffed Cabbage
TÖLTÖTT KÁPOSZTA
(tul-tot kah-poh-sta)

Stuffed cabbage is one of the glories of Hungarian home cooking, and rightly so. It varies somewhat from region to region and from family to family, but the basic ingredients are always the same: cabbage, meat and sauerkraut, paprika and sour cream. The Derecskey family recipe calls for a very sour töltött káposzta that is made only with pork and has smoked meats cooked in the pot with it. Those who do not care for that kind of tart, smoky taste, which is so characteristic of the Transylvanian culinary tradition, should skip souring the leaves and omit the piece of smoked bacon. Whether the stuffed cabbage is made sour or not, it greatly improves with age: let it stand a full 24 hours if possible. Start the sour kind two days before you plan to serve it, the plain kind the day before. Traditionally, stuffed cabbage is served as is, without potatoes or dumplings, on the principle, quite sound in this instance, that nothing should be allowed to interfere with one's enjoyment of a fine dish. Despite its humble origins, töltött káposzta deserves a good white wine, such as a Hungarian Badacsonyi Kéknyelű or Leányka. A cake or assorted pastries could be served as dessert.

[149]

3 pounds cabbage (1 large or 2 small heads) with fresh outer leaves

3 cans (12-ounce size) sauerkraut juice

¼ cup rice

Salt

3 tablespoons lard or cooking oil

2 medium onions, minced

1¼ pounds chopped pork, or beef, or a mixture of both

Pinch of freshly ground black pepper

¼ teaspoon dried marjoram

Paprika

1 egg

3 pounds fresh sauerkraut

2 ounces smoked bacon

3 cloves garlic, peeled and stuck on toothpicks

6 smoked pork chops (optional)

3 tablespoons buttermilk

½ cup sour cream

1 heaping tablespoon flour

½ pound smoked sausage (optional)

Two days before serving, wash and core the cabbage. Drop the whole head into plenty of boiling water and cook for 5 minutes. Lift the head out of the water, invert and drain it, and when it is cool enough to handle, carefully peel off the outer leaves one by one. Stop when you get to the tough white inner leaves. You should have enough to make 15 to 18 or more cabbage rolls. Put the leaves in a large glass bowl, pour the sauerkraut juice over them, and let stand overnight. When you are ready to make the dish, parboil the rice in salted boiling water for 10 minutes. Rinse under cold water, drain, and set aside. In a large heavy-bottomed pot or flameproof casserole, heat the lard or oil and sauté the onions in it until they turn translucent. Put the meat in a bowl, and season it with ½ teaspoon of salt, pepper, marjoram, and a pinch of paprika. Add the egg, the cooled rice, and half the onions and fat. Mix thoroughly. Drain the leaves, saving the juice for later, and start making cabbage rolls. Cut any very large leaves in half, count the leaves, and divide the stuffing evenly. Place each leaf on the work surface with the base or core end toward you. Spoon some stuffing into the middle of the leaf, fold the base up, the sides in, and roll carefully. Set aside, seam side up. When all the rolls are made, quickly rinse the sauerkraut in cold water, drain it, and squeeze it dry. Reheat the remaining fat and onions, and when they start to cook again, sprinkle with 1½ teaspoons of paprika. Cook for 2 minutes, then stir in ½ cup of water. Add the sauerkraut, turning it in the sauce. When it is thoroughly coated, take it off the heat. Bury the cabbage rolls, seam side down, as well as the bacon and garlic, in the sauerkraut. Pour on enough liquid (half water and half sauerkraut juice) to cover. Simmer with the lid on until the sauerkraut is barely done, about 2 hours. If smoked pork chops are to be added, put them in the pot after 1½ hours have gone by; they will cook some more when the dish is reheated. Throughout the cooking time, stir carefully and add more liquid if necessary. When the sauerkraut is nearly done, take the pot off the heat and let the contents cool to lukewarm. Transfer the cabbage rolls to a side dish, discard the garlic, and let the sauerkraut cool. Whisk the buttermilk and sour cream together, blend in the flour, and add a bit of sauerkraut and sauce. Then stir the mixture into the sauerkraut. Bring back to a simmer and cook for 3 to 5 minutes. Put the cabbage rolls and meat back into the pot, let it cool, and keep it, covered, in the refrigerator until ready to serve. About half an hour before serving time, slowly bring the káposzta back to a simmer, add the smoked sausage, and cook very gently for 10 to 15 minutes. Serve directly from the casserole or from a deep bowl.

⊷§ Transylvanian Cabbage Stew
LUCSKOS KÁPOSZTA
(lūch-kohsh kah-poh-sta)

Lucskos káposzta is a masterpiece of Transylvanian cuisine and a brassicaphile's dream, a finely seasoned thin stew that lifts cabbage right out of its patch and on up to its apogee. With two kinds of meat cooked with the cabbage, it makes a substantial meal but, happily, not one that is going to nail everybody to the chair. For the ultimate in luxury, it can be served with *smoked* loin pork chops that have been steamed on top of the stew in the last 15 minutes of cooking. All that is really needed, however, is plain boiled potatoes and a chilled bottle of white wine to drink, perhaps a Hungarian

Rizling. A good dessert to accompany this meal is almás pite (apple cake, page 222) or almás rétes (apple strudel, page 212).

> 1½ pounds fatty pork stew meat or spare ribs (if spare ribs are used, have the butcher saw the piece in half)
> 1½ pounds fresh brisket of beef (not corned beef)
> Salt
> 1 large (about 3 pounds) cabbage
> ¼ pound smoked bacon (optional)
> 3 tablespoons lard or cooking oil
> ¼ cup finely chopped purple (Bermuda) onions
> Freshly ground black pepper
> 1 tablespoon chopped fresh dill or tarragon
> 3 or 4 sprigs fresh or dried summer savory, tied together in a bouquet (optional)
> 2 tablespoons white vinegar
> 1 tablespoon flour
> ¼ cup sour cream, at room temperature

Place the pork and beef in a large pot, cover with cold water, and add 1 tablespoon salt. Slowly bring to a simmer, and continue simmering until the meat is half cooked, about 1½ hours. Remove the meat, saving the broth, and when it is cool enough to handle, cut it into 1- to 1¼-inch cubes. Meanwhile, cut the cabbage in wedges, place them on a rack in the sink, salt them, and pour boiling water over them. If that is not feasible, cook the wedges for 1 or 2 minutes in boiling salted water and drain them in a colander. If you wish to use bacon, cut it into pieces 1 inch square and ¼ inch thick. In a heavy-bottomed pot large enough to hold all the cabbage and meat, heat the lard and sauté the onions in it until they are translucent. Off the heat, place a third of the cabbage in a layer on top of the onions, salt it, and spread all the pieces of beef and half the bacon on it. Spread half the remaining cabbage on top, salt that layer, and sprinkle it with dill or tarragon. Make another layer with the pork and the rest of the bacon pieces and lay the bunch of summer savory on top. Cover with the last wedges of cabbage. Degrease the meat broth and pour on enough to cover the pork layer (about 6 cups). Cover and slowly bring to a simmer; simmer until the cabbage and meat are barely done (about 30 minutes). Add the vinegar and set the pot aside to cool. Blend the flour thoroughly into the sour cream, add a couple of tablespoons of lukewarm sauce to it, and then slowly pour the mixture into the stew. Just before serving, let the stew simmer again for 2 or 3 minutes. Remove the bunch of savory and serve immediately, preferably from the cooking pot.

✑ Poor Man's Lucskos Káposzta
SZEGÉNYES LUCSKOS KÁPOSZTA
(seh-gayn-yesh lūch-kohsh kah-poh-sta)

A true lucskos káposzta is a meal in itself; this dish can easily be stretched into one, and probably was in hard times. For the affluent, it happens to be an excellent vegetable side dish to serve with roast pork or ham.

1 small (about 1½ pounds) cabbage
Salt
¼ teaspoon caraway seeds
¼ pound smoked bacon
Additional bacon fat
2 tablespoons flour
1 teaspoon paprika
2 to 4 tablespoons sour cream
Pinch of freshly ground black pepper
Boiled potatoes (optional)

Core and clean the cabbage and slice it ¼ to ½ inch thick. Drop it into boiling salted water to which caraway seeds have been added, and cook it until half done (5 minutes). Saving about 2 cups of the water, drain the cabbage. Cut the bacon in ¼-inch dice and fry in a heavy 3-quart saucepan until golden brown, then remove to a side dish. Heat the fat that remains with additional fat to make about 2 tablespoonfuls, and stir in the flour and the paprika. Cook, stirring, for 2 or 3 minutes. Pour in ½ cup of cabbage broth, mix thoroughly, and gradually add another cup of liquid. Put the cabbage in the sauce and let it simmer for 2 or 3 minutes. Take it off the heat. Fold the bacon bits into 2 tablespoons of sour cream and season it with freshly ground black pepper. When the cabbage has cooled to lukewarm, blend 1 tablespoon of the sauce into the sour cream and bacon mixture. Slowly mix that into the cabbage. Taste for seasoning: it may need more salt or pepper or more sour cream. The sauce should not, however, be milky. Just before serving, reheat the szegényes lucskos káposzta and let it simmer for 2 or 3 minutes. Serve it as a soup-stew with plain boiled potatoes or as a vegetable side dish.

⊷ Cabbage in Tomato Sauce
PARADICSOMOS KÁPOSZTA
(*pah-rah-dee-cho-mohsh kah-poh-sta*)

Hungarians of all tribes adore paradicsomos káposzta. And no wonder! It offers a precarious balance between two esteemed vegetables, tomatoes and cabbage, two opposing textures, smooth and rough, and two flavors in tension, one sweet and one sharp. As a side dish, it goes best with beef and pork.

1 head (about 3 pounds) cabbage
¼ teaspoon caraway seeds
Salt
2 tablespoons butter
1 small onion, finely chopped
2 heaping tablespoons flour
About 1½ cups canned tomato sauce

Clean and core the cabbage and shred it ¼ inch thick. Cook the cabbage with the caraway seeds in boiling salted water for 10 to 12 minutes, until it is cooked but still quite crunchy. Drain, reserving 1 cup of the broth for the roux. Melt the butter in a heavy-bottomed saucepan over low heat, sauté the onion until the pieces wilt, and stir in the flour. Cook for 2 or 3 minutes, then slowly stir in ½ cup of the cabbage broth. Gradually add the tomato sauce. The sauce should be thick and red, not pink. Season with sugar and ½ teaspoon salt, and add ½ cup more cabbage broth. Simmer for 10 minutes, then taste for seasoning and consistency. Add the drained cabbage and let it stand. Just before serving, reheat and taste again.

৶ৡ Cabbage with Dill and Sour Cream
TEJFÖLÖS KÁPOSZTA
(tay-fu-losh kah-poh-sta)

Cabbage is not exactly known for its light touch, but this dish is surprisingly delicate in effect. In it, the cabbage is served in its own sauce, but a sauce that has been considerably brightened with dill—and a dollop of sour cream.

1 head (about 3 pounds) cabbage
Salt
¼ teaspoon caraway seeds
2 tablespoons butter
1 small onion, finely chopped
2 heaping tablespoons flour
2 tablespoons chopped fresh dill
2 tablespoons sour cream

Clean and core the cabbage and slice it ¼ to ½ inch thick. Cook in rapidly boiling salted water, to which caraway seeds have been added, until tender but still firm, about 10 minutes. Drain, reserving 2 cups of the cooking liquid for the roux. Melt the butter in a heavy-bottomed saucepan over low heat, and sauté the onion until the pieces wilt. Stir in the flour, and cook for 2 to 3 minutes. Gradually add ½ cup of the cabbage broth, then stir in up to 1½ cups more broth to make a thin but viscous sauce. Let it simmer, stirring occasionally, for 10 minutes. Taste for seasoning, and if the sauce seems floury, simmer a little longer. When the sauce is done, take it off the heat, add the drained cabbage and dill, and let it cool. When the sauce is barely lukewarm, pour a little into the sour cream, then pour the mixture slowly into the káposzta. Reheat to the simmer and taste for seasoning again just before serving.

৶ৡ Braised Red Cabbage
DINSZTELT VÖRÖS KÁPOSZTA
(deen-stelt vu-rosh kah-poh-sta)

Though red cabbage is a vegetable of limited interest, its survival is assured by the fact that it is superb with duck and goose, pot roast and game. What it needs but seldom gets anymore is a long,

[155]

slow simmer to bring out all the flavor, and some vinegar and an apple cooked with it to preserve the color. Many grandmother cooks swear by boiling up red cabbage once or even twice after it is done: reheating it just before serving seems to do the trick.

1 large head (3 to 4 pounds) red cabbage
3 teaspoons salt
1 medium onion, sliced in ¼-inch rings
¼ cup lard or cooking oil
1 tablespoon vinegar
1 tablespoon sugar
½ teaspoon caraway seeds
1 clove garlic, peeled and stuck on a toothpick
1 tart apple, quartered and seeded
2-ounce piece of smoked bacon (optional)
½ cup beef broth or water
½ cup red wine (if not available, increase the amount of broth
    to 1 cup and stir in 2 tablespoons vinegar before adding to
    the cabbage)

Choose a firm, fresh-looking head of red cabbage, allowing at least ½ pound per person. Trim and core it, and cut it in ¼-inch slices. Sprinkle the shredded cabbage with 1½ teaspoons of salt and let it stand about 20 minutes. Sauté the onion rings in the lard or oil until limp, using a heavy-bottomed casserole large enough to hold all the cabbage (not a cast-iron Dutch oven). Pour in ½ cup of water, the vinegar, sugar, caraway seeds, and 1½ teaspoons of salt. Squeeze out the cabbage and stir it into the sauce. Bury the garlic and apple pieces, as well as the piece of bacon if you wish to use it, in the cabbage. Pour on the broth or water and red wine, bring to a simmer, cover, and gently simmer until tender—about 3 hours. During the cooking, stir the cabbage from time to time with a two-pronged fork and add more water as needed to keep it moist. When the cabbage is done, remove the garlic, apple, and bacon, taste for flavoring, and set aside until ready to serve. Reheat and simmer for 10 minutes just before serving.

✌️ Baked Savoy Cabbage
RAKOTT KELKÁPOSZTA
(rah-kot kel-kah-poh-sta)

Now that Savoy cabbage is beginning to get out of its ethnic ghettos and into the supermarkets, more people, hopefully, will get to know it. It has a nutty, mellow taste quite unlike anything else, and goes equally well with pork or beef. The following two recipes seem to enhance its qualities: krumplis kelkáposzta is a hearty vegetable side dish, and rakott kelkáposzta a light Savoy cabbage pie that could be served either as a side dish with a roast or as a light supper or luncheon dish on its own. Savoy cabbage has crinkly leaves, dark green on the outside, light green to yellow on the inside. It runs large for its weight, but as with other kinds of cabbage, a good one has fresh-looking leaves and is firm to the touch.

3 pounds Savoy cabbage
3 tablespoons lard or cooking oil
½ cup minced onions
¼ cup rice
Salt
1 pound chopped meat, preferably all pork
Freshly ground black pepper
¼ teaspoon dried marjoram
1 egg
¼ pound smoked bacon, sliced (or use thick-sliced breakfast bacon)
1 tablespoon flour
1 teaspoon paprika
1 tablespoon buttermilk
¼ cup sour cream

Wash and trim the cabbage and core it. Separate the leaves: if they do not come apart easily, pour boiling water over the cabbage, invert it, and when it is cool enough to handle pull the leaves off. Set them aside. Heat the lard or oil in a skillet, and slowly sauté the onions until they wilt. Parboil the rice in boiling salted water for 10 minutes; drain and rinse with cold water. Put the meat in a bowl, season with a pinch of pepper, the marjoram, and ½ teaspoon of salt. Add the onions, rice, and egg, and work together, using a wooden spoon or your hands. Grease a high-sided baking dish that is about 10 inches across. Lay a third of the cabbage leaves, the smallest ones, in a circle on the bottom. Salt them and spread half the meat filling on top. Cover with the medium-sized leaves, salt that layer, and spread the remaining meat mixture on it. Cover with the rest of the leaves, arranging them neatly on top. Cover with slices of bacon, and place in a preheated 350° oven. Cook for 1¼ hours, basting occasionally with a bulb baster. If there is not enough juice in the pan, add ¼ to ½ cup of hot water. When the cabbage is done, transfer it to a serving platter. Discard the bacon slices. On top of the stove, make a sauce with the pan juices. Sprinkle them with flour and paprika, pour on ½ cup of hot water, and scrape the pan. Blend thoroughly and let simmer for 5 to 7 minutes. Taste for seasoning: it may need salt. If the sauce has a floury taste, simmer 2 or 3 minutes more and taste it again. Add more water if needed. Let the sauce cool to lukewarm. Blend the buttermilk into the sour cream, add a tablespoonful of sauce, and mix. Slowly stir the sour-cream mixture into the sauce in the pan. Bring back to a simmer and pour into a sauceboat. Cut the baked cabbage in wedge-shaped pieces, like a cake, spoon some sauce on each piece, and serve.

৬ई Savoy Cabbage with Potatoes
KRUMPLIS KELKÁPOSZTA
(krump-lish kel-kah-poh-sta)

This is one of the handiest vegetable dishes I know: it combines two vegetables, it can be made in advance and reheated, it is offbeat, and it comes into season just as green beans get to be a bore and salad greens hit their high in price and low in taste. If you try krumplis kelkáposzta once to plug a gap in the menu, you will be sure to serve it over and over again.

5 to 6 medium potatoes
Salt
2½ to 3 pounds Savoy cabbage
Pinch of caraway seeds
1 clove garlic, peeled and stuck on a toothpick
2 tablespoons butter

1 small onion, finely chopped
½ teaspoon paprika
2 heaping tablespoons flour

Peel the potatoes, and dice them in ½-inch pieces. Cover them with cold water, add 2 teaspoons of salt, and bring to a boil. Reduce the heat and simmer, covered. Clean and core the cabbage and shred it with a knife into pieces ¼ inch thick. When the potatoes have cooked for 15 minutes, add the cabbage, along with the caraway seeds, 1 teaspoon of salt, and the garlic, and simmer, uncovered, until done (10 to 12 minutes). Drain, reserving 1½ cups of cooking liquid. Melt the butter in a heavy-bottomed saucepan, and sauté the onion until the pieces wilt. Stir in the paprika and flour, and cook for 2 to 3 minutes. Gradually add the cooking liquid. Let the sauce simmer for 10 minutes, then taste for seasoning and consistency. Stir the potatoes and cabbage into the sauce, and let it stand until time to serve. Reheat the krumplis kelkáposzta, and let it simmer for 2 or 3 minutes before serving.

✎§ Sauerkraut
SAVANYÚ KÁPOSZTA
(shah-vahn-yū kah-poh-sta)

It should come as no surprise that so few adults like sauerkraut as served in America: it is usually raw or greasy, indigestible either way. My own first encounter with refined kraut was in Strasbourg, in eastern France, where German substance and French style have been carrying on a culinary love affair for centuries. I was a student then, but I managed to afford one good restaurant meal a week, and in retrospect it seems I ate *choucroute* every time. I even learned to cook it their way. Fortunately, good sauerkraut is made the same way from the Rhine east with only minor local variations. Here is my basic recipe with an exclusively Hungarian twist:

3 pounds of sauerkraut, fresh or in a plastic pack
2 ounces smoked bacon cut in thick slices (or substitute
    thick-sliced breakfast bacon)
Piece of smoked meat: bacon, knuckle, or ham hock
1 tart apple, quartered and seeded

2 cloves garlic, peeled and stuck on toothpicks
1 bay leaf
6 juniper berries
1 small onion, peeled
4 cloves
½ teaspoon caraway seeds
2 cups dry white wine (preferable by far) or water
2 tablespoons butter
1 small onion, finely chopped
½ teaspoon paprika
2 heaping tablespoons flour
1 cup sour cream
2 tablespoons chopped fresh dill (optional)

Rinse the sauerkraut and drain it. Taste for brininess: if it is too salty, rinse it again. Line the bottom of a very heavy pot or casserole (but not a cast-iron Dutch oven) with slices of bacon. Squeeze out the sauerkraut and spread it in the pot. Bury in the sauerkraut the piece of smoked meat, the apple, garlic, bay leaf, juniper berries, and the onion with the cloves stuck in its ends. Sprinkle the caraway seeds on the kraut. Pour in the wine or water, bring to a simmer, cover, and cook very slowly until the sauerkraut is tender, about 2½ to 3 hours. Add more wine or water as needed to keep the sauerkraut moist, and stir it from time to time with a two-pronged fork. If despite all precautions it scorches on the bottom, take care not to stir the burned kraut into the rest. When done, fish out and discard the apple, garlic, bay leaf, juniper berries, and onion; the smoked meat may be served with the sauerkraut or kept for another occasion. The sauerkraut can be served as is but to give it a Hungarian flair, continue as follows:

Melt the butter in a heavy-bottomed saucepan over low heat. Add the onions, and sauté until the pieces wilt. Stir in the paprika and flour, and cook for 2 or 3 minutes. Thin the roux with 1 cup of the cooking juices, and stir it into the sauerkraut. Simmer for 15 minutes, then let cool thoroughly. Stir some of the sauerkraut into the sour cream, then slowly add the mixture to the pot. Bring back to a simmer. Sprinkle the chopped dill over the sauerkraut and serve.

CAULIFLOWER
KARFIOL
(kahr-fee-ohl)

When I shop in the United States, the only people I ever see buying cauliflower are food freaks like myself. And yet, there are really only three groups of people who should be excused from eating cauliflower: infants under the age of one year, the elderly over eighty, and nursing mothers. But if cauliflower is to reach the heights it is capable of, it must be sauced, breaded, or baked after it is boiled.

When buying cauliflower, look for a head without any discolored patches and with fresh green leaves. A head 5 inches in diameter will serve three, an 8- or 9-inch head will serve six.

⊷§ Boiled Cauliflower

Discard the leaves and stem of the cauliflower, break it up into flowerets, all more or less the same size, and wash them in cold water. Cook in rapidly boiling salted water, uncovered, for 15 to 20 minutes, or until the stalks are tender but still firm. Drain and rinse with cold water.

⊷§ Breaded Cauliflower
RÁNTOTT KARFIOL
(rahn-tot kahr-fee-ohl)

My two sons think rántott karfiol is a dessert—it's that good—and who am I to disabuse them of the notion?

1 head cauliflower, 8 to 9 inches in diameter
Flour, preferably granular (instant-blending)
2 eggs, lightly beaten
Dry bread crumbs
Cooking oil

Prepare the cauliflower according to the preceding directions. After draining, let the cauliflower cool off a bit, then dust the flowerets with flour, dip them in the eggs, and roll them in bread crumbs. Heat about ¼ to ½ inch of cooking oil in a large frying pan, and quickly brown the cauliflower pieces on all sides. Do not crowd them in the pan. As the pieces are done, drain them on paper towels and serve as soon as possible.

⌐§ Cauliflower in Sour Cream Sauce
TEJFÖLÖS KARFIOL
(*tay-fu-losh kahr-fee-ohl*)

I have heard some people say cauliflower and sour cream do not go together, that as a combination it is too hard to digest. Others disagree, and the following recipe is a compromise: it is essentially cauliflower in a white sauce with a little sour cream added at the end, sufficient to liven it up but not enough to start a war in the alimentary canal.

1 head cauliflower, 8 to 9 inches in diameter
2 tablespoons butter
1 tablespoon chopped parsley
2 heaping tablespoons flour
1 cup milk
¼ cup sour cream

Prepare the cauliflower according to the directions on page 161. Drain, reserving the cooking liquid. Melt the butter in a heavy-bottomed saucepan over low heat. Add the parsley, stir in the flour, and cook for 2 to 3 minutes. Gradually add ½ cup of the cauliflower broth. Stir in the milk and continue cooking over low heat, stirring often, until the sauce starts to thicken. Taste it, correct the seasoning, and thin it out with more cauliflower broth if necessary. Add the drained cauliflower to the sauce and set it aside off the heat. When the sauce has cooled to lukewarm, blend some of it in the sour cream, then slowly pour the mixture into the sauce. Bring back to a simmer and serve.

✒ Cauliflower with Buttered Bread Crumbs
KARFIOL VAJAS MORZSÁVAL
(kahr-fee-ohl voi-yash mor-zhah-vul)

Cooked cauliflower can be turned into a bowl and sprinkled with buttered bread crumbs. Or for a fancier presentation, re-form the head of cauliflower.

1 head cauliflower, 8 to 9 inches in diameter
¼ cup butter
1 cup dry bread crumbs

Prepare the cauliflower as described on page 161. To re-form the cauliflower shape, warm a bowl somewhat smaller than the original head and arrange the cooked flowerets, heads down, in the dish, starting at the center and working around and up the sides of the bowl. When all the flowerets have been used, press them gently down together, place a serving plate on top of the bowl, and invert quickly. Melt the butter in a frying pan and stir in the bread crumbs. Sauté them briefly, stirring all the while, being careful not to burn them. Sprinkle the molded cauliflower head with bread crumbs and serve.

✒ Baked Cauliflower
RAKOTT KARFIOL
(rah-kot kahr-fee-ohl)

Hungarians talk about rakott karfiol as if they invented it. And it is certainly a key dish in their culinary lore, something to recall with nostalgia, to compare notes about and to ask and/or tell me how to make. Here is how I do it.

1 head cauliflower, 8 to 9 inches in diameter
4 tablespoons butter
3 tablespoons dry bread crumbs
1 tablespoon chopped parsley
2 heaping tablespoons flour
1½ cups milk
½ cup coarsely grated Swiss cheese

Prepare the cauliflower according to directions on page 161. Drain, reserving ½ cup of the cooking liquid for the roux. Butter a shallow baking dish with 1 tablespoon of the butter, and sprinkle with 1 tablespoon of the bread crumbs, shaking out the excess. Melt 2 tablespoons of the butter in a heavy-bottomed saucepan over low heat, add the parsley, and stir in the flour. Cook for 2 or 3 minutes, then gradually stir in ½ cup of cauliflower broth and the milk. Simmer, stirring constantly, until the sauce thickens. Taste for seasoning, then stir in all but 2 tablespoons of the grated cheese. Mix the other 2 tablespoons of cheese with the remaining bread crumbs, and set aside. When the cheese has melted completely in the sauce, pour a third of the sauce in the baking dish, add the drained cauliflower, and pour the rest of the sauce over it. Sprinkle with the bread crumbs and cheese and dot with the remaining butter. Bake in a preheated 375° oven for 30 minutes or until the top is golden brown. Serve immediately.

◄§ Baked Cauliflower with Ham
SONKÁS KARFIOLTORTA
(*shohn-kahsh kahr-fee-ol-tor-ta*)

This casserole is a variation on rakott karfiol, and it is very good indeed.

1 head cauliflower, 8 to 9 inches in diameter
2 tablespoons butter
3 tablespoons dry bread crumbs
2 cups sour cream
2 tablespoons flour
2 eggs, separated
½ teaspoon salt
1 cup (about ¼ pound) minced cooked ham

Prepare the cauliflower according to the directions on page 161. Butter a baking dish with 1 tablespoon of the butter and dust it with 1 tablespoon of bread crumbs, shaking out the excess. In a mixing bowl, blend together the sour cream, flour, and egg yolks, and season with salt. Beat the 2 egg whites with a pinch of salt until stiff, then fold them into the sour-cream base. Spread some of the sauce in the bottom of the baking pan, arrange half the cauliflower in it, then cover with the minced ham. Add the rest of the cauliflower, pour on the remaining sauce, sprinkle the top with the remaining bread crumbs, and dot it with the remaining butter. Bake in a 300° oven for 30 minutes or until the top turns golden brown. Serve immediately.

GREEN BEANS
ZÖLDBAB
(zuld-bab)

Now that the stringy green bean is an oddity, a mere footnote to culinary history as it were, it is rare to find anyone who actively dislikes this vegetable. Fresh green beans look clean and firm and snap easily; try to taste one or two pieces at random before buying to see if they are sweet and tender. Allow one pound of beans for every two to three persons. To prepare the beans, snap off the tips, pulling down along the seams to remove any vestigial bits of string. Wash the pieces and leave them whole or cut them into one-inch lengths.

Green beans can be braised, as in balatoni zöldbab paprikás, but are usually boiled, as follows.

❧ Boiled Green Beans

Drop the beans into plenty of boiling salted water, bring back to the boil, and simmer, uncovered. The cooking time depends on how fresh the beans are and how they will be used later on. Taste to see if they are done: they should be almost tender but still quite crunchy if they are to be cooked a second time in a roux or sour-cream sauce (about 10 minutes); they should be tender but not limp if they are going to be served in salad or with butter (about 20 minutes, less for garden-fresh beans). When the beans are done, drain and rinse them with cold water, being sure to save the cooking liquid if you are going to make a roux or sauce.

[165]

⇔§ Green Beans in Roux
ZÖLDBAB FÖZELÉK
(*zuld-bab fu-ze-layk*)

Green beans prepared in a thickened broth, flavored perhaps with fresh chopped parsley, make a versatile side dish that complements virtually any kind of meat.

2 pounds green beans
2 tablespoons butter
1 tablespoon chopped parsley (optional)
2 heaping tablespoons flour

Prepare the beans according to the preceding directions, cooking only 10 to 12 minutes. Reserve 2 cups of cooking liquid for the roux. Melt the butter in a heavy-bottomed saucepan over low heat, add the parsley if you wish, then stir in the flour. Cook for 2 or 3 minutes, then gradually add the 2 cups of bean cooking broth. Put the drained beans in the sauce, bring back to a simmer, and cook for 10 minutes or until the beans are done.

⇔§ Green Beans in Sour Cream Sauce
TEJFÖLÖS ZÖLDBAB
(*tay-fu-losh zuld-bab*)

Try this tejfölös zöldbab with roast lamb and oven-browned potatoes someday when the familiar side dishes begin to pall. It is a dramatic combination that is sure to jolt the company into a rush of compliments. Basically, it is a zöldbab főzelék with sour cream and paprika added to make it richer and spicier.

2 pounds green beans
2 tablespoons butter
½ teaspoon paprika
1 tablespoon chopped parsley
2 heaping tablespoons flour
1 clove garlic, peeled
¼ cup sour cream
Salt
White vinegar (optional)

Prepare the beans according to the directions on page 165, cooking only 10 to 12 minutes. Drain, reserving 2 cups of the cooking liquid. Melt the butter in a heavy-bottomed saucepan over low heat, add the paprika and parsley, and stir in the flour. Cook for 2 or 3 minutes, then gradually stir in the 2 cups of bean broth. Add the beans and drop in a clove of garlic. Simmer until done—about 10 minutes—then discard the garlic and let everything cool until lukewarm. Mix some beans and sauce into the sour cream, then gradually stir that mixture into the beans. Taste for flavor: additional salt may be needed as well as a few drops of white vinegar. Bring back to a simmer and cook 3 minutes longer before serving.

⇜§ Balaton Stew
BALATONI ZÖLDBAB PAPRIKÁS
(*bah-la-toh-nee zuld-bab pah-pree-kahsh*)

Hungarian cuisine abounds in filling, nourishing vegetable side dishes, but this one is exceptional. The green beans are braised and cooked with rice, and sour cream is added at the end. It is an elegant vegetable stew, exactly the kind of dish everyone looks for sooner or later to serve with things like grilled steak or lamb chops. Try it some time, at the risk of Magyarizing a few palates around the patio.

1½ pounds green beans
⅓ cup rice
Salt
½ cup cooking oil
1 medium onion, chopped fine
1 tablespoon chopped parsley
1 teaspoon paprika
1 teaspoon vinegar
½ cup sour cream, at room temperature

Clean the beans and cut them into 1-inch lengths. Parboil the rice in salted water for 10 minutes and drain. Heat the oil in a heavy-bottomed, 9-inch skillet, and sauté the onion until it wilts. Stir in the parsley, paprika, 1 teaspoon of salt, and the green beans. Cook them in the fat for about 3 to 5 minutes, stirring constantly.

Do not let them brown. Mix the vinegar in 1 cup of water and pour over the beans. Cover and simmer for 45 minutes, adding more water (up to 1 cup) as necessary to keep the beans barely covered. Add the rice and cook another 15 minutes, or until the beans are tender. Remove from the heat and let cool. Mix 2 tablespoons of the bean mixture into the sour cream, then slowly pour it all back into the pot. Simmer for 2 to 3 minutes and serve.

GREEN PEPPERS
ZÖLDPAPRIKA
(zuld-pah-pree-ka)

If soup is the soul of Hungarian cuisine, then green peppers are its heart, the sustaining force behind it. They animate the dullest dish; they perk up the most sluggish appetite. Green peppers of one kind or another can be found almost year round in the United States, though the so-called Italian peppers that are most like European varieties are only occasionally available. Use them when they are at hand; they are infinitely better than the coarse, waxy bell peppers we usually get.

✑ Green Pepper and Tomato Stew
LECSÓ
(leh-choh)

Lecsó is one of the commonplace staples of the Hungarian kitchen: green peppers and tomatoes cooked together with bacon and a pinch of paprika. It can serve as a vegetable side dish, or if sausages or frankfurters are added, a quick soup-stew. In Hungary it is canned at home to be used as a substitute for fresh peppers and tomatoes during the barren winter months. The best lecsó is, of course, made from garden-fresh vegetables: the light green (Italian) peppers and vine-ripened tomatoes. Canned tomatoes may be substituted: two one-pound cans of peeled, whole tomatoes will yield a little more than a pound of fruit. Green bell peppers are too tough for this dish.

1 pound green Italian peppers
1 pound tomatoes

⅓ cup (2 ounces) diced smoked bacon
2 tablespoons bacon fat
1 medium onion, finely chopped
1 teaspoon paprika
1 teaspoon salt
½ pound smoked sausage or frankfurters (optional)

Core the green peppers and slice them lengthwise into ½-inch strips. Core and quarter the tomatoes. (If they are fresh, scald them first to remove the skins.) Slowly cook the bacon in a 9-inch skillet until it starts to render fat. Add the additional fat, and sauté the chopped onion. When it starts to wilt, sprinkle with paprika and cook for 2 to 3 minutes. Stir in the green pepper strips and the tomatoes and salt. Cover and simmer gently, stirring occasionally, for about 30 minutes, or until the peppers are tender. If sausage or frankfurters are to be added, slice them ¼ inch thick and stir them in after the lecsó has been cooking for 20 minutes. Taste before serving: more salt may be needed.

⋑ Stuffed Green Peppers
TÖLTÖTT PAPRIKA
(*tul-tot pah-pree-ka*)

The best töltött paprika I ever ate was made by our dentist's mother in the Congo. She was an ancient lady who had left Hungary some time before to spend her declining years with her children. By the time we met the old Mrs. Fodor, her sole pleasure in life was to conjure up Hungarian specialties from what little one could then find in the Léopoldville market. Her stuffed peppers were famous. The following recipe may lack the element of triumph over nearly insuperable odds, but it does produce a first-class stuffed pepper. Töltött paprika is traditionally served with plain boiled potatoes as a lunch or light supper dish.

12 medium green peppers
Salt
¼ cup rice
½ cup chopped onions
2 tablespoons cooking oil or lard

1 pound chopped meat, either beef or pork
1 egg, lightly beaten
Pinch freshly ground black pepper
¼ teaspoon marjoram
1 tablespoon chopped parsley
About 3 cups canned tomato sauce
Boiled potatoes

Wash and core the green peppers and parboil them for 5 minutes in lots of boiling salted water to soften them and to bleach out any bitter taste. Drain the peppers and invert them until ready to stuff. Parboil the rice for 10 minutes. Sauté the onions in the oil or lard until they wilt. Using your hands, thoroughly mix together the rice, onions, meat, egg, ½ teaspoon of salt, black pepper, marjoram, and parsley. Stuff the peppers with the meat mixture and stand them up in a baking dish. Pour in enough tomato sauce to come about a third of the way up the peppers. Bake in a 325° oven for 1 hour. Serve with plain boiled potatoes.

KOHLRABI
KALARÁBÉ
(ka-la-rah-bay)

There is a cult of kohlrabi fanciers who regularly exchange information about where to find this elusive vegetable and how to prepare it. A distinguished writer we know grows kohlrabi in his penthouse garden high above Manhattan's fashionable East Side to be sure of a supply. And several times a year someone calls me up for a recipe, the conversation usually beginning, "I just found some kohlrabi and I don't know what to do with it." I am happy to oblige, for I have turned somewhat evangelical about this neglected wonder of the vegetable kingdom. It gives a sharp twist to stews and pot roast, yet when young and very fresh it can be eaten raw with salt. It makes an exotic soup and a hearty cooked vegetable, but stuffed—either the vegetable itself or the leaves—it is a delicate appetizer. In other words, full of surprises. Try it a few times, and you too will be hooked on kohlrabi. Be sure to pick small pieces: the larger, older specimens tend to get woody, and a mouthful of kohlrabi fibers would spoil everything. Allow at least 3 small kohlrabies per person or about 4 pounds to serve six.

ᴥᦥ Kohlrabi in Roux
KALARÁBÉ FŐZELÉK
(*ka-la-rah-bay fu-ze-layk*)

This is the standard way to cook kohlrabi: it is what the farmer's wife means when she says, "Oh, you cook it and make a sauce." That does not mean the dish should be dismissed: kalarábé főzelék is something very good to eat indeed. It goes best with pork, though the mild American kind of kohlrabi can also be served with poultry.

18 small kohlrabies (about 4 pounds)
Salt
2 tablespoons butter
1 tablespoon chopped parsley
2 heaping tablespoons flour
Freshly ground black pepper

Remove and discard the leaves and stems of the kohlrabies. Peel the bulbs with a small paring knife, dice them into ½-inch cubes, and drop them into a large pot of boiling salted water. Boil, uncovered, for about 30 minutes, or until the kohlrabi is nearly tender. Meanwhile, melt the butter in a heavy-bottomed saucepan over low heat. Add the parsley, then stir in the flour and cook for 2 to 3 minutes. Gradually add 1½ cups of water (kohlrabi broth is too strong). Add the drained kohlrabi and simmer for 10 to 15 minutes. Taste for consistency and salt. Season with pepper.

ᴥᦥ Stuffed Kohlrabi
TÖLTÖTT KALARÁBÉ
(*tul-tot ka-la-rah-bay*)

This is my husband's favorite way to eat kohlrabi, and though I like to please him, we seldom have it more than once a year. Finding enough kohlrabies to make it worthwhile is hard, coring them all is time-consuming, and then, of course, there is still a whole dinner to prepare. That's what I say *before*; afterwards I always say it was worth every bit of effort. Töltött kalarábé can only be an appetizer, but it must be served with boiled potatoes or rice. It would be a good opener to a meal of grilled meat and salad or a platter of cold meats, nothing more substantial than that.

[171]

18 small kohlrabies (about 4 pounds)
Salt
2 slices dry white bread (use stale bread or dry it in the oven)
½ cup milk
1 pound pork or veal, or a mixture of both, ground twice
Freshly ground black pepper
1 egg
1 tablespoon chopped parsley
½ teaspoon marjoram
½ cup sour cream, at room temperature
1½ tablespoons butter
½ teaspoon sugar
About 2 cups veal stock or water
White vinegar (optional)
Rice or boiled potatoes

Peel the kohlrabies and carefully scoop out the inside with a spoon or grapefruit knife. Chop the scooped-out parts into small pieces (¼ inch), and cut the tender leaves into ¼-inch strips. Set them aside. Parboil the hollow kohlrabies in rapidly boiling salted water for 5 minutes. Drain and turn them upside down until ready to fill. Soak the bread in the milk. Prepare the stuffing by mixing together the meat, ½ teaspoon of salt, a pinch of pepper, and the egg. Squeeze out the bread and tear it to shreds, then knead it into the meat. Add the parsley and marjoram and 2 tablespoons of sour cream, and knead again, using your hands. Stuff the kohlrabies with the meat mixture.

Butter the inside of a flameproof casserole or heavy-bottomed pot large enough to hold all the stuffed kohlrabies in one layer. (Use two pots if necessary.) Carefully arrange the kohlrabies and strew the chopped pieces and leaves around. Mix ½ teaspoon salt and ½ teaspoon sugar in 2 cups of stock. Pour in enough to come halfway up the kohlrabies. Cover and simmer gently until the kohlrabies are tender, about 45 minutes. (Or bake in a 325° oven for 1¼ hours.) Check occasionally and add more boiling stock if necessary. When done, remove the kohlrabies to a side dish and keep them warm. Let the sauce cool. Mix some of the sauce into the remaining sour cream, then gradually stir it back into the sauce. Taste for seasoning: more salt may be needed or a few drops of white vinegar to sharpen the sauce. Carefully put the stuffed kohlrabies back into the sauce and heat them up just before serving. Rice or plain boiled potatoes should accompany the kohlrabies, even though the dish is an appetizer.

ᴇᔆ Stuffed Kohlrabi Leaves
TÖLTÖTT KALARÁBÉ LEVÉL
(tul-tot ka-la-rah-bay le-vayl)

The Hungarian chef at the Hotel Continental in Kolozsvár told us that he thought of stuffing kohlrabi leaves one day when he felt in the mood to make stuffed vine leaves but didn't have any on hand. It was a brilliant improvisation, and I have served the dish as a novelty several times myself. The sole hitch is to find enough leaves: only the large but still tender ones can be used (those smaller than 3 inches across are too hard to fold). I would suggest getting a couple of bunches of kohlrabi, using the leaves first, then making soup or kalarábé főzelék two or three days later (the vegetable will certainly keep that long in the vegetable drawer of the refrigerator). Try to work out the logistics and make töltött kalarábé levél at least once: they are subtle and delicate in taste, just right for an appetizer.

To prepare töltött kalarábé levél, pick over the leaves and wash them thoroughly. Discard the large tough outer leaves and chop or shred the ones that are too small to stuff. Prepare half the amount of stuffing as for stuffed kohlrabi (preceding recipe). Place a heaping teaspoonful or less of stuffing in the middle of each leaf and fold the corners together like an envelope. Arrange the stuffed leaves, envelope seams down, in a buttered casserole or baking dish, strew them with the rest of the chopped leaves, sprinkle with ½ teaspoon salt and ½ teaspoon sugar, and pour on enough water to come halfway up the stuffed leaves. Cover and simmer about 30 minutes or bake in a 325° oven for 40 to 50 minutes. If pork was used in the stuffing, break open one of the stuffed leaves to see if the meat is done: there should be no trace of pink color in it. If the meat is not done, cook another 10 minutes. Then remove the stuffed leaves to a side dish to keep them warm. Let the sauce cool. Pour a little sauce into ½ cup of sour cream. Taste for seasoning, and carefully put the leaves back in the sauce. Just before serving, gently bring it up to the simmer. Serve töltött kalarábé levél with rice as an appetizer.

PEAS
ZÖLDBORSÓ
(*zuld-bor-shoh*)

There will come a day, I predict, when the fresh pea will be as exotic as the fresh truffle. Food writers will wax lyrical over it, and little children will learn in school about the pod in which the pea is found. Although fresh peas were a staple in my mother's kitchen when I was growing up, by now they seem to be available only to farm families and elderly millionaires. The rest of us are left to choose between the twin abominations of pale canned peas and vivid frozen ones. Occasionally I do see a bushel basket of peas at the grocer's, and even though I know those peas have been traveling across the continent for at least a week in a refrigerator car, I buy a couple of pounds. For old times' sake. Sometimes we have them just buttered, and sometimes I make a Hungarian főzelék. Whatever my intention, I always pick two or three pods at random and taste the peas before buying. They should be sweet and tender, and if they are not, I wait until next time.

⋖§ Peas in Roux
ZÖLDBORSÓ FŐZELÉK
(*zuld-bor-shoh fu-ze-layk*)

3 pounds peas
Salt
2 tablespoons butter
1 tablespoon chopped parsley
2 heaping tablespoons flour

Shell the peas and wash them under cold water. Drop them into a large pot of boiling salted water, bring it back to a simmer and cook, uncovered. Cooking time varies widely, according to the age, size and type of pea: allow at least 10 minutes for store-bought peas. Taste a couple to see if they are done. When they are, drain them, reserving 2 cups of cooking broth for the sauce. Melt the butter in a heavy-bottomed saucepan over low heat. Add the parsley and stir in the flour. Cook for 2 or 3 minutes, then gradually add the 2 cups of cooking liquid. Let the sauce simmer for 10 minutes. Add the cooked peas and let them stand until ready to serve. The főzelék may be reheated if necessary.

POTATOES
KRUMPLI/BURGONYA
(krump-lee/bur-gon-ya)

There are some regions of Hungary where the people eat a great deal of potatoes, and there are others where they eat them hardly at all. But I have yet to meet a Hungarian, whatever part of the country he came from, who did not attack a potato dish with gratifying gusto. The explanation may be that their potato dishes are so very good. In fact, I don't know how I could manage any more without krumpli paprikás and rakott krumpli in my bag of culinary tricks. All the recipes that follow can be made with either white new potatoes, which most closely approximate the all-purpose European potato, or ordinary boiling potatoes. The cooking times given are about right for either kind, but even with potatoes cooking time can vary from season to season and from sack to sack. Always taste them before serving, and above all, take care not to overcook them.

⋑ Potato Stew
KRUMPLI PAPRIKÁS
(krump-lee pah-pree-kahsh)

Krumpli paprikás is a stand-by of nearly every Hungarian household. Like so many simple, hearty dishes, it is not served to company, and that is a pity because few outsiders get to know it. Since I never felt myself bound to those rules of etiquette, I soon discovered that anyone who enjoys eating likes krumpli paprikás. Everybody is invited to verify my findings. This stew is always served with rye bread, and it does need a salad of lettuce or cucumbers on the side. In a pinch, sour pickles can be substituted for salad. Beer is definitely the thing to drink.

The best kind of potatoes to use for krumpli paprikás is firm boiling potatoes, like yellow new potatoes; so-called old potatoes taste good too, but they tend to crumble. And the best kind of frankfurters to use are the loose pairs sold at the butcher shop, or kosher frankfurters. Avoid skinless franks.

> **3 pounds (about 12 medium) potatoes**
> **1 medium onion, finely chopped**
> **¼ cup lard or cooking oil**
> **1 teaspoon paprika**
> **1 teaspoon salt**
> **¼ teaspoon caraway seeds, crushed with the back of a spoon**
> **4 frankfurters, cut in ½-inch pieces**

Peel the potatoes and cut them into half-moons ¼ inch thick. (To make half-moons, cut a potato in half lengthwise, lay each half flat, and slice it the long way.) Drop them into cold water and set aside until ready to use. In a heavy-bottomed skillet or saucepan that is large enough to hold all the potatoes, sauté the chopped onion in lard or oil until it is translucent. Add the paprika, salt, and caraway seeds and ½ cup of water. Turn the potatoes in the sauce, coating them all, then add enough water to barely cover them. Bring to a simmer, cover, and simmer gently for 15 minutes. Stir carefully, add more water if necessary, and lay the frankfurter pieces on top of the potatoes. Cover and continue simmering for 10 minutes or until the potatoes are done. Taste and add more salt if needed. Serve immediately, either from the cooking pot or from a deep bowl, in shallow soup bowls.

⋖ᶘ Potato Casserole
RAKOTT KRUMPLI
(*rah-kot krump-lee*)

I cannot fathom why rakott krumpli, the Hungarian potato casserole, is not better known in the West. It really deserves recognition. It is far easier to make than its next of kin, scalloped potatoes, and it goes with cold meats as well as roasts and chops. Since rakott krumpli is the quintessential home-cooked dish, it varies from kitchen to kitchen and from day to day. I myself use two recipes, one for everyday, the other for special occasions. It is hard to believe you could improve on the first method, and, in fact, the puffed version is in a different class altogether—almost a soufflé. The following recipes are adapted to standard-size baking dishes: rakott krumpli fits in a 1½-quart pan and serves only four; felfújt rakott krumpli fills a 3-quart pan and serves six quite generously.

2 to 2½ pounds (8 or 9 medium) potatoes (not Idaho potatoes)
Salt
1 small onion, finely chopped
Lard or cooking oil
3 hard-boiled eggs
½ cup sour cream
2 tablespoons dry bread crumbs

Scrub the potatoes and boil them in their jackets in salted water. Sauté the chopped onion in 2 tablespoons of lard or cooking oil until translucent, and set aside to cool. When the potatoes are done (when they can be pierced easily with a paring knife), drain and rinse them under running cold water and let them stand until cool enough to handle. Peel and slice them ¼ inch thick. (Cold potatoes may be used for this dish, but like potato salad, rakott krumpli seems to taste better if the dressing is put on warm potatoes.) Slice the hard-boiled eggs. Stir the cool onions and fat into the sour cream, taste it, and add salt if necessary. Fold the potato slices into the sour-cream dressing, turning carefully until all slices are coated. Grease the sides and bottom of a 1½-quart shallow baking dish (10 by 6 by 2 inches) and sprinkle with bread crumbs, shaking out the excess. Spread half the potatoes on the bottom, arrange a layer of hard-boiled egg slices on top, and cover with the rest of the potatoes. Press down with the heel of your hand, smooth the top again with a knife or spatula, and place the casserole in a preheated 300° oven for 30 minutes. Place the rakott krumpli briefly under the broiler if it has not browned on top by then. Serve directly from the baking dish or invert on a serving platter.

✑ Puffed Potato Casserole
FELFÚJT RAKOTT KRUMPLI
(fel-fu-eet rah-kot krump-lee)

2 to 2½ pounds (8 or 9 medium) potatoes (not Idaho potatoes)
Salt
8 eggs
10 tablespoons butter
2 cups sour cream
Pinch of pepper
½ cup dry bread crumbs

Scrub the potatoes, cover them with cold, salted water, and boil them in their jackets. Place 5 of the eggs in cold water, bring them to the boil, and simmer for 8 minutes. Drain and rinse under cold water, and peel immediately. Slice the eggs only when they are completely cool. Cook the potatoes until they are tender enough to be pierced with the point of a paring knife; drain them, rinse them with cold water, and let them stand until they are cool enough to handle. Peel them and slice them ¼ inch thick. Separate the 3 remaining eggs. Cream 8 tablespoons of butter, mix in the sour cream and 3 egg yolks, and season with 1 teaspoon of salt and a pinch of pepper. Using some of the remaining butter, grease a 3-quart shallow baking dish (13 by 8½ by 2 inches deep) or two 1½-quart pans (10 by 6 by 2 inches deep) and sprinkle the bottom and sides with bread crumbs, shaking out the excess. Beat the 3 egg whites with a pinch of salt until stiff. Stir 2 to 3 tablespoons of egg whites into the sour-cream mixture, then lightly fold in the rest, about a fourth at a time. Carefully fold in the sliced potatoes and eggs, and turn the mass into the baking dish. Sprinkle with bread crumbs and dot with the rest of the butter. Bake in a preheated 300° oven for about 30 minutes or until the top is golden brown. Serve immediately.

✑ Potatoes in Sour Cream Sauce
TEJFÖLÖS KRUMPLI
(tay-fu-losh krump-lee)

We Americans cream everything from corn to onions but never potatoes. Yet well-seasoned potatoes in sour cream sauce make a novel kind of side dish that goes with just about any kind of roast or grilled meat. For reasons buried deep in the cultural history of central Europe, the potatoes are supposed to be cut different ways for different flavorings. Thus, each dish is quite different from any other. Out of an infinite number of such combinations, here are three that seem particularly felicitous.

✌§ Potatoes with Marjoram
MAJORANNÁS KRUMPLI
(*mī-yo-rahn-ahsh krump-lee*)

3 pounds potatoes
1 tablespoon salt
2 tablespoons butter
¼ cup minced onions
1 teaspoon fresh marjoram (if not available, use ½ teaspoon dried marjoram)
2 heaping tablespoons flour
¼ cup sour cream

Peel the potatoes and cut them in half-moons ¼ inch thick. (To make half-moons, cut the potato in half lengthwise, lay it flat on the cutting board, and slice it the long way.) Rinse the potatoes and put them in a big pot. Pour in enough water to cover, add the salt, and put the lid on. Simmer until done (about 25 minutes), drain, and reserve 2 cups of cooking liquid. In a large, heavy-bottomed saucepan on low heat, melt the butter. Sauté the onion in it until the pieces wilt. Add the marjoram, stir in the flour, and cook for 2 or 3 minutes. Gradually stir in 1½ cups of potato broth. Simmer for 10 minutes, then taste for consistency and seasoning. If it is too floury, cook a few minutes more; if it is too thick, add more potato broth. It may also need more salt. Put the potatoes in the sauce, and let it cool. Mix a tablespoon of sauce into the sour cream, then slowly pour the sour cream into the sauce. Taste again for flavoring. Bring back to a simmer a few minutes before serving.

[179]

✑ Sour Potatoes
SAVANYÚ KRUMPLI
(shah-vahn-yū krump-lee)

3 pounds potatoes
1 tablespoon salt
1 bay leaf
2 tablespoons butter
¼ cup minced onions
2 heaping tablespoons flour
¼ cup sour cream
White vinegar
Pinch of freshly ground black pepper

Peel the potatoes and cut them in ½-inch dice. Rinse them and put them in a large pot. Cover with cold water, add the salt and bay leaf, and simmer, with the lid on, until done (about 25 minutes). Drain the potatoes, reserving 2 cups of cooking liquid, and discard the bay leaf. Melt the butter in a heavy-bottomed saucepan over low heat, and sauté the onions in it until the pieces wilt. Stir in the flour and cook for 2 or 3 minutes. Gradually stir in 1½ cups of potato broth. Simmer for 10 minutes, then taste for consistency. If it seems too floury, simmer 3 or 4 minutes longer; if it is too thick, stir in more potato broth. Add the potatoes and let cool. Stir a couple of tablespoons of sauce into the sour cream before adding it to the rest. Stir in a few drops of vinegar and grind some black pepper directly over the potatoes. Taste for seasoning: more vinegar or more salt may be needed. Reheat just before serving.

✑ Potatoes with Dill
KOLOZSVÁRI KRUMPLI
(koh-lohzh-vah-ree krump-lee)

3 pounds potatoes
1 tablespoon salt
2 tablespoons butter
1 small onion, finely chopped
1½ tablespoons chopped parsley
1 tablespoon chopped dill

2 heaping tablespoons flour
1½ cups beef or chicken stock or canned broth
¼ cup sour cream
Pinch of freshly ground black pepper

Scrub the potatoes and cook them in their jackets in boiling salted water until done (anywhere from 30 to 45 minutes). When the potatoes are cooked, cool them quickly, peel them, and quarter them. Melt the butter in a heavy-bottomed saucepan, and sauté the chopped onion until the pieces wilt. Add the parsley and dill, stir in the flour, and cook for 2 to 3 minutes. Gradually stir in the stock, and simmer for 10 minutes. Add the potatoes, and let the sauce cool to tepid. Mix some of the sauce into the sour cream, then slowly pour it back into the sauce. Grind black pepper directly into the sauce and taste for seasoning. Reheat to the barest simmer just before serving.

SPINACH
SPENÓT/PARAJ
(*shpeh-noht/pah-roi*)

Not even Popeye ("Popáj, a tengerész," as he is known in Hungarian) can rescue all the people who were traumatized as children by a mess of saltless, sandy greens. Spinach, one of the most elegant of vegetables, just cannot shake that image. Offhand I can think of ten different ways to use spinach, and none of them adds more than 30 minutes to the basic—and very short—cooking time. Three of those recipes follow some elementary directions for cleaning and cooking spinach. When buying spinach, allow 3 pounds of fresh spinach for six people, or two 10-ounce cellophane bags of cleaned spinach or two 10-ounce packages of frozen chopped spinach. One year when Swiss chard was superabundant in my neighbor's garden, I used it in some of these recipes: it lacks the subtlety of spinach, having a much sharper taste, but the hanging judges of my kitchen okayed it.

◄§ Boiled Spinach

To clean fresh spinach, discard all the wilted or yellowed leaves. Break off the stems of the small, tender leaves at the base; fold the big, tougher ones lengthwise and pull the stems down toward the tips. Rinse the spinach in a large pan of salted cold water, changing the water several times until there is no sand left at the bottom of the pan. Even so-called cleaned spinach has to be picked over and rinsed once or twice. Put the spinach in a large stainless steel or enameled pot, add salt (1 teaspoon per 10-ounce bag) and, if desired, a peeled clove of garlic. Put the lid on and steam the spinach in the water that is left on the leaves until they go limp, about 5 to 7 minutes. Discard the garlic and drain the spinach. The best way to get all the juice out—many chefs would say the only way—is to put the spinach in a stainless steel or plastic mesh strainer, press out most of the liquid, then toss the spinach up and down until it forms a compact ball and not a bit more juice comes out. Set aside to drain off those last three drops, then chop the spinach up.

For frozen spinach, break up the block of spinach, put the pieces in a stainless steel or enameled saucepan with 1 tablespoon of butter and 2 tablespoons of water, a pinch of salt, and a clove of garlic, and cook, stirring and breaking up the pieces until they melt. Boil off all the water and discard the garlic.

◄§ Spinach in Roux
SPENÓT FŐZELÉK
(*shpeh-noht fu-ze-layk*)

3 pounds fresh spinach, or two 10-ounce cellophane bags
   cleaned spinach, or two 10-ounce packages frozen chopped
   spinach
2 tablespoons butter
2 heaping tablespoons flour
1 cup milk
1 teaspoon salt
Dash of nutmeg

Prepare the spinach according to the preceding directions. Reserve the spinach cooking broth, and add enough water to make 1 cup of liquid. Chop the spinach coarsely. Melt the butter in a heavy-bottomed saucepan over low heat, then stir in the flour and cook for 2 to 3 minutes. Gradually stir in the milk and the cup of spinach broth. Season with salt and nutmeg, and simmer gently for at least 10 minutes, stirring now and then. Add the spinach, taste, and serve.

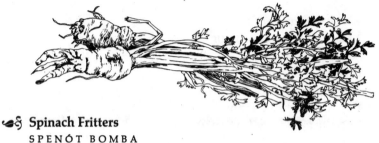

⌇ Spinach Fritters
SPENÓT BOMBA
(*shpeh-noht bohm-bah*)

"Kató néni's spenót bomba was round like a ball," my husband said, looking suspiciously at my pancake-like product. I cannot seem to duplicate Aunt Kate's effect, but in defense of *my* spenót bomba, let me say that it is light, fluffy, and delicious, and it tastes just right with roast pork, roast beef, or grilled steak.

> 1½ **pounds fresh spinach, or 1 cellophane bag (10 ounces)**
>   **cleaned spinach, or 1 package (10 ounces) frozen chopped**
>   **spinach**
> 3 **eggs, separated**
> 5 **tablespoons cooking oil**
> 3 **tablespoons flour**
> ½ **teaspoon salt**

Prepare and cook the spinach according to the directions on page 182, and chop it as finely as possible. Mix together the egg yolks and 1 tablespoon of oil. Stir in the flour and salt and enough water to make a thick, creamy batter. Stir in the chopped spinach. Beat the egg whites until stiff. Blend a spoonful of egg whites into the batter to lighten it, then carefully fold the rest in. Heat the remaining oil in a frying pan and drop the batter in by the tablespoonful. Brown well on both sides, drain on paper towels, and serve.

✑ Baked Spinach
RAKOTT SPENÓT
(*rah-kot shpeh-noht*)

3 pounds fresh spinach, or 2 packages (10 ounces each) fresh
  cleaned spinach, or two 10-ounce packages frozen chopped
  spinach
7 eggs
4 tablespoons butter
1 heaping tablespoon flour
Salt
Pepper
Nutmeg
Dry white bread crumbs
2 smoked sausages (optional)

Prepare the spinach according to the directions on page 182, chopping the cooked spinach very finely. Hard-boil 3 of the eggs and let them cool. Melt 2 tablespoons of the butter in a heavy-bottomed saucepan over low heat. Stir in the flour, and cook for 2 to 3 minutes. Separate the remaining 4 eggs. Mix the roux and the egg yolks into the spinach. Beat the egg whites with a pinch of salt until stiff, stir a spoonful into the spinach, and then fold the rest in quickly and lightly. Butter a baking dish 10 by 6 by 2 inches and sprinkle the sides and bottom with bread crumbs, shaking out the excess. Slice the 3 hard-boiled eggs. If sausage is to be used, slice it into ¼-inch rounds. Spread a layer of spinach on the bottom of the dish, then a layer of egg slices, a layer of spinach, a layer of sausage slices, and a layer of spinach on top. Dot with the remaining butter, and bake in a preheated 350° oven for half an hour, until the spinach puffs and browns slightly on top. Serve immediately.

SQUASH AND ZUCCHINI
TÖK
(*tuk*)

Squash and zucchini are such versatile and plentiful summer vegetables that every culture has found a few special ways to prepare them. Tök főzelék, for example, strikes me as quintessentially

Hungarian, and yet it appeals to even the most parochial palate. The soufflé bears a lighter Hungarian touch, and it too is liked by all. In my opinion, both dishes go best with ham, pork, or chicken, but we have a friend who invariably serves tök főzelék with barbecued steak: she reaps praise from her guests all summer long.

⋘ Squash in Sour Cream Sauce
TÖK FŐZELÉK
   (*tuk fu-ze-layk*)

2 pounds zucchini, patty pan, or yellow summer squash
Salt
1 medium onion, finely chopped
2 tablespoons cooking oil
½ teaspoon white vinegar
2 tablespoons flour
½ teaspoon paprika
½ cup sour cream at room temperature
2 tablespoons chopped fresh dill

Peel the squash and cut it into long, thin spaghetti-like strips. Put them in a glass bowl, sprinkle with ½ teaspoon salt, and let stand for 20 minutes. In a 2- or 3-quart enameled saucepan, sauté the chopped onion in oil until it starts to wilt. Squeeze the liquid out of the squash, and add the strips to the cooked onions. Sprinkle with vinegar. Continue cooking until the squash goes limp. Dust with flour, paprika, and ½ teaspoon of salt, and cook another 3 minutes, turning often so that the squash is evenly coated. Slowly pour in 1 cup of tepid water and let simmer, uncovered, for 5 minutes. Taste sauce: if it seems floury, simmer another 2 or 3 minutes. Remove from heat and let cool. Blend 2 tablespoons of sauce into the sour cream, then gradually stir that mixture into the sauce. Add the chopped dill, taste for seasoning, reheat, and serve.

◄§ Squash Soufflé
TÖK PUDDING
(*tuk pud-ding*)

1½ pounds zucchini or yellow summer squash
1 tablespoon vinegar
Salt
4 tablespoons butter
2 heaping tablespoons flour
2 tablespoons chopped fresh dill
2 cups milk
3 eggs, separated
½ cup bread crumbs

Peel the zucchini and cut in ½-inch cubes. Boil until almost tender—about 10 minutes—in 3 quarts of water to which the vinegar and about 2 teaspoons of salt have been added. (Squash needs plenty of salt: do not undersalt it.) Drain the squash and set it aside. Meanwhile, prepare a soufflé base as follows: Melt 2 tablespoons of butter in a heavy-bottomed saucepan. Add the flour and dill, and let it all foam together. Slowly pour in the milk, stirring constantly, and add ½ teaspoon salt. When the sauce thickens, remove from the heat and beat in the egg yolks. Then stir in the cooked and drained squash. Beat the egg whites until stiff, and carefully fold them into the mixture. Grease a six-cup soufflé dish with some of the remaining butter, dust it with 2 tablespoons of bread crumbs, and shake out the excess. Pour in the batter, sprinkle the top with the rest of the bread crumbs, and dot with the rest of the butter. Bake in a 350° oven until the top is browned, about half an hour. Serve immediately.

Salads

Saláták

(SHA-LAH-TAHK)

$\mathcal{S}$alad with the meal is a canon of Hungarian eating, and the wisdom of eating something fresh and sour with spicy, fat foods should need no explaining. While some combinations are traditional (cucumber salad with csirke paprikás, for example), lettuce is always good. I always have something on hand in the refrigerator to make a quick salad, as well as a jar of pickles, which have the same salutory effect as salad. For the rest, the best guide is always to use what is in season and looks good in the vegetable stall.

৺§ Hungarian Salad Dressing
SALÁTALÉ
(*sha-lah-ta-lay*)

Many northern and central Europeans fancy a kind of salad in which the ingredients are essentially marinated in vinegar. Except for cucumbers—with which the effect is magical—this kind of salad is definitely an acquired taste. Limp, sour lettuce leaves are just not for everyone. The following recipe makes 1 cup of dressing, enough for 2 large cucumbers or a medium-sized head of Boston lettuce.

½ **cup vinegar**
½ **cup water**
1 tablespoon sugar
½ **teaspoon salt**
Dash of freshly ground black pepper

Blend all the ingredients together in a large glass bowl, add the vegetables, and let the salad stand for at least 1 hour before serving. Serve in individual glass salad bowls.

⊷ French Sauce Vinaigrette
FRANCIA SALÁTALÉ
(*frahn-see-ya sha-lah-ta-lay*)

Although some Magyar purists actually crave a pungent, limp Hungarian salad with their meal, most people seem to prefer a somewhat milder and crisper version. Every cook has his or her own favorite salad dressing; mine is a simple French sauce vinaigrette to which I add different herbs according to the ingredients and the rest of the meal. The following recipe makes ½ cup of sauce, enough for 2 medium heads of Boston lettuce. A larger quantity may be made at one time and stored in the refrigerator for several days.

½ teaspoon dry mustard
¼ teaspoon salt
Pinch of black pepper
2 tablespoons wine vinegar
6 to 8 tablespoons olive oil or cooking oil

Blend the mustard, salt, and pepper, add the vinegar, and mix thoroughly with a fork. Add the oil and stir or shake vigorously. Just before serving, mix the sauce thoroughly again and pour it over the salad vegetables. Turn quickly and carefully until all the pieces are coated. Serve in individual salad bowls.

⊷ Mayonnaise
MAJONÉZ
(*mī-yu-nayz*)

Mayonnaise, of course, is not Hungarian at all, although it is an important element in Hungarian cuisine. And it really should be in the repertoire of every self-respecting cook, simply because no bottled preparation can approach the sublime taste of homemade mayonnaise. This is a sauce that can grace just about anything, from an artistic cold buffet for forty to an improvised cold supper for the family. I have tried many mechanical ways of making mayonnaise, but in the end I always go back to a pretechnological method that I have found foolproof. It was taught to me by Muteba Jean, our Congolese cook, and he learned it at a Belgian mission school deep in the equatorial bush. The following recipe will make at least 2 cups of mayonnaise.

> 3 egg yolks
> 4 to 5 teaspoons lemon juice or white vinegar
> ¾ teaspoon salt
> ¼ teaspoon mustard
> 1½ to 2 cups cooking oil
> 1 tablespoon boiling water

Have all ingredients at room temperature. Beat the egg yolks lightly with a stainless steel table fork in a flat soup dish. (The sauce may splash, but the fork-dish combination is far easier to handle than a wire whisk and deep bowl, especially at the beginning.) Beat in 3 teaspoons of lemon juice or vinegar, the salt, and the mustard. Then place a wooden spoon handle under one side of the dish—the left if you are right-handed—to tilt it. Slowly dribble the oil into the high end of the dish while beating the yolks constantly to absorb the oil as fast as you are pouring it. Once the sauce has started to thicken, beat the oil in a tablespoonful at a time. (At this point, you may quickly transfer the sauce to a warm deep bowl and use a wire whisk for beating if you prefer, or continue with the dish and fork.) If the sauce gets too thick and hard, beat in a few drops of lemon juice or vinegar, then continue with the oil. Three egg yolks can hold 2 cups of oil, even more, particularly if all the ingredients and the kitchen are warm, but you should proceed very carefully once the first 1½ cups of oil have been absorbed, beating in less than a full tablespoonful of oil each time. Stop pouring in oil at any point between 1½ and 2 cups, whenever you think the yolks cannot take any more. Then beat in 1 teaspoon of lemon juice or vinegar and 1 tablespoon of boiling water to guard against curdling. Taste the sauce, and add more lemon juice or vinegar and salt if need be. Makes about 2 cups.

To rescue a curdled mayonnaise, beat 1 tablespoon of it into 1 teaspoon of prepared mustard (or ½ teaspoon dry mustard) in a warm bowl. Very slowly beat the rest of the curdled mayonnaise into this mixture.

ᴇᴊ Lettuce Salad
FEJES SALÁTA
(*fay-esh sha-lah-ta*)

European lettuce is much like our own Boston or Bibb and has nothing to do with the ubiquitous California iceberg. Others may disagree, but I find that the crunchy rabbit-food salads made with iceberg, Romaine, and/or escarole lettuce—good as they might be with a grilled steak or bowl of spaghetti—just don't go with Hungarian food. It needs a softer green salad, made with Boston or Bibb or some of the curly garden varieties. Since their leaves are sometimes delicate, they should be individually washed and dried and carefully torn into smaller pieces by hand. The greens can be prepared in advance and kept in the refrigerator until mealtime; just before serving, toss them with French sauce vinaigrette (page 190). (To make a limp Hungarian salad, marinate the leaves in Hungarian salad dressing, page 189, for an hour before serving.)

ᴇᴊ Lettuce and Cucumber Salad
UBORKA-FEJES SALÁTA
(*ū-bor-ka fay-esh sha-lah-ta*)

2 medium heads of Boston lettuce
1 medium cucumber
1 tablespoon chopped fresh dill
1 tablespoon finely chopped scallions or chives
½ cup French sauce vinaigrette (page 190)

Wash and dry the lettuce leaves, tear them in half or in thirds, and place in a glass or wooden salad bowl. Peel and slice the cucumber very thin and wrap the pieces in paper toweling. Just before serving, squeeze the juice out of the cucumber slices and add them to the lettuce. Sprinkle with dill and scallions or chives. At the last possible moment, pour on the sauce vinaigrette and turn the salad quickly but thoroughly until every piece of lettuce is coated with sauce. Serve in individual salad bowls.

❧ Cucumber Salad

UBORKA SALÁTA
(ŭ-bor-ka sha-lah-ta)

There is nothing more refreshing than cucumber salad, and the Hungarians are so right to make it an obligatory course with many of their main dishes (csirke paprikás, for instance). It cuts the fat, as they would say, aids digestion, and leaves you with a virtuous feeling even after a huge helping, since it is almost calorie-free. In a good cucumber salad, the slices are paper thin and limp and they are swimming in sauce. To make the slices thin, use a special cucumber slicer (some graters have a blade for slicing cucumbers or potatoes) or use a vegetable peeler. To make the slices limp, let them stand in the sauce for at least an hour or even overnight. And, of course, be sure to make enough sauce. For six people allow at least 2 large cucumbers (peeled and sliced) and 1 cup of Hungarian salad dressing (page 189). A tablespoonful of chopped fresh dill should be sprinkled on top if it is available.

❧ Tomato Salad

PARADICSOM SALÁTA
(pah-rah-dee-chohm sha-lah-ta)

6 medium-size, firm ripe tomatoes (about 1½ to 2 pounds)
About ½ cup French sauce vinaigrette (page 190)
2 tablespoons finely chopped parsley, preferably the flat-leaved Italian kind
6 tablespoons finely chopped scallions

Cut out the stems of the tomatoes, removing a cone-shaped piece of core. Standing the tomato on the stem end, cut ¼-inch slices. (Sliced this way, the tomatoes seem to stay firmer and absorb more sauce than they do when sliced conventionally from blossom to stem.) They may also be quartered and then cut across the quarters into eighths. Put the tomatoes in a large glass or porcelain bowl, pour on the sauce, and mix thoroughly. Stir in half the parsley and scallions, and refrigerate for an hour or two, turning the salad once or twice. Just before serving, turn the salad again and sprinkle the rest of the parsley and scallions on top.

[193]

ᥦᢓ Green Bean Salad
ZÖLDBAB SALÁTA
(*zuld-bab sha-lah-ta*)

2 pounds green beans, cooked and cooled
2 tablespoons chopped scallions
1 tablespoon chopped parsley
½ cup French sauce vinaigrette (page 190)

Put the green beans, scallions, and parsley in a glass or porcelain bowl and pour the sauce vinaigrette over them. Mix thoroughly and refrigerate for at least an hour before serving.

ᥦᢓ Mixed Salad
VEGYES SALÁTA
(*ve-djesh sha-lah-ta*)

1 pound tomatoes
1 large sweet onion
1 medium green pepper, about 3 inches across the top
½ cup French sauce vinaigrette (page 190)

Cut out the stem of each tomato. Stand each tomato on that end, and cut slices ¼ inch thick. Peel and slice the onion about ⅛ inch thick. Remove the stem and core of the green pepper and cut it carefully in rings not more than ¼ inch thick. Put all the vegetables in a large glass or porcelain salad bowl, pour on the sauce vinaigrette, and turn the salad once. Refrigerate for at least an hour. Turn again just before serving.

ᥦᢓ Asparagus Salad
SPÁRGA SALÁTA
(*shpahr-ga sha-lah-ta*)

2 pounds asparagus, cooked and cooled
1½ tablespoons chopped scallions
1 tablespoon finely chopped parsley
½ cup French sauce vinaigrette (page 190)
1 hard-boiled egg yolk

Arrange the asparagus stalks in an oblong glass dish. Mix the scallions and parsley into the sauce vinaigrette, and pour it over the asparagus. Refrigerate for at least 30 minutes. Crumble the egg yolk rather coarsely so that it resembles blossoms of mimosa or goldenrod. Just before serving, baste the asparagus with the sauce and sprinkle the crumbled egg yolk on top.

◄§ Pickled Beets
CÉKLA SALÁTA
(*tsayk-la sha-lah-ta*)

2 pounds fresh beets
Salt
½ cup white vinegar
Bay leaf
3 cloves
6 peppercorns
Pinch of caraway seeds
1 large sweet onion, thinly sliced (optional)

Scrub the beet roots with a vegetable brush, place them in a large enameled or stainless steel pot, add 1 tablespoon of salt, and cover with cold water. Bring to a boil, reduce the heat, and simmer, covered, until the beets are done, at least 1 hour. (They are done when they can be pierced easily with a knife. The cooking time varies a great deal, depending on how large and how fresh the beets are.) Meanwhile, put the vinegar, bay leaf, cloves, peppercorns, caraway seeds, and ½ teaspoon of salt in a small enameled saucepan. Add ½ cup of cold water. Simmer, uncovered, for 20 minutes. Let the sauce cool. When the beets are done, drain them and rinse them under cold water. As soon as they are cool enough to handle, slip off the skins and slice the beets ¼ inch thick. Put them in a glass or porcelain bowl with the optional onion rings, and pour the sauce over them. Refrigerate at least overnight.

[195]

✑ Potato Salad with Mayonnaise
MAJONÉZES BURGONYA SALÁTA
(mi-ju-nay-zesh bur-gon-ya sha-lah-ta)

3 pounds (about 12 medium) new potatoes
Salt
1 cup mayonnaise (page 190)
½ cup sour cream
1 tablespoon lemon juice or white vinegar
Pinch of freshly ground black pepper
2 tablespoons chopped chives or ¼ cup chopped scallions
2 hard-boiled eggs, sliced or chopped
1 green pepper, cored and cut in ⅛-inch rings
4 radishes, thinly sliced, or 6 radish roses

Scrub the potatoes and put them in a large pot with 1 table-spoon of salt and cold water to cover. Bring to a boil, reduce heat, and cook, covered, until the potatoes are barely done, 35 to 45 minutes. (They should be firm but not hard when pierced with a knife.) Meanwhile make the dressing by mixing together the mayonnaise and sour cream. Beat in the lemon juice or vinegar by drops, taste, and add more if need be, as well as salt and pepper. When the potatoes are done, drain and rinse them under cold water and start peeling as soon as they can be handled. Slice them ¼ inch thick while still warm. Pour the salad dressing over the warm sliced potatoes and turn gently but thoroughly until all pieces are coated. Refrigerate for several hours or overnight to give the flavors a chance to meld. Before serving, garnish with chives or scallions, hard-boiled eggs, pepper rings, and radishes.

Desserts and Cakes
Édességek és Torták
(AY-DE-SHAY-GEK AYSH TOR-TAHK)

$\mathcal{G}$enerally speaking, Hungarian meals end with something sweet; in fact, they often seem to anticipate it. That might be a custard or sweetened noodles or palacsinta or rétes or even a spectacular cake. What I have tried to suggest here, given the limits of time and space, is the diversity and the virtuosity of the Hungarian dessert kitchen. A full list of desserts would be terrifying in its length and breadth; truly the mind boggles.

Each recipe is self-contained except for the following general information.

• EGGS. Large Grade-A eggs were used throughout. Remember that it is easier to separate eggs when they are cold, and it is best to beat them at room temperature. Preferably, beat the yolks and sugar with an electric mixer; if you don't have one, use a fast rotary egg beater. The whites should not contain a speck of grease or egg yolk. If you beat them stiff with an electric mixer, make that your first step; otherwise, beat them just before folding them into the batter.

• FLOUR. All-purpose flour was used in all these recipes. I prefer unbleached flour, but bleached flour can be used as well. Measuring the flour by volume instead of weight is always tricky: my method is to sift it directly into a measuring cup and then level it off. If the flour is to be measured by the tablespoon, dip it into sifted flour and use a rounded spoonful, unless the recipe notes otherwise. Always sift the flour into the batter.

• NUTS. Fresh nuts or canned whole nutmeats were used interchangeably for these cakes (but not cellophane-packed shelled nuts, which are often stale and sometimes even rancid). Grind the nuts by hand in a manual nut grinder or food chopper, using the medium blade. Wipe away the oil as it collects on the chopper. Nuts can also be ground in a blender, but they tend to be too fine and, of course, the oil is mixed in with the nuts.

• POPPY SEEDS. If possible, buy poppy seeds in a food specialty shop where they grind them for you. Otherwise, you have to get whole poppy seeds and do it yourself with a special grinder or in the blender, a little at a time at high speed. Store the ground seeds in a closed jar in the refrigerator; if they have been standing for a while, taste them before using to be sure they are not rancid (*avas* in Hungarian).

• SUGAR. Granulated sugar or confectioners' sugar (10-X powdered sugar) were used as specified. Confectioners' sugar should be sifted before measuring, like flour.

• VANILLA SUGAR. Vanilla granulated sugar or vanilla confectioners' sugar should be used as indicated. It gives a much more delicate flavor than sugar plus vanilla extract. If you have no vanilla sugar on hand, substitute plain sugar and a few drops of pure vanilla extract. If you intend to do much serious baking, prepare two jars of vanilla sugar, one for granulated and one for powdered: bend a vanilla bean in two places and put it in a jar; fill it with sugar, and screw the cap on firmly. Keep replacing the sugar as you use it until the vanilla bean loses its flavor; then start with a new one.

⊷ Witches' Froth
BOSZORKÁNYHAB
(*buh-sor-kahny-hab*)

To my mind, this is the company dessert *par excellence*: a sweet, fluffy counterpoint to the groaning-board kind of meal I tend to offer my guests. Besides, this is a dessert that does not require the cook's undivided attention, and if it is made in the morning, it will be at the height of perfection by dinner time. Served in a sher-bet or parfait glass, it is lovely to look at and virtually evanescent.

> **4 Roman Beauty baking apples (about 2 pounds)**
> **2 egg whites**
> **¾ cup granulated sugar**
> **¼ cup light rum**

Wash the apples and bake them until done (about 45 minutes at 350°). Let them cool, peel and core them, and purée the pulp. (If you have a mixer with a heavy-duty attachment, use that; if not, use a food mill or a potato ricer or an old-fashioned potato masher. Do not use a blender or fine sieve to make the apple purée perfectly smooth and even: this dessert tastes better with small bits and pieces of apple in it.) Stir in the egg whites and sugar and beat the mixture until fluffy and rather thick (about 10 minutes with an electric mixer). Add the rum, and continue beating for another 5 minutes. Spoon into serving glasses and keep in the refrigerator until ready to serve.

⮂§ Floating Island
MADÁRTEJ
(*ma-dahr-tay*)

Madártej means "bird's milk" in Hungarian, which is one of those gastronomic puns that defy explaining. Floating Island it is called in English, a soft custard topped with poached meringues, light and airy and, indeed, ephemeral as bird's milk. The last time we visited Hungary, we heard how the simple people of the Balaton would leave gifts outside the door of the great contemporary poet Gyula Illyés—a bottle of wine, a couple of eggs, a bowl of madártej. Could any offering be more loving?

THE CUSTARD
> **3 eggs**
> **3 egg yolks**
> **⅔ cup sugar**
> **1 teaspoon flour**
> **2½ cups milk**

¼ teaspoon salt
1 teaspoon vanilla extract

Beat the eggs and egg yolks lightly with a fork, and strain them (to remove the cords) directly into the top of a glass or stainless steel or enameled double boiler. Stir in the sugar; sift and stir in the flour. Scald the milk in a separate saucepan, heating it just until bubbles form around the edges. Gradually stir the milk into the egg mixture, and cook over simmering but not boiling water, stirring constantly with a wooden spoon until the mixture coats a metal spoon. Remove from the heat immediately, stir in the salt and vanilla, and pour into a large shallow bowl. Stand the bowl in cold water to cool it rapidly, then chill it in the refrigerator.

THE MERINGUE

2 egg whites
⅛ teaspoon cream of tartar
Dash of salt
½ teaspoon vanilla extract
¼ cup sugar
2 cups milk

Beat the egg whites with the cream of tartar and salt until frothy. Add the vanilla, then add the sugar 1 tablespoon at a time, beating well after each addition. Continue beating until stiff and shiny. Heat the milk in a frying pan. When bubbles start to form around the edges, drop in the egg white mixture, a tablespoonful at a time. Do not cover. Cook over low heat until the meringues are firm but not hard, about 5 minutes. Using a slotted spoon, lift them carefully out of the milk and slide them onto the custard. Chill until ready to serve.

৵ Chestnut Purée
GESZTENYE PÜRÉ
(geh-sten-ye pu-ray)

Some would say that gesztenye püré is an acquired taste, but I fell in love with it at first sight. All those faintly sweetened and flavored chestnuts served with a portion of whipped cream make the ultimate in desserts. Unfortunately, there is no way to tinker with it or cut corners—it must be made from scratch with whole fresh chestnuts, laboriously peeled and slowly simmered. It can be made only in the fall when chestnuts are in season; large and shiny chestnuts that are rather heavy for their size are the right kind. Peeling them is a dismal job, no matter what technique you use. Some say you should mark the shells with an x before boiling, others prefer making a slit; still others contend neither is necessary. It doesn't seem to make much difference. But fresh chestnuts they must be: canned chestnut purée is too sweet and has a metallic aftertaste. If you are offering gesztenye püré to novices, serve it in individual sherbet glasses. Old-timers will know how to handle a large serving platter full of the stuff.

3 pounds chestnuts
Milk
1½ cups granulated sugar, more if necessary
2 cups heavy cream
6 tablespoons rum
¼ cup vanilla confectioners' sugar

Slit or make a cross in the shell of each chestnut or leave it intact. Put them all in a saucepan and cover with cold water. Bring the water to the boil and cook for 3 to 5 minutes. Drain, and remove the chestnut shells and the bitter inner skin while warm. Set aside any that cannot be peeled, and boil them a second time. When all the chestnuts are peeled, place them in a clean saucepan and add enough cold milk to cover. Stir in the granulated sugar and slowly bring to a simmer, stirring occasionally until the sugar is dissolved. Simmer very gently, uncovered, until the chestnuts are tender (this may take as long as 1 hour, depending on how fresh they are). Add more warm milk if needed to keep the chestnuts covered. When they are done, drain them and put them through a food mill. Taste and add more sugar if needed. Moisten the chestnut purée with 3 or 4 tablespoons of heavy cream, then gradually beat in the rum. Press the paste through a potato ricer. With everything very cold—the cream, the bowl, and the beater—start whipping the rest of the heavy cream. Gradually add the vanilla confectioners' sugar, and continue beating until the cream forms soft peaks. Arrange the dessert on a large platter with the chestnut purée heaped up in the middle and surrounded by a ring of whipped cream. Or prepare individual serving glasses with the chestnut purée on the bottom and the whipped cream on top.

⌘ Plum Dumplings
SZILVÁS GOMBÓC
(*sil-vahsh gom-bohts*)

Szilvás gombóc is not a food, it is a vice. Grown men daydream and reminisce about plum dumplings they have known; they brag about how many they can eat at one session. They feel gloomy and deprived if the season passes without a plum-dumpling orgy. In earthbound reality, a szilvás gombóc is a potato dumpling with a pitted purple plum inside it, and a melted sugar cube inside that. To the initiate, the moment of revelation comes even before the first bite, namely when he jabs his fork into the dumpling and hot plum juice squirts out. From then on, it is a riot of sensations, gluey versus chewy, sweet versus bland—a unique item in anyone's repertoire. Although szilvás gombóc can be served as a dessert, it usually shows up as a snack on a Sunday afternoon in late summer. The following recipe is for 18 dumplings of the drier type (some aficionados prefer a moister dumpling that is kneaded, not rolled). It will serve six as a dessert; for a snack, count 5 or 6 dumplings per person.

> 6 medium potatoes (about 1½ to 2 pounds)
> Salt
> 18 purple plums (the kind called Italian or Hungarian plums)
> 3 cups sifted all-purpose flour
> 3 eggs
> 8 tablespoons (1 stick) butter, at room temperature
> 18 small sugar cubes
> ¾ cup dry bread crumbs

The night before, cook the potatoes in their jackets in salted water until done (when they can be pierced easily with the point of a paring knife) and drain. As soon as they are cool enough to handle, peel them and force them through a ricer. Spread the riced potatoes out on a cookie sheet and let them stand overnight in a cool place to dry them out. When you are ready to make the gombóc, pit the plums and set them aside. Transfer the riced potatoes to a mixing bowl (there should be about 3 cups, loosely packed), and mix in the flour and 1½ teaspoons of salt. Add the eggs, and work the dough together with a wooden spoon and your floured hands. Beat in 5 tablespoons of butter, a tablespoonful at a time, and continue to work the dough with your hands until it is smooth. Let it rest for 20 minutes, then roll it out ¼ inch thick on a floured board and cut it into 3- or 4-inch squares. To form the dumplings, flour your hands, place a square of dough in your left palm, put a plum in the middle of it and a sugar cube into the pit cavity. Pinch the dumpling closed, and roll it into a round smooth ball. Place it, pinched side up, on a floured board until ready to cook. Just before serving, drop the dumplings one at a time into plenty of rapidly boiling salted water. Do not crowd them in the pot. After a minute, give the dumplings a jog with a wooden spoon to keep them from sticking to the bottom. Let them cook 12 to 15 minutes uncovered after they rise to the surface. Taste one: the plum should be hot and the dough firm but not gummy when done. Do not overcook. While boiling the dumplings, quickly brown the bread crumbs in the remaining 3 tablespoons of butter. As the dumplings are ready, lift them carefully out of the water with a slotted spoon, roll them in the browned bread crumbs, and keep them warm until all are done. Serve immediately.

NOODLE DESSERTS
ÉDES TÉSZTÁK
(ay-desh tay-stahk)

Noodle desserts are very Hungarian: in one cookbook I've seen, there are twelve of them right in a row, not to mention the ones scattered throughout the text. And only recently, some friends of ours who were eating in a home-style restaurant in New York's Magyar quarter found themselves being urged by the waitress to order mákos tészta rather than the fancier and more expensive palacsinta dessert they thought they wanted. They took her advice and were pleasantly surprised: it was sweet and unpretentious, just the right thing after their main course of gulyás. The three sweet noodle dishes that follow have that quality of pleasant simplicity in common.

[205]

✎ Noodles with Poppy Seeds
MÁKOS TÉSZTA
(mah-kohsh tay-sta)

½ pound egg noodles, ¼ inch wide
¼ cup (½ stick) butter, at room temperature
3 tablespoons ground poppy seeds
Vanilla confectioners' sugar

Prepare the noodles and toss them with the butter. Fold in the poppy seeds, dust with confectioners' sugar, and serve immediately.

✎ Noodles with Walnuts
DIÓS TÉSZTA
(dee-ohsh tay-sta)

3 tablespoons butter
½ cup (2 ounces) roughly chopped walnuts
½ pound egg noodles, ¼ inch wide
Vanilla confectioners' sugar

Melt 2 tablespoons of butter in a skillet and briefly sauté the walnuts. Meanwhile, cook the noodles according to the package directions, drain them, and toss them with the remaining butter. Scrape the nuts out of the frying pan into the noodles, toss thoroughly, and sift the powdered sugar over them. Serve hot.

✎ Noodle Pudding
STÍRIAI METÉLT
(stee-ree-oyi me-taylt)

3 tablespoons butter
2 tablespoons bread crumbs
½ pound egg noodles, ½ inch wide
⅓ cup sugar
3 eggs, separated
Grated rind of ½ lemon
1 cup sour cream
½ cup yellow seedless raisins

½ cup chopped nuts (optional)
½ cup apricot jam (optional)
Vanilla confectioners' sugar

Lightly grease a 1½-quart oblong baking dish with some of the butter, and sprinkle the bottom and sides with bread crumbs, shaking out the excess. Cook the noodles according to the package directions, drain them, and toss them with the rest of the butter. Beat the sugar and egg yolks together, and add the lemon rind. Stir in the sour cream, then the raisins and the nuts if you wish. Add the noodles and turn them carefully so all are coated. Preheat the oven to 350°. Beat the egg whites until stiff, and fold them into the noodles. Pour them into the baking dish, or, if you want to add jam, pour only half the noodles in, spread the layer with jam, then pour the rest on top. Bake for 30 minutes or until the pudding is set and the top is golden brown. Dust with vanilla confectioners' sugar, and serve hot from the casserole.

PALACSINTA DESSERTS
PALACSINTÁK
(pah-lah-chin-tahk)

The thin pancake called palacsinta in Hungarian is surely the most protean dessert of all. It can be served alongside dishes of jam and chopped nuts with powdered sugar as a do-it-yourself dessert. It can be rolled around a stuffing and heated up in the oven. A stack of palacsinta can be layered with filling and baked like a cake. And there is no limit to the number of fillings to choose from. We ourselves often have palacsinta: as a family treat, as an after-theater snack, as a dinner-party dessert.

The basic palacsinta recipe will be found on page 37. For dessert palacsinta, add 1 tablespoon of sugar to the flour.

✑ Stuffed Palacsinta
TÖLTÖTT PALACSINTA
(tul-tot pah-lah-chin-ta)

The simplest way to serve palacsinta is to spread them with filling and fold each one in four or roll it up into a cylinder. They taste best freshly filled, but it is possible to prepare a quantity somewhat in advance and heat them in the oven just before serving. Three folded or rolled palacsinta make a good helping, and they should be sprinkled with powdered sugar or a mixture of ground nuts and powdered sugar just before being served.

Jam Fillings
GYÜMÖLCSÍZ TÖLTELÉKEK
(dju-mulch-eez tul-te-lay-kek)

A thin layer of jam makes a very pleasant filling for palacsinta. Apricot jam is most popular, but strawberry jam and red currant jelly are also very good. The jam should be thinned a bit with warm water or a few drops of brandy and the fruit mashed up if the pieces are very large. Sprinkle the filled palacsinta with powdered sugar or a mixture of ground nuts and powdered sugar.

Walnut Filling
DIÓS TÖLTELÉK
(dee-ohsh tul-te-layk)

Palacsinta may also be filled with walnuts (or hazelnuts). To make enough filling for 18 palacsinta, cook 1½ cups of coarsely ground nuts and 6 tablespoons of sifted confectioners' sugar with ¾ cup of milk until you have a thick mush. Spread some on each palacsinta, roll or fold it, and dust with powdered sugar.

Pot Cheese Filling
TÚRÓS TÖLTELÉK
(tū-rohsh tul-te-layk)

Sweetened pot cheese (or small-curd cottage cheese) makes a delicious filling for palacsinta. The palacsinta should be rolled and arranged in a single layer in shallow baking dishes and heated through just before serving. One pound of cheese will yield enough filling for 18 palacsinta.

1 pound pot cheese or small-curd cottage cheese
3 eggs, separated
½ cup sifted vanilla confectioners' sugar

Grated rind of 1 lemon (1½ to 2 teaspoons)
¼ cup yellow seedless raisins
¾ cup sour cream
3 tablespoons buttermilk

Lightly butter shallow oval or oblong dishes (as many as you need to hold all the palacsinta rolls in one layer). Strain the cheese and force it through a potato ricer. Mix well with the egg yolks, confectioners' sugar, and grated lemon rind. Stir in the raisins. Beat the 3 egg whites until stiff and fold them in. Spread some of the filling on each palacsinta, roll it, and place it in a baking dish. Thin the sour cream with the buttermilk, whisk it with a fork, and spread it on the palacsinta rolls. Half an hour before serving, place in a preheated 325° oven for 20 to 25 minutes. Serve immediately.

⊷§ Layered Palacsinta
RAKOTT PALACSINTA
(*rah-kot pah-lah-chin-ta*)

Rakott palacsinta is one of the loveliest desserts there is, and it never fails to please. It is a many-layered palacsinta cake, and as a company dessert, it has a great advantage over the rolled or folded palacsinta: it can be made a few hours in advance and popped into the oven while the main course is being served. To make rakott palacsinta, lightly butter an 8-inch springform pan. Place a palacsinta in the bottom, spread it with filling, place another palacsinta on top of that, spread that one with filling, and so on until the pan is filled, ending with a palacsinta. Top it with a meringue made from 3 egg whites stiffly beaten with ½ cup of sugar, and place the pan in a preheated 300° oven for 25 to 30 minutes, or until the top is lightly browned. Or simply sprinkle the top palacsinta with sugar, dot it with butter, and bake the rakott palacsinta in a 375° oven for 20 to 25 minutes. Remove the sides of the pan and transfer the palacsinta cake to a serving platter. Cut into thin wedges to serve. Rakott palacsinta tastes best warm. It seems to come off particularly well when made with diós töltelék (walnut filling) and topped with meringue. Another very good cake can be made by alternating apricot jam and chopped walnuts with powdered sugar for filling. It could have either a meringue topping or a plain sugar topping. If made with a sugar topping, this rakott palacsinta can be flambéed: once at the table, pour a generous quarter-cup of warmed barack (Hungarian apricot brandy) or cognac over the cake and light it. Two more elaborate versions of rakott palacsinta follow: both are quite out of the ordinary—and very sweet.

⋐§ Armenian Palacsinta Cake
ÖRMÉNY RAKOTT PALACSINTA
(*ur-mayny rah-kot pah-lah-chin-ta*)

1 recipe palacsinta batter (page 37), with 1 tablespoon of sugar added to flour

FILLING 1
½ cup (2 ounces) coarsely chopped walnuts
1 to 2 tablespoons honey

FILLING 2
1 cup ground poppy seeds
2 tablespoons honey

FILLING 3
¼ cup Damson plum jam
¼ cup coarsely chopped walnuts

FILLING 4
2 squares (2 ounces) semisweet chocolate, grated
¼ cup yellow seedless raisins
1½ tablespoons chopped candied orange peel
2 tablespoons rum

TOPPING
2 tablespoons granulated sugar
1 tablespoon butter

Cook the palacsinta and keep them warm while making the fillings. Prepare each filling in a separate dish, combining the listed ingredients and stirring with a fork to get four different kinds of thick mush. Butter an 8-inch springform pan and place a palacsinta in the bottom. Spread it with the nut filling (number 1) and cover it with another palacsinta. Spread the second one with the poppy seed filling (number 2) and cover that. Next use the jam filling (number 3), cover it, and lastly the chocolate filling (number 4). Continue in this fashion until you reach the top of the pan, ending with a palacsinta. Sprinkle it with sugar and dot with butter. About half an hour before serving, place the pan in a preheated 375° oven and bake for about 20 minutes. Remove the sides of the pan and transfer the rakott palacsinta to a platter. Cut in wedges like a cake to serve.

ৰ্঵ Gala Palacsinta Cake
TRIPLA RAKOTT PALACSINTA
(*treep-lah rah-kot pah-lah-chin-ta*)

1 recipe palacsinta batter (page 37), with 1 tablespoon sugar added to the flour

FILLING 1
2 squares (2 ounces) semisweet chocolate, grated
1 cup (4 ounces) coarsely chopped walnuts
½ cup sifted vanilla confectioners' sugar

FILLING 2
½ cup apricot jam
1 to 2 tablespoons brandy or water

FILLING 3
1 cup pot cheese or small-curd cottage cheese
1 egg, separated
4 tablespoons sifted vanilla confectioners' sugar
1 teaspoon grated lemon rind
2 tablespoons yellow seedless raisins

TOPPING
3 egg whites
½ cup vanilla sugar

Make the palacsinta and set them aside while preparing the fillings in separate dishes. Mix the grated chocolate with the chopped walnuts and confectioners' sugar. Set it aside. Thin the jam with brandy or water, and mash up any large pieces of fruit. Put that to one side. Strain the pot cheese and force it through a potato ricer. Mix it well with the egg yolk, confectioners' sugar, and lemon rind, and stir in the raisins. Beat the egg white until stiff, then fold it into the pot-cheese mixture. To form the rakott palacsinta, lightly butter an 8-inch springform pan and place a palacsinta on the bottom. Spread it with some nut and chocolate filling (number 1), and cover with a second palacsinta. Spread that with a thin layer of apricot jam (number 2), and cover it with another palacsinta. Spread it with the pot cheese filling (number 3), and cover with a fourth palacsinta. Repeat and continue the layering process until you reach the top of the pan; end with a palacsinta. Three-quarters of an hour before serving, preheat the oven to 300° and beat the egg whites with the sugar until stiff and shiny. Pile the meringue on the top palacsinta and place the pan in the oven to bake for 30 minutes or more, or until the meringue is lightly browned ("pink"). Remove the sides of the pan and transfer the rakott palacsinta to a platter. Serve hot, cut in wedges like a cake.

STRUDEL
RÉTES
(ray-tesh)

Rétes is *the* Hungarian confection, a fine, flaky pastry wrapped around a filling of fruit or nuts or cheese or even cabbage. It always seems wrong to me to call it strudel, which conjures up an image of Herr Professor and Frau Doktor having a hearty snack after their Sunday stroll in the woods. And it has nothing in common with that sodden mass of dough and apples sold at the corner deli. A true rétes is neither brittle nor soggy—it is as light and as fragile as the wings of an angel. It is now possible to find ready-made strudel sheets (or phyllo leaves) in a grocery or butcher shop with a large European following, and these are excellent. Consult the package directions for handling them, and use one of the following recipes for the filling. Making rétes from scratch requires considerably more time and talent, but it is the only way to get the real thing in most parts of the country. For best results, use special flour with a high gluten content, which can be bought at some food specialty shops or directly from a good bakery. Rétes made from all-purpose flour is nothing to be ashamed of either. As you make your own rétes, remember that it has to be kneaded aggressively and stretched lovingly. Like all good things in life, it needs care and attention or it will go awry.

◄§ Strudel Dough

A RÉTES TÉSZTÁJA
(*ah ray-tesh tay-sti-ya*)

2 cups sifted flour
¼ teaspoon salt
1½ teaspoons vinegar
1 cup (½ pound) butter
1 egg
2 to 3 tablespoons fine, dry bread crumbs
Confectioners' sugar

Sift the flour and salt into a large bowl. Pour the vinegar into a measuring cup and add enough lukewarm water to make ½ cup. Melt the butter. Make a well in the flour and add the egg, slightly beaten, the vinegar water, and 1½ teaspoons of butter. Mix with a wooden spoon and your hands to make a mass of dough (add a few more drops of warm water if absolutely necessary to make it stick together). Turn the dough out on a floured wooden surface and knead until it is smooth and elastic and blisters start to form on the surface. Then pick the dough up and slap it down hard on the surface over and over again for at least 5 minutes or 100 times. Form the dough into a ball, brush it with melted butter, and cover it with an inverted bowl; let it rest for 30 minutes. Prepare the filling (see following recipes) while the dough is resting.

Cover a small rectangular kitchen table (about 30 by 45 inches) with a cloth: use one with a design so you can see if you are stretching the dough thinly and evenly enough (a printed cotton bedsheet is ideal for the purpose). Sprinkle the cloth with flour, and set the ball of dough in the middle. Roll it as thin as possible with a rolling pin, lifting and turning it around so it doesn't stick. Brush lightly with melted butter and begin to stretch the dough by hand. Slide the backs of your hands and wrists under the dough and start stretching from the center outward. When the dough is twice its original size or is too awkward to handle, put it back down on the cloth. Reach under the dough, and with the tips of your fingers (or the back of your hand if that is easier) stretch the dough very gently from the center outward. Walk around and around the table as you work to stretch the dough evenly. Continue the stretching operation until the dough is as thin as tissue paper and covers the table, with the excess hanging over the edges of the table. An expert rétes maker can stretch the dough gossamer thin without any tears or holes; if you have some, leave them—patching does more harm than good. Cut off the excess dough with kitchen shears, and let the rest stand to dry for no longer than 5 minutes.

Preheat the oven to 400° and grease a heavy baking sheet or jelly roll pan. Brush the dough with melted butter and sprinkle lightly with some of the bread crumbs. Fill the dough at the narrow end: leaving a 3-inch margin on the bottom and both sides, spread the rest of the bread crumbs in a thin, even layer about 2½ to 3 inches wide, and spread the filling evenly over that. Fold over the margins and start to roll the rétes. Pull the cloth toward you and up to make each turn: do not roll the rétes too tightly. Carefully place the rétes in the pan, seam side down. If it is too large for the pan, bend it into a horseshoe or cut it in two. Brush the top lightly with melted butter and place the pan in the preheated oven. Bake for about 30 minutes, brushing the top every ten minutes with melted butter, or until the rétes is golden brown. Let it cool for at least 20 minutes before serving. Then dust with powdered sugar and cut into 2½-inch slices. Rétes may be eaten cold, but it tastes best warm; it can be reheated.

◦§ Strudel Fillings
RÉTES TÖLTELÉKEK
(ray-tesh tul-te-lay-kek)

The classic fillings for rétes are apple, sour cherry or cherry, cheese, poppy seed, and nuts. There is even a sweet cabbage filling for rétes. They are all so good it is hard to make a choice. When making rétes, always have the filling ready before the dough is stretched.

Apple Filling for Strudel
ALMÁS TÖLTELÉK
(ahl-mahsh tul-te-layk)

1 medium lemon
4 or 5 medium-size green cooking apples (about 1½ pounds)
½ cup sugar, more if necessary
½ cup (2 ounces) coarsely ground walnuts
½ teaspoon cinnamon

Grate the rind of the lemon and set aside, then squeeze the lemon and set the juice aside. Peel, core, and thinly slice the apples, and sprinkle with lemon juice to keep them from discoloring. Mix together the sugar, ground nuts, cinnamon, and grated lemon peel, and set aside. Just before filling the rétes, toss the apples with the nuts and sugar mixture. Taste, and add more sugar if the apples are very tart.

Sour Cherry Filling for Strudel
MEGGY TÖLTELÉK
(medge tul-te-layk)

2 cups pitted sour cherries (fresh or canned)
¾ cup sugar
¼ cup coarsely ground walnuts

Drain the cherries and let them stand in the strainer until just before filling the rétes. Then, toss with the sugar and ground nuts. (Rétes may also be filled with pitted sweet cherries or a mixture of sweet and sour cherries. In either case, use less sugar to sweeten the filling.)

Pot Cheese Filling for Strudel
TÚRÓS TÖLTELÉK
(tū-rohsh tul-te-layk)

1 pound pot cheese or small-curd cottage cheese
½ cup sifted vanilla confectioners' sugar

3 egg yolks
1½ teaspoons grated lemon peel
¼ cup yellow seedless raisins

Strain the cheese and press it through a potato ricer. Mix it with the sugar, egg yolks, and lemon peel, and stir in the raisins.

Poppy Seed Filling for Strudel
MÁKOS TÖLTELÉK
  (*mah-kohsh tul-te-layk*)

2 cups water
1 cup sugar
2 tablespoons yellow seedless raisins
3 cups ground poppy seeds
1 tart apple, grated

Heat the water and sugar in a saucepan and add the raisins to plump them. When the syrup comes to the boil, pour it over the poppy seeds and mix thoroughly until all are moistened. Stir in the grated apple and set aside until ready to use. Makes enough filling for one large rétes.

Walnut Filling for Strudel
DIÓS TÖLTELÉK
  (*dee-ohsh tul-te-layk*)

2 cups (8 ounces) chopped walnuts
½ cup sugar
3 tablespoons apricot jam
Juice of ½ lemon
1 tart apple, grated

Mix all the ingredients together to make a thick mush. Taste for sweetness and add more sugar if needed. Set aside until ready to use. Makes enough filling for one large rétes.

Cabbage Filling for Strudel
KÁPOSZTÁS TÖLTELÉK
(kah-poh-stahsh tul-te-layk)

1 medium head (about 2 pounds) cabbage
Salt
2 tablespoons lard or cooking oil
1 tablespoon sugar
Freshly ground black pepper

Core the cabbage and clean it, then grate it. Put it into a large glass bowl, sprinkle liberally with salt, and turn it. Let it stand for 20 minutes to half an hour, then squeeze it out. Heat the lard or oil in a heavy-bottomed skillet and cook the sugar in it until it turns dark brown. Add the cabbage and sauté it until it is brown and limp: this takes nearly half an hour. Season to taste with pepper and salt, and let it cool before filling the rétes.

YEAST CAKES
ÉLESZTŐS TÉSZTÁK
(ay-les-tush tay-stahk)

The tempo of modern life is not kind to yeast cakes, which require the presence of the cook at several crucial points over a period of time. It is a pity, because they are fun to make and everyone seems to like them. Somehow, though, it seems easier to find a block of time to make a torta or some palacsinta that can be set aside if necessary and finished at the cook's convenience. But aranygaluska and darázsfészek are so very special that it would be a shame not to include recipes for them. As always when baking with yeast, it is essential to work in a warm place that is free from drafts. To avoid the worst kind of disappointment, make sure the yeast is alive by dissolving it in warm water first, no matter what the manufacturer says about mixing the dry yeast with the flour. And for best results, add just as much flour as the dough can absorb and give it all the time it needs to rest and to rise.

[217]

ᥱᵹ Golden Dumpling Coffeecake
ARANYGALUSKA
(ah-rahny gah-lūsh-ka)

Many people who can pass by a tray of pastries and other sweets with equanimity simply cannot deny themselves a piece of coffeecake. Somehow they manage to convince themselves that it isn't fattening. I ought to know: I am one of them. And with those credentials, I can honestly report that this Hungarian concoction is *prima inter pares:* a spectacular hilly ring of sugary golden dumplings. The orthodox way to serve it is to break it apart with forks and eat the dumplings one by one; more fastidious eaters may prefer to slice it like any other coffeecake. Either way, it is utterly delicious.

THE DOUGH

2 packages dry yeast
1 tablespoon sugar
½ cup warm water (110° to 115°)
½ cup (1 stick) butter
½ cup sugar
1½ teaspoons salt
½ cup milk
4½ to 5 cups sifted all-purpose flour
2 eggs

Sprinkle the yeast and the tablespoon of sugar on the warm water. Let it stand 2 or 3 minutes, then stir to dissolve. Put it in a warm, draft-free place (an unlighted oven is ideal) for 5 to 10 minutes, or until the yeast bubbles and doubles in volume. In a very large mixing bowl, cream the butter together with ½ cup of sugar and the salt. Scald the milk by heating it in an enameled or stainless steel saucepan until bubbles form around the edges (do not let it boil); pour the scalded milk over the butter-sugar mixture right away. Work it in, then add ½ cup of flour and beat until the dough is smooth. Stir the yeast solution and mix that in. Add 2 cups of flour and beat until the dough is smooth again. Using a fork, beat the eggs till they begin to froth, then add them to the dough. Next work in 2 cups or more of the flour (enough to make a soft dough),

[218]

turn the dough out onto a lightly floured surface, and let it rest for 5 to 10 minutes. Lightly grease a large bowl and set it aside in a warm place. Knead the dough for about 10 minutes until it is smooth and elastic. (To knead dough, form an oblong and fold it in half, flipping the opposite end over toward you. Using the heel of your hands, gently push the dough away from you. Give it a quarter-turn, clockwise, and repeat. Continue in this way for 8 to 10 minutes, always turning the dough in the same direction, until it is smooth and elastic.) Form the dough in a large ball and place it in the greased bowl, then turn it over so the greased surface is on top. Cover the bowl with a kitchen towel and place it in a warm place—again an unlighted oven is ideal—to rise until the dough has doubled in volume (about 1 hour). Punch it down, fold the corners over into the middle, then turn the ball over smooth side up, and let it rise again until nearly doubled (about 1 to 1½ hours). The sweet dough is now ready to shape and fill.

ARANYGALUSKA FILLING

    1 cup (4 ounces) walnuts
    1 cup sugar
    1½ teaspoons cinnamon
    ½ cup (1 stick) butter, melted, more if needed
    ½ cup yellow seedless raisins

Chop the walnuts by putting them through a food or meat chopper, using the medium blade: they should be fine but not pulverized. Mix the nuts, sugar, and cinnamon together in a shallow bowl. The melted butter should also be in a shallow bowl. Set the raisins aside. Grease a 10-inch tubed springform pan. When the dough (see above) has risen sufficiently, flour your hands and tear off bits of dough to form balls about 1 to 1¼ inches in diameter. Rolling the balls in the melted butter, coat them on all sides completely, then roll them in the nut mixture. Arrange half the balls in the bottom of the pan, close together but not touching. Sprinkle with the raisins. Arrange the rest of the balls on top, and if there is any of the nut mixture left, sprinkle it on top. About 2 tablespoons of melted butter should be dripped on top: use what is left, melt more if necessary. (This is to keep the sugar from caramelizing and burning in the rather hot oven. Do not put raisins on top; they will burn.) Cover the pan with a towel and let the cake rise for about 45 minutes. Preheat the oven to 375°, place the cake in the middle, and bake 35 to 40 minutes or until golden brown. Remove the sides of the pan immediately and the tubular piece as soon as it is cool enough to handle. Let the cake cool thoroughly on a wire rack, then transfer it to a plate. To serve, break the cake apart with forks or slice it 1 to 1½ inches thick.

✑ Wasps' Nest Coffeecake
D A R Á Z S F É S Z E K
(dah-rahzh-fay-sek)

Darázsfészek is my husband's *madeleine*, a piece of cake that can evoke memories long hidden behind the veil of time. The cake itself is made up of individual pinwheels of dough with nut filling that puff up as they bake to resemble little wasps' nests. The way to eat it is to break off one of the nests and work your way from the outside in; in other words do not cut it. Even without the sentimental associations, darázsfészek turns out to be an exceptionally good coffeecake that gets even better with time as the filling slowly soaks into the yeast cake.

THE DOUGH
  1 package dry yeast
  1 teaspoon sugar
  ¼ cup warm water (110° to 115°)
  4 tablespoons (½ stick) butter
  ¼ cup sugar
  1 teaspoon salt
  ¼ cup milk
  2¼ cups sifted all-purpose flour
  3 egg yolks

Sprinkle the yeast and a teaspoon of sugar on the warm water and let it stand for 2 or 3 minutes. Stir to dissolve, and put it in a warm, draft-free place, such as an unlighted oven, for 5 to 10 minutes, or until the yeast bubbles and doubles in volume. Cream the butter with ¼ cup of sugar and the salt in a large mixing bowl. Scald the milk in an enameled or stainless steel pan just until bubbles form around the edges. Pour it over the creamed butter immediately and work it in. Add ¼ cup of flour and beat vigorously. Beat the yeast solution in, then add 1 cup of flour and beat that in. Whisk the egg yolks with a fork and beat them in. Next work in as much of the remaining cup of flour as you need to make a soft dough. Turn it out on a lightly floured surface, and let it rest for 5 to 10 minutes. Knead the dough for 8 to 10 minutes until it is smooth and elastic. Form it into a large ball and place it in a greased bowl. Grease the top of the dough and cover the bowl with a kitchen towel. Place it in a warm place (the unlighted oven is perfect), and let it stand until the dough has doubled in volume (about 1 hour). Punch it down, fold the corners over into the middle, and turn the ball over smooth side up. Cover it with the towel and let it rise again until nearly doubled (about 1½ hours). Roll out the dough in a rectangle ½ inch thick, and fill it as follows.

DARÁZSFÉSZEK FILLING
    ½ cup (1 stick) butter
    1 cup sifted vanilla confectioners' sugar
    ½ cup (2 ounces) coarsely ground walnuts
    ½ cup yellow seedless raisins
    1 tablespoon sugar
    ½ cup warm milk

Cream the butter with the sugar until light and fluffy. Add the nuts and raisins and mix well. Spread the filling on the dough and roll it up like a long jelly roll. Cut the roll into 1-inch slices and place them, cut side down, in a buttered baking pan. They should be close together but not touching. A 10-inch round springform pan is the right size, but a square or rectangular pan large enough to hold all the pieces in one layer could be used. Cover with the towel and place in a warm place to rise for about 45 minutes. Bake in a preheated 375° oven for 35 to 40 minutes or until golden brown. Twice during the baking time, dribble a sugar-milk topping (1 tablespoon sugar dissolved in ½ cup of warm milk) over the cake. When it is done, remove the pan sides and let it cool. (If a springform pan is not used, remove the cake by inverting the pan. Turn the cake right side up to let it cool.) Darázsfészek may be served either warm or cold, sprinkled with confectioners' sugar or not. The protocol is to break off individual wasps' nest buns, never to slice them.

SHORT CAKES
PITÉK
(pee-tayk)

The cakes called piték are made with various kinds of short dough or 1-2-3 dough, so called because the original proportions, by weight, are 1 sugar to 2 fat (usually butter) to 3 flour. The dough is difficult to handle at first, but an experienced cook will acquire the knack quickly. The main point to remember is to keep everything cold and to work fast so as not to melt the butter in the dough or "burn" it, as they say. A pite can be made over a period of days: the dough will keep in the refrigerator, and a half-baked shell can be made in advance, loosely wrapped and stored in a cool dry place until it is time to fill it. Although pite-type cakes are usually rectangular and rather flat, they are often made square or round at home. The following recipe gives the right amounts for a home-style pite, 1½-inch high, 9-inch round or 8-inch square, which would serve six people quite generously. To fill a standard jelly-roll pan (about 15 by 10 by 1 inch in size) double the entire recipe.

✑ Hungarian Apple Pie
ALMÁS PITE
(ahl-mahsh pi-te)

Finding a light dessert to go with a Hungarian meal does not always come easy; fortunately, almás pite is there. This delectable closed apple cake is neither too sweet nor too flat, neither too dry nor too creamy. It is just right. As always with a new kind of cake, though, I would recommend trying out the recipe on a compassionate jury before presenting it to the supreme court. This simple cake can be ticklish to handle the first time.

THE DOUGH
>   2¼ cups sifted all-purpose flour
>   ¼ teaspoon salt
>   ½ teaspoon double-acting baking powder
>   ½ cup vanilla sugar
>   ¾ cup butter (cold)
>   2 egg yolks (cold)
>   1 teaspoon grated lemon peel

Sift together the flour, salt, and baking powder, either into a mixing bowl or directly onto a large floured clean surface (like the kitchen table or a pastry board). Stir in the sugar and make a well. Drop in the butter, egg yolks, and lemon peel. Using your floured fingertips or a pastry blender, work all the ingredients together as quickly as you can until they are rather evenly mixed. Then try to squeeze all the pieces and crumbs together into a smooth ball. This can take some doing, and you may have to resort to sprinkling some ice-cold water on the dough to bind it. Work as quickly as you can to avoid "burning" or overworking the dough by causing the butter to melt. Flatten the ball with the heel of your hand by pushing from the center out in all directions. Fold the edges in to make a ball again, wrap it in waxed paper or plastic wrap, and refrigerate it for at least 1 hour. (The dough will actually keep in the refrigerator for several days.) When you are ready to make the pastry shell, take the dough out of the refrigerator and give it about ½ hour to come to room temperature. Divide it more or less in half. Put the smaller portion back in the refrigerator, and turn the oven on to 400°. Roll out the larger half ¼ inch thick, and shape it for the pan you intend to use. Butter the pan and line it with the dough, prick it in several places with a fork, and place it in the preheated oven to bake for 10 minutes. Let the shell cool off before filling it.

APPLE FILLING

> 3 medium green cooking apples (about 1 pound)
> 2 teaspoons lemon juice
> 1 teaspoon grated lemon peel
> ½ cup sugar
> ½ teaspoon cinnamon
> ½ cup (2 ounces) chopped walnuts
> 2 egg whites
> Salt
> 2 tablespoons bread crumbs
> 1 whole egg, lightly beaten

Remove the rest of the dough from the refrigerator and let it come back to room temperature while you make the filling. Peel the apples and grate them, using the large hole of the grater. (You should have about 3 cups of apple pieces that look like broken matchsticks.) Immediately sprinkle with lemon juice to keep the apples from turning brown. Flavor with the lemon peel, cinnamon, and ¼ cup of the sugar. Stir in the chopped walnuts. Roll out the dough ¼ inch thick and in the appropriate shape. Preheat the oven to 400°. Quickly beat the egg whites with a pinch of salt, then gradually add the remaining ¼ cup of sugar and continue beating until stiff. Fold the beaten whites into the apple mixture. Sprinkle the half-baked pastry shell with bread crumbs and fill it with the apples. Carefully put the upper crust in place, seal the edges, and prick it with a fork in several places. Paint the crust with the beaten egg, and place the pite in the middle rack of the oven to bake for 20 minutes or until the crust is a shiny golden brown.

৺৳ Cottage Cheese Cake
TÚRÓS PITE
(tū-rohsh pi-te)

Túrós pite is a very pleasant dessert, falling somewhere between a sweet quiche and a light cheesecake. It is supposed to be a closed cake, but the upper crust is sometimes dispensed with. Our neighborhood baker does so all the time, selling the product as Hungarian cheese cake for a googol of a price. A very good túrós pite can be made by following the directions for almás pite (preceding recipe) but substituting the following cottage cheese filling:

Press 1 pound of pot cheese or small-curd cottage cheese through a potato ricer. Some milky liquid will come through the ricer first: wipe this off and throw it away. Lightly mix the riced cottage cheese with 4 egg yolks and 1 cup of vanilla sugar. Stir in 1½ teaspoons of grated lemon peel. Use as soon as possible.

৺৳ Lady's Whim
NŐI SZESZÉLY
(nu-i se-say-y)

Női szeszély has an extra-rich cake base spread with raspberry jam and topped with a nut meringue. In the realm of pastry, at any rate, a lady's whim is painfully sweet—and her lovers keep coming back for more. Serve it with tea in the afternoon or as a dessert along with another kind of pastry, almás pite, for example, which is more on the tart side. Be sure to let női szeszély cool thoroughly before cutting it, and do not cover it, not even with waxed paper, or the meringue will collapse. The cake bottom is so rich it will stay moist for days without being wrapped or refrigerated.

> 3 cups sifted all-purpose flour
> ¼ teaspoon salt
> 1½ teaspoons baking powder
> ½ pound butter
> 1 cup vanilla sugar
> 6 egg yolks
> About 1 cup (12-ounce jar) raspberry jam
> 9 egg whites
> 1½ cups confectioners' sugar
> 1½ cups (6 ounces) coarsely ground walnuts or hazelnuts

Preheat the oven to 350°. Sift together the flour, salt, and baking powder. Cut the butter into small pieces and work them into the flour, using your hands or a pastry whisk. Work in the vanilla sugar and the egg yolks, and squeeze the dough together into a mound. Pat it into an unbuttered jelly-roll pan (15½ by 10½ by 1 inch), place it in the preheated oven, and bake for 10 minutes. Let the cake cool for 10 minutes, then spread the jam evenly over the entire surface. Turn the oven down to 300° and beat the egg whites until frothy. Add the confectioners' sugar ¼ cup at a time, and continue beating until very stiff. Fold in the ground nuts and spread the mixture evenly over the jam. Bake in the preheated 300° oven for 20 minutes or more, until the meringue is lightly browned. Remove from the oven, cool in the pan, and cut into neat squares. Do not cover the cake.

◄§ Poppy Seed Roll
BEIGLI
(bī-glee)

Beigli is a slang word for several kinds of poppy seed cake rolls. There is village beigli made from sweetened yeast dough with a high proportion of cake to filling. There are the Pozsonyi kifli (crescent rolls) and tekercs (cake roll), which originated in Pozsony,

as Bratislava, Czechoslovakia, used to be known. These are made
with a yeast dough that is handled in a special way to keep the cake
thin; its characteristic mark is a shattered golden-brown glaze on
top. And then there is a fine beigli that can be made easily at home
with a variation of the old 1-2-3 dough. This one is relatively easy
to handle, and it can be rolled up quite tightly to get in many turns
and plenty of filling. Filled with poppy seeds, the cake may also
be called mákos tekercs; with chopped walnuts, diós tekercs. The
same dough can be used for cookies or for almás pite; it is just as
rich but not quite as sweet as the one on page 222.

THE DOUGH

    2 cups (1 pound) butter
    9 cups (2 pounds) all-purpose flour, sifted once
    3 egg yolks
    1 whole egg
    Pinch of salt
    1 teaspoon sugar
    1½ to 2 cups sour cream

THE GLAZE

    ¼ teaspoon powdered instant coffee
    1 egg yolk

Work the butter into 7 cups of the flour with your fingertips
until you have dime-sized morsels of flour-coated butter. Make a well
and add the egg yolks, whole egg, salt, and sugar, and work the
dough until the eggs are evenly distributed. Add as much of the
sour cream as necessary to make the dough stick together. Knead
it, sprinkling more flour on the board and dough as needed to keep
it from sticking, until it is smooth and firm. Divide the dough into
four parts, and knead each one briefly. Then form each portion into
a ball, wrap it in waxed paper, and refrigerate for 1 hour. Make the
fillings (following recipes) while the dough is resting. Preheat the
oven to 400°. Roll the balls out one at a time into rectangles ¼ inch
thick and spread each with filling. Start at the long side to roll each
one up, pinching the first turn together and ending up with a roll
about 3 inches wide. Mix the instant coffee and the egg yolk together for a glaze, and paint the top of the cake with it. Make sev-

eral swirls with a table fork, and puncture the roll down the middle once every 3 inches with an ice pick. Tuck in the ends and place on a baking sheet. Put it in the hot oven and immediately reduce the heat to 350°. Bake for 30 minutes or until dark golden brown on top. Cool thoroughly before serving.

Poppy Seed Filling for Beigli
MÁKOS TÖLTELÉK
  (*mah-kohsh tul-te-layk*)

2 cups water
1 cup sugar
2 tablespoons yellow seedless raisins
3 cups ground poppy seeds
1 tart apple, grated

Heat the water and sugar in a saucepan, add the raisins to plump them, and bring the syrup to a boil. Pour the syrup and raisins over the poppy seeds and mix thoroughly until all are moistened. Stir in the grated apple. Set aside until ready to use. Makes enough for one beigli roll.

Walnut Filling for Beigli
DIÓS TÖLTELÉK
  (*dee-ohsh tul-te-layk*)

2 cups (8 ounces) chopped walnuts
½ cup sugar
3 tablespoons apricot jam
Juice of ½ lemon
1 tart apple, grated

Mix all the ingredients together to make a thick mush. Taste for sweetness and add more sugar if needed. Set aside until ready to use. Makes enough for one beigli roll.

FANCY CAKES
TORTÁK
(tor-tahk)

Hungarians love to eat cake, and they have invented, adapted, and adopted some of the world's best. Every town has its cukrászda, or pastry shop, and every family boasts of one member who makes cakes as fine as the best pastry chef around. To keep that tradition alive, I tried in this section to choose several kinds of tortes and to make them attainable.

✑ Sponge Cake
PISKÓTA TÉSZTA
(peesh-koh-ta tay-sta)

The unadorned sponge cake is the epitome of elegant simplicity, and yet how complicated it has become as the experts vie to point out the one and only true way to make it. Until persuaded otherwise, I will stick to the ancient formulation: it was perfected generations ago, but it works in a modern home kitchen. Changed a bit here and there, it is the basis for most of the tortes or fancy cakes in this collection. And it can, of course, stand on its own with a simple apricot or chocolate glaze or merely a light dusting of powdered sugar. The key to a successful sponge cake is technique, and with so few steps, there is not much margin for error:

• The egg yolks and sugar need to be beaten together with an electric mixer until they turn light yellow and very creamy. They are done when volcanic bubbles rise to the surface and pop when you stop beating or when the batter folds back on itself like a ribbon when you lift the beater out of the bowl. Avoid overbeating, which causes the mixture to turn grainy.

• The egg whites must be beaten to stiff peaks, as for a soufflé. For the maximum effect, the bowl and beaters have to be free of any grease or specks of egg yolk. Many cooks prefer to beat the whites with a rotary beater or a whisk just before folding them in; others use the electric mixer, beating the whites first to skip washing the beaters in the middle of cake making.

• All folding has to be done with a light and deft hand. The egg whites should be evenly distributed but not broken up too much: it is better to err on the side of a lumpy batter.

8 eggs, separated
Salt
8 tablespoons vanilla sugar
1 teaspoon cooking oil
1½ teaspoons grated lemon rind
8 tablespoons sifted all-purpose flour

Preheat the oven to 350°. Prepare a rectangular cake tin or a 9-inch springform pan or two 8- or 9-inch layer cake tins by buttering the insides, laying a piece of waxed paper or brown paper in the bottom and buttering that. Beat the egg whites with a pinch of salt until they form stiff peaks. Using an electric mixer, beat the yolks, gradually adding the sugar, until the mixture is light yellow and very creamy. Stir in the oil and lemon rind. Sift 2 tablespoons of flour on top of the yolks and sugar mixture and quickly fold it in, using a spatula. Repeat until all the flour is folded in. Stir 2 tablespoons of beaten egg whites into the batter to lighten it, then fold in the rest of the egg whites a fourth at a time with a quick light hand. Pour the batter into the prepared pans or pan and bake in the preheated oven for 25 minutes or more. The cake is done when a wooden toothpick inserted near the middle comes out clean. Place the cake pan on a rack and let it cool for 10 minutes. Then invert to remove the cake and quickly peel off the paper. Finish cooling the cake: if it is to be iced, leave it upside down; otherwise, turn it right side up.

Apricot Glaze
BARACK MÁZ
    (*bah-rahtsk mahz*)

½ cup apricot jam
2 tablespoons sugar

Mash up any large pieces of fruit in the jam. Heat the jam and sugar together over low heat for a few minutes, stirring constantly with a wooden spoon. The glaze is done when it thinly coats the spoon. Let it cool slightly before icing the cake. Leftover glaze may be kept in a jar in the refrigerator and reheated when needed.

Chocolate Glaze
CSOKOLÁDÉ MÁZ
(*cho-ko-lah-day mahz*)

6 ounces semisweet chocolate
3 tablespoons strong black coffee
4 tablespoons sugar
2 tablespoons butter

Melt the chocolate, coffee, and sugar together over very low heat, stirring constantly with a wooden spoon until the mixture is smooth and shiny. Remove from the heat and beat in the butter. Frost the sides and top of the cake with the glaze. Store any leftover glaze in a jar in the refrigerator: let it come back to room temperature and beat it again before using it.

⋙ Jelly Roll
ÍZES TEKERCS
(*ee-zesh te-kayrch*)

Many cakes are proud—and disappointing. The jelly roll, on the other hand, may be humble, but it never lets you down. Now that all but the very best bakeries have taken to filling theirs with chemical muck, it is socially acceptable to serve a jelly roll to company. In fact, I have found it the ideal dessert for many Hungarian meals, where an elaborate torta would be too much and a light cream too insubstantial. And it is virtually effortless: not a mean consideration if the rest of the menu requires a great deal of attention. The main points to remember with a jelly roll are to work fast when you roll it up and to sprinkle it with powdered sugar to keep the cake soft.

6 eggs, separated
Salt
6 tablespoons vanilla sugar

Grated rind of ½ lemon
1 teaspoon cooking oil
6 tablespoons sifted all-purpose flour
About 1 cup (12-ounce jar) jelly or jam

Butter a 15½ by 10½ by 1-inch jelly-roll pan, line it with waxed paper or brown paper, and butter that too. Preheat the oven to 350°. Beat the egg whites with a pinch of salt, slowly at first and then very fast until they are stiff. Beat the yolks with an electric mixer, gradually adding the sugar, until the mixture is light yellow, thick, and creamy. Fold in the lemon rind and oil. Sift the flour over the egg-yolk mixture and fold it in. Lightly and quickly fold the whites into the yolk mixture: first mix a big spoonful of whites in the batter to lighten it, then fold the rest. Do not overwork the batter. Turn it into the prepared jelly-roll pan and spread it out evenly to the edges. Bake in a 350° oven for 17 to 20 minutes until golden brown. While the cake is in the oven, warm the jelly or jam, mashing up any large pieces of fruit. Remove the cake from the oven, invert it immediately onto a warm damp towel, and tear off the paper. Spread the cake with jam and roll it up, using the towel to turn it, to make a 15½-inch jelly roll. Sprinkle with confectioners' sugar and place on a cake rack to cool.

⮌ Chocolate Log
FATÖRZS
(fah-turzh)

There is something very friendly about a chocolate log. Besides, it gives the cook a rare chance for a bit of artistic self-expression. To make it, fill a jelly roll with apricot jam and frost it with the filling for diós torta (page 239). Make the frosting look rough, like bark, and decorate it with meringue mushrooms and colored sugar for moss, dusting it with powdered sugar for snow. To enhance the fatörzs, serve a bit of Tokay Aszú wine afterwards.

৩ Dobos Torte
DOBOS TORTA
(doh-bosh tor-ta)

A musician friend of ours from Budapest insists, historical evidence to the contrary notwithstanding, that this cake got its name because it looks like a drum (*dob* in Hungarian). But he is wrong: this is one of the few desserts that was named for its creator and not its appearance or the celebrity it was created to honor. József Dobos was a well-known nineteenth-century pastry chef and gourmet who owned a famous delicacy shop in Budapest. Some say he invented the torta in answer to a challenge that he make a cake that would become famous the world over. The story has to be apocryphal, for that is exactly what happened. Dobos torta, six thin layers of sponge cake with light sweet chocolate cream between them and hard caramel on top, has lived to be nearly a hundred. It first won international acclaim when Dobos served it at a restaurant he opened near the Városliget park in Budapest in time for the National Exhibition which was held there in 1885, and it has been imitated everywhere, ever since. Though the original recipe has long been available, Hungarian chefs and cooks treasure their own individual versions. This one, which works exceptionally well with American ingredients, was developed by my friend Margaret Simon, who makes the best Dobos torta I have ever tasted this side of the Danube. Here or there, the pleasure of eating Dobos torta can be prolonged by a sip of Tokay Aszú after the cake.

To make a Dobos torta at home takes a light hand and a lot of patience. The results are sensational, a clear case of culinary virtue amply rewarded. For a full measure of success, I would advise the home cook to take three precautions with this cake: one, do a dress rehearsal for the family before making it for company; two, make some extra batter so that any layers that curl can be discarded; and three, bake the layers one at a time, since most home ovens heat very unevenly. That first try may produce layers that look like warped phonograph records, but the cake will still taste good, and with a little practice any reasonably skilled cook should be able to put on a pastry-shop performance and produce a cake that is quite mystifyingly rich and light at the same time. (The following recipe is for a round cake. To make an oblong Dobos strip, increase the ingredients to 9 eggs, 1 scant cup of vanilla sugar, and 1½ cups plus 1 tablespoon of flour. Spread the dough very thinly in two jelly-roll pans, bake it, and when it is done, cut each cake across in three even pieces. Fill and top it as in the master recipe, but score the top layer in rectangles about 2 by 4 inches in size.)

THE CAKE

Butter
6 eggs, separated
Salt
Scant ⅔ cup vanilla sugar
1 cup sifted all-purpose flour

Prepare six 9-inch cake tins for baking: cut 6 circles of waxed paper, brown paper, or baking parchment to fit the bottom of the pans, grease the bottom of each one with butter, place the paper in, and grease that as well. Set the pans aside until ready to use. Preheat the oven to 400°. Beat the egg whites with a pinch of the salt until foamy; continue beating until stiff peaks are formed. Set aside. Using an electric mixer, beat the egg yolks and the remaining sugar together until lemon-colored and very thick. About ¼ cup at a time, sift the flour on top of the egg yolk and sugar mixture and fold it in. Mix a tablespoonful of beaten egg whites into the batter to lighten it, then gently fold in the rest of the whites. Keep a light touch throughout, handling the batter just enough to make sure it is evenly blended. Take a prepared pan and spread one-sixth of the batter on the bottom as evenly as possible. (One technique is to place the pan flat on the counter and twirl it counterclockwise with your left hand while spreading the batter clockwise with a knife or short spatula held in your right hand.) Let the batter touch the sides of the pan at several points. Place it in the middle of the preheated oven. Bake for 10 to 12 minutes or until the cake hardens and begins to turn color. Remove from the pan with a spatula, invert, and quickly but carefully tear off all the paper. Cool on a cake rack. Continue in this fashion until all the layers are baked. During the baking time, prepare the filling as follows.

CHOCOLATE CREAM FILLING
  6 ounces semisweet chocolate (6 squares or 1 small package
    chocolate bits)
  3 tablespoons strong coffee
  1 cup (½ pound) butter
  1 cup sifted vanilla confectioners' sugar
  3 eggs

Melt the chocolate with the coffee in a double boiler or over very low heat. Cream the butter with the sugar and beat until fluffy. Add the melted chocolate and beat until it is well blended. Beat in the eggs, one at a time, and continue beating until the cream is light and fluffy. Keep the filling in the refrigerator until ready to use.

CARAMEL GLAZE
  ¾ cup granulated sugar

When all the layers are ready, pick the best one for the top. Place it on a piece of waxed paper and set it aside. Spread filling on the first four layers and stack them; put the fifth layer on top. Saving enough filling for the fifth layer plus a little extra, frost the outside of the cake and then the fifth layer. Meanwhile, melt the sugar in a light-colored heavy skillet over low heat. Continue cooking until the caramel is smooth and quite brown. Do not touch or taste the caramel: it is very hot. When it is ready, pour it quickly over the sixth layer, spreading it evenly with a spatula. With a buttered knife, quickly cut the caramel-topped layer into 12 or 16 wedges before the caramel hardens. As soon as it dries, place the wedges on top of the cake and use the rest of the filling to frost the outside of the fifth and sixth layers. If there is enough filling left, put it in a pastry bag and pipe a design along the top edge of the torta. Leave the cake in a cool place until ready to serve. Keep any leftovers in the refrigerator.

◄§ Russian Cream Torte
OROSZ KRÉM TORTA
(o-ros kraym tor-ta)

Orosz krém torta has presence, star quality, call it what you will. As a company dessert, it is nothing less than spectacular. Two very thin sponge layers support a rum-flavored cream, which is made with just enough gelatin to give it body. When the torta is unmolded, it is not a rigid mass, but rather a delicate, trembling temptation to the vice of gluttony.

THE CAKE
Butter
4 eggs, separated
Salt
¼ cup vanilla sugar
Scant ½ cup sifted all-purpose flour

Prepare two 8- or 9-inch layer-cake tins: they should be slightly smaller than the mold or springform pan you will use to form the torta. Butter the sides and bottom of each tin, line the bottom with brown paper or waxed paper, and butter that. Preheat the oven to 400°. Beat the egg whites with a pinch of salt until they are stiff but not dry. Beat the egg yolks, using an electric mixer, and gradually add the sugar. Continue beating until the mixture is light yellow, thick, and creamy. Sift and fold the flour into the egg yolk and sugar batter, about 2 tablespoons at a time. Stir in 1 tablespoon of egg whites, and then fold in the rest, a quarter at a time. Do not handle the batter too much; at the same time, be careful not to leave any large lumps of egg white. Divide the batter between the two cake tins, spread it out evenly, and place in the preheated oven to bake for 10 to 12 minutes, or until golden brown. Remove from the oven, loosen the sides of each layer from the tin if necessary, and invert over a cake rack. Quickly remove all the paper from the bottom of the layers and let them cool completely.

THE CREAM
½ cup yellow seedless raisins
5 tablespoons rum
1 tablespoon (1 envelope) gelatin

8 egg yolks
1½ cups sifted vanilla confectioners' sugar
1 cup milk
2 cups heavy cream
Cooking oil
1 ounce semisweet chocolate, shaved

Soak the raisins in the rum and sprinkle with gelatin. Set aside. Using an electric mixer, beat the egg yolks and gradually add 1 cup of the vanilla confectioners' sugar, continuing to beat until the mixture is light yellow and very creamy. Meanwhile, scald the milk. Dribble the milk into the yolks and sugar, beating all the while. Transfer this custard to a saucepan and cook over very low heat, stirring constantly with a wooden spoon, until it starts to thicken and coats the spoon. Be sure to keep the heat low, and stir constantly to keep the eggs from curdling. Remove from the heat and beat in the raisins-rum-gelatin mixture. Pour the custard into a large clean bowl and set it aside to cool. Stir it occasionally. When it is cold but not yet set, whip the heavy cream, gradually sifting in the remaining ½ cup of vanilla confectioners' sugar, until it is quite stiff and peaky. Stir the custard thoroughly until smooth, then fold in the whipped cream. Thinly oil a mold or round springform pan slightly larger than the cake layers. Pour half the custard cream into the mold, then gently place one of the layers on top of the cream. Pour in the rest of the custard cream and place the second layer on top of it. Chill for at least 4 hours. Just before serving, unmold the torta and sprinkle the top with shaved chocolate.

⊷§ Rigó Jancsi
RIGÓ JANCSI
(ree-goh yahn-chee)

Chocolate upon chocolate upon chocolate upon chocolate—this is the cake called Rigó Jancsi. It would steal your heart away, just as the passionate dark eyes and soulful violin playing of the gypsy primás Rigó Jancsi won the love of the fair Princess Chimay at the turn of the century. She heard him play and soon left her husband and children to follow the song of a wild bird: it was the scandal of the day. Their affair caught the popular imagination, and in time a pastry chef concocted this magnificent chocolate cake to honor it. The cake too caught on, and it survived long after the primás and his princess were forgotten. Appearances to the contrary, Rigó Jancsi is not too difficult a cake to make at home. The two pitfalls are the layers and the whipped cream filling. The layers of chocolate cake will come out light and airy if you follow the special folding instructions. The chocolate whipped cream must be beaten until it is very stiff so that it will stand firm and high. Be sure to use the very best-quality cocoa: everything depends on it.

THE CAKE

Butter
6 eggs, separated
Salt
6 tablespoons vanilla sugar
3 tablespoons sifted cocoa
4 tablespoons sifted all-purpose flour

Butter a 15½-inch jelly-roll pan and line the bottom with waxed paper. Butter the paper too. Preheat the oven to 400°. Beat the egg whites with a dash of salt until frothy, continue beating until they are stiff. Beat the egg yolks together with the sugar, using an electric beater, until the mixture is light yellow and very thick. Sift the cocoa on top of the egg yolk mixture and fold it in. Stir in a heaping tablespoon of egg whites to lighten the batter, then sift the flour on top and fold that in. Lastly, carefully fold in the rest of the whites. Pour the batter into the prepared pan and smooth it out evenly. Put it in the oven and bake until done, about 12 minutes: the cake should spring back when pressed with the finger. Invert the pan on a cake rack and remove the cake. Quickly tear off any paper that is stuck to the bottom. Let the cake cool thoroughly before filling it.

CHOCOLATE WHIPPED CREAM FILLING

4 tablespoons sifted confectioners' sugar
4 tablespoons sifted cocoa
2 cups heavy cream

Sift the sugar and cocoa together. With everything ice cold—

the cream, the bowl, and the beater—beat the cream until it starts to thicken. Sift in the sugar and cocoa mixture, beating all the while, and continue beating until the cream is very thick. Cut the cake in half to make two layers 10 by 7½ inches, and pile the chocolate whipped cream on one of them. Level it off on top, then refrigerate immediately.

CHOCOLATE GLAZE

4 ounces semisweet chocolate
½ cup sugar
1 tablespoon butter

Heat the chocolate, sugar, and 3 tablespoons of water over very low heat until all is melted and looks very smooth and shiny. Remove from the heat and beat in the butter. Spread this topping on the other layer and let it harden. When the topping has set, cut the layer into twelve 2½-inch squares. Remove the first layer from the refrigerator and set the squares on top of the whipped cream. Put the cake back in the refrigerator immediately. When you are ready to serve the Rigó Jancsi, cut the cake all the way through.

Date Cake

DATOLYA TORTA
(*dah-toy-ya tor-ta*)

Leafing through some old Hungarian cookbooks, I came across two recipes for datolya torta. It looked like something that would turn out to be very good, so I worked out my own recipe from the other two and tried it. The result was a very sweet, moist cake quite unlike any other we had ever had before. Three of my most trusted tasters judged it delicious: one Magyar gourmand ate a quarter of the cake in one sitting. For special occasions, datolya torta could be served with a sweet dessert wine: a Tokay Furmint would be just right.

THE CAKE

Butter
Flour
½ pound pitted dates

9 egg whites
2 cups sifted vanilla confectioners' sugar
2 cups (½ pound) coarsely ground blanched almonds
2 tablespoons bread crumbs

Butter the bottom and sides of two 9-inch layer cake tins and sprinkle with flour, shaking out the excess. Preheat the oven to 350°. Set aside 5 dates to decorate the cake, and chop the rest coarsely. Beat the egg whites until frothy, then gradually add the sugar and continue beating until stiff. Mix the almonds and bread crumbs together and fold them into the egg whites. Fold in the dates. Pour the batter into the cake tins and spread it evenly around, keeping a light touch. Bake for 25 to 30 minutes or until the top is lightly browned. Loosen the layers and invert the pans on a cake rack. Remove them and let the cake cool thoroughly before filling it.

CHOCOLATE NUT FILLING
1 ounce semisweet chocolate
½ cup (1 stick) butter, at room temperature
1 cup sifted vanilla confectioners' sugar
½ cup (2 ounces) coarsely ground blanched almonds

Melt the chocolate in a double boiler or over very low heat. Cream the butter with the confectioners' sugar, add the melted chocolate, and beat until fluffy. Fold in the ground almonds. Refrigerate until ready to use. When the layers are thoroughly cooled, take the better-looking one for the top. Decorate it with the dates: cut four in half lengthwise and place them near the outer edge of the cake; cut the fifth date across and put half in the center. Spread the other layer with filling, set the decorated layer on top, and dust with powdered sugar.

◄§ Walnut Cake
DIÓS TORTA
(*dee-ohsh tor-ta*)

A couple of fancy bakeries in town would have lost my patronage years ago if I had known how easy it is to make this kind of cake—and how much better it is when homemade. Diós torta is a moist cake that stays fresh for days. And since it is so very rich, a 9-inch torta will serve 10 to 12 people. On special occasions, it might be followed by a sweet dessert wine like a Tokay Aszú. This cake, by the way, can also be made with hazelnuts: simply substitute ground hazelnuts for walnuts. It would then be called a mogyorós torta in Hungarian.

THE CAKE
Butter
7 eggs, separated
Salt
¾ cup sugar
¾ cup (3 ounces) coarsely chopped walnuts
¼ cup fine bread crumbs

Butter two 9-inch layer-cake tins, place a circle of waxed paper or brown paper in the bottom, and butter that. Set the tins aside. Preheat the oven to 375°. Beat the egg whites with a pinch of salt until foamy; continue beating until very stiff. With an electric mixer, beat the egg yolks with the sugar until light yellow and very creamy. Blend the walnuts and bread crumbs together, and fold them into the egg yolk mixture. Mix a heaping tablespoon of the beaten egg whites into the batter to lighten it, then lightly fold in the rest of the whites. The batter should be evenly mixed but not overworked. Pour it into the cake tins and bake for 20 minutes or until the cake springs back when touched. Cool them for 10 minutes in the tins, then invert them on a cake rack and quickly remove all the paper from the bottom of the layers. Cool completely before filling and frosting the cake.

CHOCOLATE FILLING
¼ pound semisweet chocolate (4 squares or ½ cup of chocolate bits)
½ cup sugar
½ cup (1 stick) butter
2 eggs

Melt the chocolate and sugar in the top of a double boiler until satiny smooth. Remove from the heat and beat in the butter a tablespoon at a time. Beat in the eggs, one at a time. Refrigerate until ready to use. If the filling gets too hard, let it come back to room temperature and beat it briefly. Fill and frost the walnut cake layers and keep the cake in a cool place until ready to serve.

✺ Chestnut Cake
GESZTENYE TORTA
(*geh-sten-ye tor-ta*)

Most people who like chestnuts would agree that if you take the trouble to find and peel, cook and mash, flavor and rice a couple of pounds of chestnuts, you should eat the end product, not bury it in a cake. In this case, you can save a fabulous cake from oblivion by replacing the homemade stuff with a canned substitute. The cake is most easily made and served in one piece with a topping of whipped cream and gestenye püré, as I describe. Or the cake can be split into two layers (or made in two layers in the first place) and filled and frosted. Whipped cream and chestnuts are inseparable: fill and top the cake with it, or fill it with the chocolate and nut filling for datolya torta (page 238) and top it with whipped cream.

THE CAKE
1¼ cups (packed) chestnut purée (about ¾ of a 440-gram can of unsweetened chestnut purée, or see recipe on page 202)
4 ounces semisweet chocolate
½ cup (2 ounces) chopped blanched almonds
½ cup fine bread crumbs
8 eggs, separated
Salt
1½ cups vanilla sugar

Force the chestnut purée through a potato ricer and set it aside. Grate the chocolate, using the grater attachment of your electric mixer if you have one, or a food chopper. Grated, the chocolate will amount to about 1¼ cups. Mix the almonds together with the bread crumbs. Preheat the oven to 325° and prepare a 9-inch springform pan for baking: butter the sides and bottom of the pan, then dust it with flour and shake out the excess. Beat the egg whites with a pinch of salt until stiff but not dry. Then beat the egg yolks with an electric mixer, gradually adding the vanilla sugar until it is well blended and the mixture is light yellow in color and very thick and creamy. Fold in the riced chestnut purée and then the grated chocolate. Carefully fold in the ground nuts and bread crumbs. Stir 1 tablespoon of beaten egg whites into the batter, and then fold the rest in, a fourth at a time. Pour the batter into the prepared pan, spread it around evenly, and place it in the center of the preheated oven to bake for 50 minutes to 1 hour. The cake is done when it shrinks away from the sides of the pan and turns brown on top. Take it out of the oven and let it cool somewhat in the pan. Remove the sides of the pan and let it cool thoroughly before serving.

THE TOPPING
>   1 cup heavy cream
>   2 to 3 tablespoons sifted vanilla confectioners' sugar
>   Remaining canned chestnut purée (about ½ cup)
>   2 tablespoons vanilla confectioners' sugar
>   1 tablespoon rum

Whip the cream in a cold bowl with a cold beater. Gradually sift in the confectioners' sugar and continue beating until stiff and peaked. Refrigerate until ready to use. Mash the chestnut purée with a fork, then work in 2 tablespoons of confectioners' sugar. Beat in the rum and taste for flavoring. When ready to serve the cake, pile the whipped cream on top and force the sweetened chestnut purée through a potato ricer directly onto the whipped cream.

Shopping Guide

In the past, the best and often the only source for special ingredients for Hungarian dishes was one of those Hungarian butcher shops (Magyar Hentes) that used to be found in every ethnic enclave around the nation. These shops, usually small family operations, carried a full line of bacon, kolbász, smoked meats, paprika, noodles and tarhonya, pickles and other delicacies. They are still to be found, and they are still the best source, but their numbers have been decreasing.

Instead what we now find on the urban landscape is gourmet supermarkets, such as Sutton Place Gourmet in Washington, D.C., Food Emporium in New York City, and Bildner and Sons in Boston. These shops stock special ingredients, both imported and domestic, for every kind of cuisine. In addition, many department stores have expanded their food shops and, of course, their housewares departments in response to greater interest in food. All over the United States there are shops that carry specialty foods and equipment; Williams-Sonoma has outlets in dozens of cities, as well as a mail-order department. Other companies specialize in catalogue sales to the serious cook.

There are more health-food stores now than there used to be; these are always a good source for nuts, flour and stoneground cornmeal. And you should always check your local supermarket: Hungarian paprika, usually in a red square can, seems to be on the shelf everywhere. A list of shops around the country that carry a wide range of Hungarian cooking ingredients follows. Some accept mail orders, but it is always advisable to check in advance about minimum orders, prices, charges and such.

CALIFORNIA

Los Angeles and Vicinity

Alex & Ella's European Pastry Shop, 7356 Melrose Ave., Los Angeles 90046. Tel: (213) 651-3165

Ernie's Continental Delicatessen, 8400 8th Ave., Inglewood 90305. Tel: (213) 752-8194

Gastronom, 7859 Fairfax Ave., Los Angeles 90046. Tel: (213) 654-9456

Hickorysweet Meats, 8768 S. Main St., Los Angeles 90003. Tel: (213) 759-9935

Ludvig's Village Market, 2713 W. Olive Ave., Burbank 91505. Tel: (818) 848-1858

Otto's Magyar Import Uzlet, 2320 W. Clark Ave., Burbank 91506. Tel: (818) 845-0433

Tibor's European Meat Market, 7862 Santa Monica Blvd., Los Angeles 90046. Tel: (213) 654-3434

Valley Hungarian Sausage and Meat Company, 8809 Pearblossom Hwy. (138), Littlerock 93543. Tel: (805) 944-3190

Victor Benes Bakery, 8718 W. Third St., Los Angeles 90048. Tel: (213) 276-0488

San Francisco and Vicinity

Aidell's Sausage Company, 618 Coventry Rd., Kensington 98707. Tel: (415) 526-6377

CANADA

Montreal, Quebec

Vieille Europe Charcuterie, 3855 St. Lawrence Blvd., Montreal. Tel: (514) 842-5773

Toronto, Ontario

Bourret Pastry and Delicatessen, 5771 Victoria Ave. Tel: 733-8462

Elisabeth Delicatessen and Meat Market, 410 Bloor St. W. Tel: (416) 921-8644

Hungarian Honey Bear, 249 Sheppard Ave. E. Tel: (416) 733-0022

Open Window Bakery, 1125 Finch Ave. W. Tel: (416) 665-8242

Tuske Meat and Delicatessen, 566 Bloor St. W. Tel: (416) 533-3453

World Delicatessen and Meat, 557 St. Clair Ave. W. Tel: (416) 656-6259

DISTRICT OF COLUMBIA

Washington and Vicinity

Cafe Mozart, 1331 H St., NW, Washington 20005. Tel: (202) 347-5732

Kitchen Bazaar, 4455 Connecticut Ave., NW, Washington 20008. Tel: (202) 244-1550. *Kitchen equipment only. Accepts mail orders: (202) 363-4625*

La Cuisine, 323 Cameron St., Alexandria, VA 22314. Tel: (703) 836-4435

Someplace Special, Giant Gourmet, 1445 Chain Bridge Rd., McLean, VA 22101. Tel: (703) 448-0800

Sutton Place Gourmet, 3201 New Mexico Ave., NW, Washington 20016. Tel: (202) 363-5800, and 10323 Old Georgetown Rd., Bethesda, MD 20814. Tel: (301) 564-3100. *Accepts mail orders: (800) 468-7638*

Tell's Apple, 3251 Prospect St., NW, Washington 20007. Tel: (202) 338-7277

Wenzel's, 7185 Lee Hwy., Falls Church, VA 22046. Tel: (703) 534-1908

ILLINOIS

CHICAGO AND VICINITY

Bende and Son Salami Company, 114 W. Fay St., Addison 60101. Tel: (312) 543-0763. *Accepts mail orders.*

Black Forest Meat Market, 2002 W. Roscoe, Chicago 60618. Tel: (312) 348-3660

Delicatessen Meyer, 4750 N. Lincoln Ave., Chicago 60618. Tel: (312) 561-3377

European Sausage House (Szalai Brothers), 4361 N. Lincoln Ave., Chicago 60618. Tel: (312) 472-9645

H & E Meat Market, 3534 W. Irving Park Rd., Chicago 60618. Tel: (312) 583-9786

Joe's Homemade Sausage, 4452 N. Western Ave., Chicago 60625. Tel (312) 478-5443

Kuhn's Delicatessen, 3051 North Lincoln Avenue, Chicago 60618, Tel: (312) 525-9019; 749 W. Golf Rd., Des Plaines 60016, Tel: (312) 640-0222; and 116 S. Waukegan Rd., Deerfield 60015, Tel: (312) 272-4197

Lalich Delicatessen, 4206 W. Lawrence Ave., Chicago 60630. Tel: (312) 545-3642

Meyer Import Delicatessen, 3306 N. Lincoln Ave., Chicago 60657. Tel: (312) 281-8979

Stingaciu International Imports, 4812 N. Oakley Blvd., Chicago 60625. Tel: (312) 275-9523.

MARYLAND

BALTIMORE

Egon Binkert's Meat Products, 8805 Philadelphia Rd., Baltimore

21237. Tel: (301) 687-5959

Old European Delicatessen, 117 N. Eutaw St., Baltimore 21201. Tel: (301) 752-7545

MINNESOTA

MINNEAPOLIS-ST. PAUL

Gleason's Specialty Shoppe, 382 St. Peter St., St. Paul 55102. Tel: (612) 222-6914

Kramarczuk Sausage Company, 215 E. Hennepin Ave., Minneapolis 55414. Tel: (612) 379-3018

NEW MEXICO

ALBUQUERQUE

Alpine Sausage Kitchen, 2800 Indian School, NE, Albuquerque 87110. Tel: (505) 266-2853

Fremont's Fine Foods, 556 Coronado Center, Albuquerque 87110. Tel: (505) 883-6040

NEW YORK

NEW YORK CITY AND VICINITY

Andrew's Hungarian Strudel and Pastries, 100–28 Queens Blvd., Forest Hills 11375. Tel: (718) 830-0266

European Meat Center, 458½ S. Broadway, Yonkers 10705. Tel: (914) 968-7315

European Meat Company of Flushing, 4141 Main St., Flushing 11355. Tel: (718) 358-7459

Hungarian Meat Center, 1592 Second Ave., New York 10028. Tel: (212) 650-1015

Hungarian Pastry Shop, 1030 Amsterdam Ave., New York 10025. Tel: (212) 866-4230

Hungarian Rigo Pastries, 318 E. 78th St., New York 10021. Tel: (212) 988-0052

Kleine Konditorei, 234 E. 86th St., New York 10028. Tel: (212) 737-7130

Paprikas Weiss, 1546 Second Ave., New York 10028. Tel: (212) 288-6117. *Accepts mail orders.*

Tibor Meat Specialties, 1508 Second Ave., New York 10021. Tel: (212) 744-8292

Zabar's, 2245 Broadway, New York 10024. Tel: (212) 787-2000

OHIO

CLEVELAND
>Magyar Áruház, 11802 Buckeye Rd., Cleveland 44120. Tel: (216) 991-3737
>
>The Cheese Shop, 1979 W. 25th St., Cleveland 44113. Tel: (216) 771-6349

TEXAS

DALLAS
>Simon David, 7117 Inwood Rd., Dallas 75209. Tel: (214) 352-1781

WASHINGTON

SEATTLE
>Bavarian Meat Products, 2934 Western, Seattle 98101. Tel: (206) 448-3540
>
>Continental Store, 4014 Roosevelt Way, NE, Seattle 98105. Tel: (206) 523-0606
>
>Market Spice, 85A Pike Place Market, Seattle 98101. Tel: (206) 622-6340. *Accepts mail orders: P.O. Box 2935, Redmond 98073. Tel: (206) 883-1220*

Hungarian Index

General Index

About the Author

Susan Derecskey was born in New York City and educated at Brooklyn College and the University of Strasbourg. She worked in publishing and journalism until she met a transplanted European journalist named Charles Derecskey, by origin a Hungarian from Transylvania, and embarked on the globe-trotting uncertainties of life with a foreign correspondent. Already an accomplished cook in the French mode, she began to cook Hungarian, first as a treat for her husband, then as a parlor trick, finally as an obsession.

When the Derecskeys returned to the United States, Susan already had an extensive collection of notes and recipes she had accumulated and tested wherever they were: the Congo, Paris, Germany and—as culmination—Hungary. Here, in the fine restaurants of Budapest and the more modest establishments and homes of Transylvania, she learned how the classic dishes should be made and developed that instinct for the cuisine that separates the gifted cook from the merely skillful one.

Her husband and two young sons cheered her on through the writing of *The Hungarian Cookbook*. They still gather every summer in the big kitchen at Ledgewood in the Adirondack Mountains, where many of the recipes in the book were put to the test. This annual ceremony of renewal is bound to feature such enshrined favorites as kohlrabi soup and chicken paprikash and one or more of those fabulous Hungarian desserts.